Seven Congregations in a Roman Crucible

Seven Congregations in a Roman Crucible

A Commentary on Revelation 1–3

RICHARD E. OSTER JR.

WIPF & STOCK · Eugene, Oregon

SEVEN CONGREGATIONS IN A ROMAN CRUCIBLE
A Commentary on Revelation 1–3

Wipf & Stock
An Imprint of Wipf and Stock Publishers
199 W. 8th Ave., Suite 3
Eugene, OR 97401

www.wipfandstock.com

ISBN 13: 978-1-62032-105-8

Manufactured in the U.S.A.

As many scholars know, their families usually have spouses and parents who are not always available as they should be. That was also true in my circumstance. It might not provide much consolation, but I dedicate this work to my family, Sandy and our three children, Molly, Grant, and Bradley, to express thanks for an unreasonable amount of love and joy they provide.

Contents

Preface

THE WRITING OF THIS book has not only been protracted, but its scope and aims have undergone many metamorphoses. In the mid-1980s my wife, Sandy, and our three children moved to Germany for an eight-month Sabbatical. During that period we met with other Christians who worshiped at the *Gemeinde Christi* in Cologne, Germany. They encouraged me to teach a Sunday morning Bible study on the book of Revelation. A very rudimentary English manuscript was provided so that the study could be bilingual. This manuscript was hardly more than an embellished outline for a study of the book of Revelation, but it did provide to me the opportunity to introduce to some in the congregation new perspectives about the book of Revelation, including its structure and background.

Now some twenty years later the manuscript has evolved into something significantly different, both in size and focus. My work on this commentary has also benefitted from interaction with students in an English exegesis course I teach on the book of Revelation. By design it is no longer the same kind of commentary that I was working on even a few years ago. In addition to the obvious need to interact with others portions of Scripture, I have attempted to incorporate appropriate Graeco-Roman and Jewish materials, including literary sources, epigraphical, architectural, and numismatic artifacts.

In an attempt to stay engaged with the author of Revelation and his outlook, and since I regard Revelation as a part of Scripture, I have occasionally remarked about the contemporary significance of the prophet John's message for Christianity in the West. I have felt the need to expand an argument or two in appendices at the end of the book or use an appendix to give the reader additional resources. For further information and conversation go to richardoster.com.

Acknowledgments

I WOULD LIKE TO acknowledge the assistance provided to me by many others. I express appreciation to Steve and Margaret Bills who made it possible one summer to have release time to work on the manuscript. The library staff under the direction of Mr. Don Meredith, Head Librarian, has provided invaluable assistance over the years with interlibrary loans, the purchase of required books, and checking the manuscript for possible faults. My focus in the manuscript has changed significantly in the past few years with the incorporation of graphics and visual materials; this was no small change. There have been some graduate assistants who deserve special thanks for their tireless efforts in assisting me in doing research for this book in recent years, especially Wes Kuryluk, James Mitchell, and Clint Burnett. Special thanks goes to my friend and colleague Prof. Allen Black, who read the entire manuscript and made many helpful suggestions, especially regarding infelicitous wording.

Abbreviations

BA   *Biblical Archaeologist.*

BDAG   Bauer, W., F. W. Danker, W. F. Arndt, and F. W. Gingrich. *Greek-English Lexicon of the New Testament and Other Early Christian Literature.* 3rd ed. Chicago: University of Chicago Press, 1999.

IG   *Inscriptiones Graecae.* Editio minor. Berlin, 1924–.

IGRR   *Inscriptiones Graecae ad Res Romanas Pertinentes.* Edited by Cagnat, Rene. Chicago: Ares, 1975.

ILS   *Inscriptiones Latinae Selectae.* Edited by Hermann Dessau. Chicago: Ares, 1979.

JAC   Jahrbuch für Antike und Christentum.

JBL   *Journal of Biblical Literature.*

JRS   *Journal of Roman Studies.*

LSJ   Liddell, H. G., R. Scott, H. S. Jones, *A Greek-English Lexicon.* 9th ed. with revised supplement. Oxford: Oxford University Press, 1996.

LXX   Rahlfs, Alfred and Robert Hanhart, eds. *Septuaginta.* 2nd rev. ed. Stuttgart: Deutsche Bibelstiftung, 2006.

NA27   *Novum Testamentum Graece*, Nestle-Aland, 27th ed.

NETS   *A New English Translation of the Septuagint, and Other Greek Translations Traditionally Included Under That Title.* Oxford: Oxford University Press, 2007.

NTS   *New Testament Studies.*

NRSV   New Revised Standard Version.

RAr   *Revue archéologique.*

ResQ   *Restoration Quarterly.*

SEG   *Supplementum epigraphicum Graecum.* 25 vols. Edited by J. J. E. Hondius and A. G. Woodhead. Alphen aan den Rijn, The Netherlands: Sijthoff & Noordhoff, 1923–71. Reprint, Amsterdam: J. C. Gieben, 1984. Vol. 26 to date. Edited by H. W. Pleket and R. S. Stroud. Amsterdam: J. C. Gieben, 1979–.

SIG   *Sylloge inscriptionum graecarum.* Edited by W. Dittenberger. 4 vols. 3d ed. Leipzig, 1915–24.

UBS4   *The Greek New Testament,* United Bible Societies, 4th ed.

WUNT   Wissenschaftliche Untersuchungen zum Neuen Testament.

ZPE   *Zeitschrift für Papyrologie und Epigraphik.*

1

Introduction

INTRODUCTION

CONTROVERSY HAS BEEN A constant companion of the Revelation of John.[1] One has to go no farther than John's own day to see this. At the time of John's writing there were clearly Christians in some of his congregations that were so intimidated by his rhetoric and threats and upset by aspects of his message, that they were willing to challenge him and to change the content of his prophecies (22:18–19). John's concern about other Christians altering his prophecies demonstrates the presence of believers who regarded Revelation as perhaps too controversial, or perhaps too trenchant, or possibly just too unreasonable for those wanting to be at peace with the aspirations and mores of the surrounding urban cultures. While there are many things that scholars have argued about in John's book, there can be no doubt that it was a book that contained beliefs and rhetoric subversive to the surrounding cultures.

Those Christians in Roman Asia looking for a message less radical than the message of the enthroned Messiah did not flounder without leadership. In particular, those who disavowed John, his ministry, and

---

1. Wainwright, *Mysterious Apocalypse*; Newport, *Apocalypse*, gives a history of interpretation as found outside critical circles, from the sixteenth century to the tragedy at Waco, TX; Beckwith, *Apocalypse*, 318–36; Barr, *Revelation*, 151–61.

the spiritual perspectives he taught existed in identifiable coteries labeled by John as Nicolaitans (2:6,15), followers of Balaam (2:14), and children of Jezebel (2:20, 23). Given the diversity of nascent Christianity, it might even have come as a shock to some when they learned of John's disapproval of their own Christian lifestyles. If so, the severity of his censure probably alienated some of them even more.

Following the earliest years of its influence among Christian congregations, Revelation began to be exploited by heretics in the church.[2] Disagreement and controversy followed it so doggedly that the later deliberations and decision about its place in the Christian canon were contentious.[3] Why admit a book into Scripture that, like the Trojan horse, secretly brought problems into the city of God? Even pre-Reformation Catholics were at times in conflict about the correct use of Revelation, and there was certainly a lack of consensus regarding the meaning of its symbols.[4] Even all these centuries later, it still has an uneven acceptance in Christendom. In the Eastern Orthodox churches of today, "Revelation is the only New Testament book not publically read in [their] services." This decision seemingly gives Revelation a stepchild status, although the book is regarded as both inspired and canonical by the Eastern Orthodox churches.[5]

With the advent of Protestantism there was naturally a pervasive proliferation of new doctrines and perspectives. This new diversity also impacted the interpretations and controversy surrounding this book. Revelation was a rich resource for both Protestants and Catholics, and it provided a plethora of verses with which to attack one another. Radical factions of the Reformation also employed it, but in their case the book of Revelation was frequently utilized to enhance apocalyptic fanaticism and millenarian hopes. The ease with which Revelation was used to promote fanaticism may have contributed to the fact that often it was either selectively used or ignored[6] by some of the mainstream voices in the Protestant Reformation.

---

2. Wainwright, *Mysterious Apocalypse*, 21–31.

3. Collins, "Revelation," 695; Carson and Moo, *Introduction*, 717; Eusebius writes, "Of John's writings, besides the gospel, the first of the epistles has been accepted as unquestionably his by scholars both of the present and of a much earlier period: the other two are disputed. As to the Revelation, the views of most people to this day are evenly divided" (*Hist.* 3.24.17–18).

4. Backus, *Reformation Readings*, xvii–xviii.

5. *Orthodox Study Bible*, 1711.

6. Parker, *Calvin*, 107; Backus, *Reformation Readings*, 29.

In the oft-quoted "Preface to the Revelation of St. John" in his 1522 edition of the New Testament, Martin Luther judged that:

> I say what I feel. I miss more than one thing in this book, and it makes me consider it to be neither apostolic nor prophetic. First and foremost, the apostles do not deal with visions, but prophesy in clear and plain words . . . For it befits the apostolic office to speak clearly of Christ and his deeds, without images and visions. . . . Again, they are suppose to be blessed who keep what is written in this book; and yet no one knows what that is, to say nothing of keeping it. This is just the same as if we did not have the book at all. . . . My spirit cannot accommodate itself to this book. For me this is reason enough not to think highly of it: Christ is neither taught nor known in it.[7]

Figure 1

Unfortunately modern students of the book of Revelation are often not told that these were not Luther's final thoughts on Revelation. A more thoughtful and better informed Luther expressed much more favorable opinions in the replacement "Preface" written eight years later in his 1530 edition. After coming to peace personally with the type of "prophecy" in the book of Revelation, Luther gives a lengthy summary of the chapters of John's work and then observes: "We can profit by this book and make good use of it. First, for our comfort! . . . Second, for our warning! . . . As we see here in this book, that through and beyond all plagues, beasts, and evil angels Christ is nonetheless with his saints, and wins the final victory."[8] Rather than letting his initial personal biases and problems with this part of Scripture dominate his theology, Luther decided in the end to place himself under the authority of this part of Scripture also.

In light of the polyvalent symbolism of the book, most denominations in Christendom have been allured, to one degree or another, into foisting personal preferences and doctrines onto the texts of John's prophecies. Some have been more successful than others in resisting this temptation. It continues to be the case, nevertheless, that tendentious and anachronistic perspectives often twist the message of Revelation into something that John would not even recognize as his own work. This makes it all the more

7. *Luther's Works,* 398–99.
8. *Luther's Works,* 409–11.

important that modern interpreters should strive to be aware of their own assumptions toward this book.

It is often thought that bizarre explanations and interpretations of Revelation only arise from extreme groups such as the Münster, Germany sect of the sixteenth century,[9] the Millerites of the nineteenth century,[10] or the Waco, Texas Branch Davidians of the twentieth century.[11] History, however, teaches that very influential and erudite people have been associated with eccentric views about Revelation. Most twenty-first-century students of Revelation, for example, would not readily associate absurd or sectarian interpretations of Revelation with the perspectives of influential individuals like Christopher Columbus and Sir Isaac Newton, to cite two brief examples.

Figure 2

While my own academic record from elementary school would attest that I did not give my full attention to my teachers, I am relatively confident that when I was learning the words, "In fourteen hundred and ninety-two Columbus sailed the ocean blue," the teacher did not mention that the Catholic explorer Columbus held a highly developed and futuristic eschatology, including the defeat of the Muslims, the coming of the Antichrist, and the discovery of the New World.[12]

In fact, I find that most undergraduate and graduate students have never been taught that Christopher Columbus and his voyages were closely connected to his personal millenarian and apocalyptic beliefs, including controversial interpretations of the book of Revelation. Columbus believed that his voyages and discoveries were an explicit and direct fulfillment of Scripture and Christian eschatological hopes and, furthermore, a harbinger of the "last generations" before the return of Christ.[13] Spe-

---

9. Stayer, "John of Leiden," 350–51; Kirchhoff, "Münster," 97–98; Krahn, *Dutch Anabaptism*, 135–64.

10. Lippy, "Millennialism," 834–36; Stein, "Apocalypticism," 115–17; Boyer, "Growth," 145–47.

11. Pitts, "Davidians," (2000), 113–17.

12. Columbus, *Prophecies*, 24–25. Helpful summary and bibliography is also given in Hubers, "'Strange Thing," 333–53.

13. The eschatological reckoning of Columbus is contained in his following words,

cifically, Columbus wrote: "Of the new heaven and the new earth, which Our Lord made—as St. John writes in Revelations [sic]—following the words given to Isaiah, "He made me the messenger and he showed me where to go"--all men were incredulous. But the Lord gave to my Lady the Queen the spirit of understanding and great courage, and He made her His dear and much beloved daughter, heiress to it all. I took possession of all these lands in her royal name."[14] In another work entitled *Book of Prophecies*, Columbus remarked, "Our Lord wished to make something clearly miraculous of this voyage to the Indies," to which he later added, "I have already said that for the voyage to the Indies neither intelligence nor mathematics nor world maps were of any use to me; it was the fulfillment of Isaiah's prophecy."[15]

Isaac Newton, famous scientist of the seventeenth and eighteenth centuries and namesake of Newton's "Three Laws of Motion," is less well known for his hermeneutical perspectives on Christian eschatology, the Revelation of John, and his putative scientific explanation for the imminent arrival of Christ and the end of the world. Though not in vogue today, it appeared very scientific to Newton to envision the return of Christ and the end of the world in terms of his own view of natural causes in the galaxy. Furthermore, according to one historian, "Isaac Newton, for example, thought that his scientific discoveries would, by laying nature bare, hasten the rule of Christ."[16] Again, many modern Christians would be surprised to explore the thoughts of Isaac Newton on the book of Daniel, the book of Revelation, and the controversial nature of his teachings in these matters.

The point of all of this is to say that mistaken interpretations of Revelation are not something reserved only for marginal members of society

---

"St. Augustine said that the world would end in the seventh millennium after its creation; the holy theologians agree with him, in particular, the cardinal Pierre d'Ailly in Statement XI and in other passages, as I will indicate below. From the creation of the world or from Adam until the coming of Our Lord Jesus Christ there are 5,343 years and 318 days, according to the calculation made by King Alfonso (the Wise), taken to be the most accurate by Pierre d'Ailly in statement X of his *Elucidario astronomice concordie cum theologica et historica veritate*. Adding to this number 1,500 years, and one not yet completed, gives a total of 6,845 years counted toward the completion of this era. By this account, only 155 years remain of the 7,000 years in which, according to the authorities cited above, the world must come to an end. Our Redeemer said that before the consummation of this world all that had been written by the prophets would have to be fulfilled." Columbus, *Prophecies*, 71–73. For additional discussion see Watts, "Prophecy," 73–102.

14. Cohen, *Four Voyages*, 265.

15. Columbus, *Prophecies*, 69, 75.

16. Webb, "Eschatology," 503.

or for those associated with fundamentalist sectarian groups. Accordingly, the contemporary reader of Revelation should strive to identify his own assumptions about the appropriate methods for interpreting Revelation. There is no school of interpretation, and certainly no denomination or seminary, that does not approach Revelation with its own distinctive presuppositions, hermeneutical preferences, and occasional circular reasoning. What seemed patent and obvious to the mind of Columbus, of Newton, and of David Koresh strikes most believers and interpreters today as ludicrous and foolish, or at best naive. Our own views might appear similar to others at a later date.

What, then, are the assumptions of this work? The working assumptions of this study include the conviction that John's prophecies contain recognizable goals and purposes, an authorial intention, and that the modern student, with focused effort, can place himself within reasonable earshot of the authorial intention of John. Thus, it seems to me that it is possible to understand Revelation generally to the same degree as other biblical prophetic books.

This is not intended to deny that John's language is polyvalent in many instances. I would say, though, that just because a symbol can have more than one meaning does not imply it can have every meaning. In light of the stated importance of better understanding the meaning of words and symbols in Revelation, it is highly unlikely that John would intentionally want to promote obfuscation. To state the obvious, the book begins by stating that it is intended to be a "revelation."

There are, of course, those who doubt the possibility of recovering an author's original intent, since subjectivity abounds in all communication and since we are far removed from John's culture and time period. If that were the whole truth, then there will be little to gain in reading this study, since discovering the intent of my ideas would also be improbable. Furthermore, all of the historical, cultural, and archaeological materials employed in this study would be similarly unintelligible due to the cultural and temporal remoteness of these historical materials.

In some regards this task of the interpretation of Revelation is no different than attempting to place oneself within reasonable earshot of other ancient authors such as Homer, Moses, Plato, Hosea, Suetonius, Josephus, or Luke. From this perspective the initial directive for us is to hear the text, not to force the text to hear us.

For many interpreters like myself standing within earshot of Revelation has a different significance than merely placing oneself within earshot of Plato. Specifically, many interpreters are drawn into the sphere of sacred Scripture when they study the text of Revelation. Once Revelation is recognized as Scripture, interpreting John's words now presupposes the use of paradigms not necessarily used when interpreting the words of Homer or Josephus. In particular, convictions about the truthfulness of Scripture, the authority of Scripture, and Scripture's fundamental coherence provide additional paradigms that bring clarification, perspective, and significance to the message of Revelation.

Naturally every new study runs the risk of merely adding another discordant voice that interferes with the voice of John. This study hopes to employ methodologies and to introduce ancient resources that will help the reader to hear, to understand, and to appreciate Revelation itself, and furthermore to see the significance of Revelation both in the context of its culture and in the context provided by other Scriptures. This study, after all, can have no greater goal than to help the reader hear what the Spirit says to the contemporary church through what it spoke to the seven churches of Roman Asia.

THEOLOGICAL CONCERNS

As an interpreter who is sympathetic with the idea of "authorial intention," it is important to acknowledge the distinction between an individual's or a church's systematic theology on the one hand and the theology expressed in Scripture itself on the other hand. As the eighteenth century was drawing to a close and hard won political freedoms were appearing in France, the United States, and other places, another type of freedom was also being advocated in academic and ecclesiastical circles of Europe. The name of Johann Philipp Gabler is often associated with the advocacy of this other type of freedom, namely the freedom to stand within earshot of Scripture and to hear its melody without the imposition of louder and possibly distracting ecclesiastical chords. Since Gabler's ideas constituted a watershed moment in the study and interpretation of Scripture, his actual words are noteworthy: "Also one need not discuss at length that unfortunate fellow who heedlessly dared to attribute some of his own most insubstantial opinions to the sacred writers themselves—how he increased the unhappy fate of our religion! There may even be some like him who would like to solidify the frothiness of such opinions about the divine authors; for it is certainly something to give a divine appearance to their human ideas.

Those completely unable to interpret correctly must inevitably inflict violence upon the sacred books."[17]

One conspicuous example of this general problem addressed by Gabler well over two hundred years ago is seen in the number of ideas and doctrines that scholars have sometimes foisted upon the book of Revelation. In some instances these doctrines and concepts are either totally absent from Revelation or have little significance in the overall message of the book. This often occurs when scholars use methods to interpret Revelation that they themselves would find unacceptable if employed in the interpretation of other parts of Scripture.

One is reminded of the Greek story of a certain man named Procrustes (Diodorus, *Hist.* 4.59.5). When strangers would pass by his house he forced them to fit exactly into one of his two beds, either by chopping their legs off if they were too tall or by stretching them out with weights if they were too short. No matter what the realities of the size of the passersby, each of them had to fit into the prescribed size of Procrustes's beds. Sometimes interpretations of the book of Revelation of John have achieved their successes on the basis of exegetical and hermeneutical techniques that resemble the technique of the Procrustean bed.

The following are some of the most obvious examples of forcing ideas onto the text of Revelation when they are not necessarily an appropriate fit. These types of problems seem to abound in the area of Christian eschatology and the study of Revelation. There are many long cherished and widely embraced doctrines that ostensibly derive from Revelation, but in fact have often achieved their status primarily by the forceful intrusion of ecclesiastical dogma into exegesis and descriptive theology.

Antichrist

The term "antichrist," the *sine qua non* for many interpretations of Revelation, is not found even a single time in the book of Revelation.[18] In theory, at least, this problem might be overcome if one posits, as Stephen Smalley does,[19] that John's and his community's situation "is reflected in the Johannine Corpus as a whole." Smalley's position facilitates a "synoptic" reading of Revelation, the epistles, and the Fourth Gospel. Thus, the problem of the absence of the term "antichrist" in Revelation would supposedly be

17. Sandys-Wunsch and Eldredge, "J. P. Gabler," 134–44.

18. Peerbolte, "Antichrist, ἀντίχριστος," 62–64.

19. Smalley, *Revelation*, 4.

solved by the fact that the term does occur in the epistles of John. Few scholars, however, embrace the approach taken by Smalley. And even if one were to adopt Smalley's views, there are still major problems that it does not solve.

As a study of a concordance reveals even though the term "antichrist" is indeed found in the epistles of John, and only in the epistles of John, (1 John 2:18–22, 4:3; 2 John 1:7), its significance there has little resemblance with the themes and issues usually associated with the figure of the "antichrist" in later Christian eschatological views. There is, for example, no concern in the epistles of John with issues such as the Jews and Israel, Zion, one-world government, unified Europe, the Rapture, the number 666, Armageddon, or even the political oppression of believers.

> "Children, it is the last hour! As you have heard that **antichrist** (*antichristos,* ἀντίχριστος) is coming, so now many **antichrists** (*antichristoi,* ἀντίχριστοι) have come. From this we know that it is the last hour" (1 John 2:18).
>
> "Who is the liar but the one who denies that Jesus is the Christ? This is the **antichrist** (*antichristos,* ἀντίχριστος), the one who denies the Father and the Son" (1 John 2:22).
>
> "And every spirit that does not confess Jesus is not from God. And this is the spirit of the **antichrist** (*antichristos,* ἀντίχριστος), of which you have heard that it is coming; and now it is already in the world" (1 John 4:3).
>
> "Many deceivers have gone out into the world, those who do not confess that Jesus Christ has come in the flesh; any such person is the deceiver and the **antichrist** (*antichristos,* ἀντίχριστος)" (2 John 7)!

Figure 3

Rather, these rare occurrences of the term "antichrist" in the New Testament explicitly teach that there is not just one "antichrist," but in fact many "antichrists" and that they had already arrived in John's churches in the late first century AD (*nun antichristoi polloi gegonasin,* νῦν ἀντίχριστοι πολλοὶ γεγόνασιν). John's "antichrists" did not have to wait for the creation of the modern state of Israel in order to appear. Moreover, since there were many "antichrists" (*antichristoi,* ἀντίχριστοι) in the epistles of John, one is left to wonder what happened to all the rest of the "antichrists," since later doctrinal embellishments of John's "antichrist" have tended to focus on only one "antichrist" in Revelation.

Based upon the clear information from the Johannine Epistles, the singular identifying characteristic of the "antichrists" was the heretical doctrine of docetism, a doctrine that denied the incarnation of Jesus (1 John 2:18, 22; 4:3; 2 John 1:7), his coming in the flesh (*hoi mē homologountes Iēsoun Christon erchomenon en sarki,* οἱ μὴ ὁμολογοῦντες Ἰησοῦν Χριστὸν ἐρχόμενον ἐν σαρκί).[20] One's search for a docetist among the letters to the seven churches of Roman Asia or elsewhere in Revelation ends in vain. There seems to be no shred of evidence of docetism either among the heresies of the seven letters of Revelation or in the robust imagery of Revelation.

In light of these facts, one quite naturally wonders how it came about that so many later interpreters in Christian history have embraced the idea of the "antichrist" in the Revelation of John when John himself never mentioned one.[21] Irenaeus is usually acknowledged as the first Christian author to have insinuated the term "antichrist" into John's prophecies.[22] We can most certainly be sure that the prophet John himself, unlike most of his later interpreters, had no awareness of or need for such a term in his own theology. The historical evidence, or lack of evidence, rather, for this term in Revelation is well summarized by C. Clifton Black: "It is remarkable to learn from the elder that antichrist has come—more than one, in fact. Thus described, this figure is unprecedented in the apocalyptic literature of 1 John's day, surprisingly absent from the Revelation to John, and rare in early Christian writings."[23]

Millennial Reign of Christ

In addition to the misnomer of the antichrist, there is an equally profound misunderstanding in the matter of the millennial reign of Christ. The term "millennium" is mentioned only six times in the entire New Testament, and all of these can be found in one six-verse section of Revelation (20:2–7).[24] In the first place, there is simply no exegetical or doctrinal justification for elevating the significance of these six verses to the status they have achieved. Only by using some doctrinal alchemy has it been possible to turn this issue into something seemingly far more valuable than anything imagined by John and his first audience.

---

20. Strecker, *Johannine Letters,* 69–76; Wright, "Docetism," 306–9.

21. From a futurist's perspective see Mounce, *Revelation,* 220; Osborne, *Revelation,* 521–2. From another perspective see Charles, *Revelation,* 332–33.

22. Peerbolte, "Antichrist, ἀντίχριστος," 62.

23. Black, "Letters of John," 403.

24. For discussion of millennialism see Lerner, "Millennialism," 326–60; Dodd, "Millennium," 738–41.

As surprising as it might seem in light of centuries of mistaken emphasis, a careful examination of these six specific verses reveals that there is in fact no explicit reference to a temporary millennial enthronement of Christ in Revelation (20:4, 6). Furthermore, if this traditional view were true, then this millennial interregnum of Christ would stand in clear contradiction to the teachings of the rest of the New Testament regarding Christ's cosmic enthronement.

According to John and the rest of the New Testament (e.g., Acts 2:22–36; Eph 1:18–22; 4:7–10; Phil 2:5–11), Christ was enthroned once, and only once (Rev 12:4b–5): "Then the dragon stood before the woman who was about to bear a child, so that he might devour her child as soon as it was born. And she gave birth to a son, a male child, who is to rule all the nations with a rod of iron. But her child was snatched away and taken to God and to his throne." This enthronement took place following God's redemptive work in conjunction with Christ's death, burial, resurrection, and ascension. This is a necessary part of the New Testament's use of the Royal Davidic Psalm where Christ is told to sit at the right hand of God (Ps 110:1).

For Paul, Peter, and the author of Hebrews, the enemies of God, those inimical beings of the universe, remain subdued only because Christ is on the throne. For John and those believers whom he consoled, the enthronement of the Messiah had already taken place (3:21). The enthronement of the Messiah did not lie in some future time, either near or distant.

If Christ's reign is not delimited by a millennium, then to what does the phrase "a thousand years" refer? If one consults the Greek text of Rev 20:4, it becomes clearer that John does not refer to a millennial "reign of Christ," but rather to a millennial "reign of saints." John writes that "They came to life and [they] reigned a thousand years with Christ." The words of the Greek text reveal that the grammatical subject of "reigned a thousand years" is always plural. If John were describing the millennial reign of Christ [a singular subject], then a singular verb would be the most natural construction. John, however, employs a plural verb to go with a plural subject. This plural points to the fact that the "millennial reign" is of saints, particularly their co-reign with Christ's eternal reign.

While the Greek phrase for one thousand years, *chilia etē* (χίλια ἔτη), occurs six times in Rev 20:1–7 (20:2, 3, 4, 5, 6, 7), the Greek verb for reign, *basileuō* (βασιλεύω), occurs only twice (20:4, 6). In both instances it reads "they reigned with Christ/him for one thousand years," with no contextual evidence for the later idea that it was the Messiah who reigned for one thousand years. When these verses of Rev 20 remain uncontaminated by anachronistic views, begun in the patristic era, then John's view in Rev 20 is completely compatible with the remainder of the New Testament in its proclamation of the once-for-all enthronement of the Christ at the behest of the Father, "Sit at my right hand."

> "The LORD says to my lord, 'Sit at my right hand until I make your enemies your footstool'" (Ps 110:1).
>
> "[Jesus] said to them, 'How is it then that David by the Spirit calls him Lord, saying, "The Lord said to my Lord, Sit at my right hand, until I put your enemies under your feet"?'" (Matt 22:43-4; cf., Mark 12:36; Luke 20:42).
>
> "You have said so. But I tell you, from now on you will see the Son of Man seated at the right hand of Power" (Matt 26:64a; cf., Mark 14:62; Luke 22:69).
>
> "For David did not ascend into the heavens, but he himself says, 'The Lord said to my Lord, "Sit at my right hand"'" (Acts 2:34; cf., 5:31; 7:55).
>
> "Who is to condemn? It is Christ Jesus, who died, yes, who was raised, who is at the right hand of God" (Rom 8:34a; cf., Eph 1:20; Col 3:1).
>
> "But to which of the angels has he ever said, 'Sit at my right hand'" (Heb 1:13; cf., 1:3; 8:1; 10:12; 12:2).
>
> "Who has gone into heaven and is at the right hand of God, with angels, authorities, and powers made subject to him" (1 Pet 3:22).

Figure 4

In light of the above evidence, there seems to be no justification for the desire to locate this scene of a millennial co-enthronement with Christ in an earthly Jerusalem. Views differ among scholars regarding who participates in this millennial co-enthronement. For many interpreters the reading, "They had not worshiped the beast or its image and had not received its mark on their foreheads or their hands" (20:4) points decisively to all faithful Christians, those who followed the Lamb and were among the overcomers. Other commentators note the emphasis upon the wording "souls of those who had been beheaded" (20:4) and are led to conclude that only those who experienced martyrdom were co-enthroned for a millennium with Christ.[25]

25. For a discussion concerning the identity of those enthroned see Osborne, *Revelation*, 704–5; Aune, *Revelation 17–22*, 1084–90; Beale, *Revelation*, 996–97.

Rapture

Those interpreters whose eschatology requires a "Secret Rapture" are at a disadvantage in comparison with those interpreters whose mistake is to believe that the "antichrist" is in the book of Revelation. At least those who insinuate the antichrist figure into Revelation can find support in the patristic era. The "Secret Rapture" and its attendant system of Premillennial Dispensationalism can trace it beliefs back no farther than the early nineteenth century, concretely to the trans-oceanic preaching ministry of John Nelson Darby.[26] That explains why there is such a deafening silence in Revelation when it comes to the concept of the "Secret Rapture."[27] Nobody in the scenes and narratives of Revelation is "Left Behind." To be sure, the prophet himself was "in the Spirit" and his personal transport between heaven and earth, like that of his prophetic forefathers (e.g., Ezek 2:2; 3:12, 14, 24; 8:3; 11:1, 24; 37:1; 43:5), was associated with his reception of divine revelation. There is no support in Revelation, however, for the notion that John's visit to heaven (Rev 4) was intended to be a model for the church being secretly raptured, while the others are "left behind."[28]

One must question whether the "secret rapture" is even part of any direct eschatological teaching of the New Testament. The Apostle Paul is certainly aware of a public rapture, which will occur at the end of time when the Messiah returns (1 Thess 4:13–18). This rapture, it seems, will not create stranded, perplexed, and confused unbelievers, nor chariots running amuck without drivers in the streets and alleys of ancient Rome or Ephesus.

The Pauline rapture includes the audible sound of the trumpet of God and the coming to life of deceased believers, all of whom "will be caught up together . . . to meet the Lord in the air." For the Apostle Paul, and he is the single source for any New Testament doctrine of the rapture,[29] there is only a single rapture. There is one "Day of the Lord" at which time God's wrath is revealed (1 Thess 5:1–11) and when everyone, both friend

26. Boyer, "Growth," 152.

27. The wording for "left behind" was adapted from Matt 24:40–41, but the scenes there fit very easily into Paul's view of the rapture as depicted in 1 Thess 4:13–18, which is clearly not furtive.

28. Most futurist scholars rightly reject this misuse of Rev 4:1, thought it is still believed by futurist laypersons and a part of their theology of the "raptured church"; "There is little reason to posit this [Rev 4:1] as the rapture of the church," notes Osborne, but rather it is a command to John to "see the revelation of the majesty of God on his throne, not a call to the church to ascend to heaven." *Revelation*, 243.

29. Ladd, *Theology*, 609–11.

and foe, both saved and lost, must appear before God's judgment tribunal (2 Cor 5:10–11).[30] With Paul's clear references to a shout, the archangel's voice, the trumpet of God, and mighty angels with flaming fire, it is difficult to imagine this taking place in stealth mode. The belief in multiple eschatological judgments and raptures is very problematic exegetically and theologically.

To be sure, Revelation clearly contains a brief scene that is traditionally viewed as the final judgment of humankind (Rev 20:11–15). Significantly, however, this scene and the surrounding verses contain no direct reference to a rapture, not even the kind portrayed in Paul's theology. To the point, this graphic judgment scene of Rev 20 in fact "makes no mention of the return of Christ."[31]

Clearly then, the notion of the "secret rapture" needs to be removed from the paradigm and vocabulary of those who seek a theology of Revelation based on an exegetical study of John and his prophecies. What needs to be "left behind" are the apocalyptic fantasies of these millenarian perspectives. In reality these fantasies are often little more than nineteenth-century Anglo-American nationalistic and apocalyptic ideologies dressed up as exegesis.[32]

Conclusion

One cannot help but notice the continuation of end time speculation, both Christian and non-Christian, in the modern era.[33] A perusal of any of the informative books that trace the history of the interpretation of Revelation shows that the contemporary church has yet to learn many of the important lessons of church history on this issue.[34] In every instance (and there have been so many) over the past two thousand years, when someone has predicted or sensed the end was near, they have been demonstrably wrong and their prophecies were patently false. Lamentably, even though this apocalyptic plane has crashed every single time it has attempted to take off, there still seems to be no difficulty in finding passengers for promised

---

30. Garland, *2 Corinthians*, 265; Martin, *2 Corinthians*, 115.

31. Dodd, "Millennium," 741.

32. Boyer, "Growth," 141–48.

33. See, for example, contemporary films such as *Independence Day*, *Armageddon*, *Day After Tomorrow*, *Deep Impact*, and *2012*.

34. Kyle, *Last Days*.

future flights. This will continue, as long as dogma continues to masquerade as exegesis.

JOHN AND HIS PROPHECY

Although the academic arguments have been refined and the terminology has been made more exact, scholars have still not yet reached a consensus about the meaning of the terms "apocalypse" and "apocalyptic."[35] Indeed, scholars are not even united on whether these are appropriate designations for John's work.[36] The term "apocalypse" in reality is actually nothing more than an English transliteration, not translation, of the first word in the Greek text of John's Revelation (*apokalupsis*, ἀποκάλυψις). This transliteration has in fact little to do with the analysis of a genre. Regarding exegetical methodology, the transliteration of this initial word, which is a *hapax legomenon* in the book of Revelation, hardly seems to be a meaningful criterion for determining the message, the characteristics, and genre of this work.[37]

Rather than relying principally upon the terminology of apocalyptic and apocalypse, I have chosen to follow John's lead and employ the terms prophet/prophecy/prophesy since this is the explicit terminology used by John himself. The author writes that the text of his work consists of "words of prophecy," that these words are to be read and heard as prophecy among the churches (1:3), and that the churches must regard his material collectively as a "book of prophecy" (22:7, 10, 18, 19).

John's sense of his own ministry and calling is focused in the concept of prophet. This is the crucial term that he uses for himself (Rev 22:6); his ministry is one of prophesying (Rev 10:11; 19:10); and what John writes are prophecies (Rev 1:3; 22:7, 10, 18–19). While the Greek term *apostolos* (ἀπόστολος) occurs only at Rev 2:2; 18:20; 21:14, the Greek term *prophētēs* (προφήτης) is found in Rev 10:7; 11:7–18; 16:6; 18:20, 24; 22:6; 22:9. With all its cognates the term "prophet" occurs almost twenty times.

John highlights the divine authority he attributes to this prophetic book, these words of prophecy, by means of threatening brutal retribution from God for anyone who tampers with its contents (22:18–19). While there is no easy answer to the question whether a particular ancient author

---

35. Collins, "Apocalypses, Jewish," 282–88; Collins, "Apocalypses, Christian," 288–92.

36. Aune, *Westminster*, 401–2.

37. The opposite view is expressed by Aune, "Apocalypse," 169–70.

knew that he was writing Scripture, Christopher Rowland suggests that "Here for the first time is a Christian text that comes close to portraying itself as sacred scripture on a par with the writings of the old covenant."[38] Paganism encompassed notions of divine revelation, preservation of revelation as *lex sacra* (sacred law), and threats of punitive action if the sacred revelation was ignored or disobeyed. In this instance, however, John's idea stems from his Jewish heritage. As H. B. Swete noted, "The words are based on two passages in Deuteronomy, and they practically place the Apocalypse on a level with the Torah and anticipate for it a place among the Scriptures of the Church."[39]

That said, it must still be decided what is meant by prophecy in Revelation, since prophecy was a diverse phenomenon in paganism and Judaism.[40] Many individuals in the Hebrew Scriptures were called prophets,[41] and clearly the word "prophet" had varying meanings in the Judaism of John's day. There is, fortunately, internal evidence within Revelation to provide some guidance for the interpreter's assessment of John's use of this terminology. There are three important features of Revelation that serve as guideposts in helping to establish John's use of prophetic language and therefore the genre of this book: A. Old Testament heritage that most influenced the prophetic content of Revelation; B. Contours of prophetic ministry; and C. John's depiction of false prophets and anti-prophets.

A. Old Testament Heritage

It is clear that the prophet John drank at the well of Old Testament prophets, and certainly the bulk of the prophetic messages from the Jewish Scriptures dealt with contemporary situations intended to be interpreted in the light of the near historical horizon. This study adopts the hermeneutical perspective that Mark Allan Powell calls historical, meaning that the book should be viewed from "the time and place in which it was written."[42]

---

38. Rowland, "Revelation," 568.

39. Swete, *Apocalypse*, xcviii.

40. Aune, *Prophecy*; Huffmon, "Prophecy," 477–82; Schmitt, "Prophecy," 482–89; Barton, "Prophecy," 489–95; Boring, "Prophecy," 495–502.

41. Abraham (Gen 20:7), Aaron (Exod 7:1), Moses (Deut 18:15–18; 34:10), Samuel (1 Sam 3:20), Gad (1 Sam 22:5), Nathan (2 Sam 7:2), Elijah (1 Kgs 18:36), Elisha (2 Kgs 9:1), David (Acts 2:29–30), and former prophets (Zech 1:4; 7:7, 12) and canonical major and minor prophets.

42. Powell, *Introducing*, 525.

It remains to be established, however, which concepts from the diverse prophetic messages of the Hebrew Scriptures affected John the most.

For John the concept of prophet was not a designation for an "end times" ministry. There clearly is "end times" material in Revelation (e.g., Rev 20:7–15), but this appears principally toward the end of Revelation and in no way captures the focus of John's ministry. John's own concept of prophet was, rather, a comprehensive paradigm for the spiritual and historical circumstances that evoked his ministry. Specifically, John's prophetic calling comes from his malice toward the pagan vortex in which the churches of Roman Asia find themselves. These believers are the true Jews of God (Rev 2:9; 3:9), the twelve tribes of Israel (Rev 7:3–8; cf. Jas 1:1), and they must have, as did their Jewish ancestors, a prophetic voice to rescue them from the threat of assimilation to their pagan milieu.

Before turning to those most influential parts of the Jewish Scriptures, it is necessary to comment on John's general use and adaptation of Scripture. It is well known that the Jewish Scriptures had a dramatic and thoroughgoing influence on the book of Revelation.[43] Sometimes Revelation draws upon well-known Old Testament materials (e.g., plagues against Egypt), while at other times it relies upon the minutiae of Jewish Scriptures (e.g., key of David). As scholars have generally pointed out, texts from Jewish Scriptures are never explicitly quoted and unlike other parts of the New Testament Old Testament themes in Revelation are not introduced with formulae.[44]

This lack of direct quotation, however, should not belie the relationship between John and the Jewish Scriptures. John's contextual and prophetic needs truly control his adaptation of the Old Testament. In commenting on this phenomenon, Swete observed: "But the Apocalyptist's use of his Old Testament materials is artless and natural; it is the work of a memory which is so charged with Old Testament words and thoughts that they arrange themselves in his visions like the changing patterns of a kaleidoscope. . . . There is not a single instance in which the Christian prophet of the Apocalypse has contented himself with a mere compilation or combination of Old Testament ideas. . . . he does not allow his Old Testament author to carry him a step beyond the point at which the

43. The recent literature on this topic is extensive and diverse. For the nature and extent of the influence of the Old Testament on the book of Revelation see, for example, Moyise, *Old Testament*; Fekkes, *Isaiah*; Beale, *Use of Daniel*; Ruiz, *Ezekiel*.

44. Some interpreters of Revelation believe that the exception to this is Rev 2:27 and its "quoting" of Ps 2:9, according to Fekkes, *Isaiah*, 67.

guidance ceases to lend itself to the purpose of his book."[45] Even with only a glance at Revelation and the Jewish Scriptures, a reader observes how freely John adapted and contextualized the Scriptures when he employed themes, imagery, and scriptural idiom from texts such as Ezekiel, Daniel, Psalms, Zechariah, Isaiah, and Jeremiah.

With the phantasmagoric narrative of John's style, he intends the hearers to interact, automatically and at times subliminally, with the underlying power of the theology associated with the particular scriptural narratives and idiom of the Old Testament. In this regard John is far more artistic in his use of Scripture than either Jesus or Paul. Jesus and Paul often cited Scripture using introductory formulae. At times they employed argumentation and propositional reasoning to interpret Scripture, while John's style of rhetoric and hermeneutics—demanded in my judgment by his circumstances—was more picturesque, emotive, and resonant with his Scriptures. It is inappropriate that some interpreters have aborted the function of the pregnant symbolism of Revelation by suggesting that John at times employed difficult Scripture symbolism to obscure his message from outsiders, just in case this book fell into the wrong hands. John alluded to Scripture rather to draw upon the power of its imagery for application to his own circumstances, without strict or rigid conformity to only its original and literal meaning.

Much of the later confusion about the ostensibly difficult and opaque symbolism of Revelation has come about because a large percentage of post-apostolic Christianity has been characterized by an abysmal ignorance of the text, theology, and idiom of the Old Testament. Therefore, modern readers often find it difficult to understand the basic idioms that Revelation uses and that animate its words and theology. After all, the book is entitled "revelation," and later readers who do not experience the text of John as revelatory probably owe that to their own unfamiliarity with Scripture, rather than to John's supposed choice of esoteric and mysterious words and images.

What is also noteworthy in distinguishing John's use of the Hebrew Scriptures from other authors in the New Testament is that unlike Romans, Hebrews, and the Gospel of Matthew, Revelation is not significantly impacted by the Pentateuch. Moyise's work, *The Old Testament in the Book of Revelation*, observes that, "It would appear that his [John's] primary

---

45. Swete, *Apocalypse*, cliv.

interest was not the Torah but the prophetic literature, along with the worship language of the Psalms."[46]

Indeed, the modern reader will miss much of John's prophetic hermeneutic and selection of Scripture if he fails to notice that John's primary interest is focused upon prophetic literature that was engendered by anti-assimilationist messages. Those Old Testament texts that reveal a struggle with domination by pagan cultures, exile, oppression, and assimilation adumbrate the future paradigm of John's prophetic ministry. In particular, passage after passage in Revelation is guided by the argot of Old Testament anti-assimilationist theology and pastoral guidance. Even when Moses or Mosaic themes appear, e.g., bringing plagues, the themes chosen reveal no interest in Moses as giver of the Torah or founder of a new nation, but rather Moses as one who stands in opposition to an oppressive regime dominating the people of God. This is obviously similar to some of John's concern for his own congregations.

The theological outlook and anti-assimilationist spirituality that shaped John's theology and ministry came from mentors such as Moses, Elijah, Jeremiah, Ezekiel, Isaiah, and Daniel. These were the voices and ministries that forged John's prophetic consciousness and innervated his ability to be a "brother who share with you in Jesus the persecution and the kingdom and the patient endurance" (Rev 1:9). John's messages project a vibrant intertextuality with the stories of these Old Testament mentors, since all of them, in fact, labored to keep God's elect people free from the polluting sins found in the surrounding sea of paganism.[47]

These anti-assimilation heroes and the contours of their lives and ministries also explain and illumine the nature and extent of John's rhetoric of violence,[48] a rhetoric that has been very troublesome to many later believers. Long before John's time, all these spiritual mentors of Israel spoke unashamedly and frequently about the doom and violence that awaited both disobedient pagan nations[49] and also the erring elect of God who were being assimilated to paganism.[50]

---

46. Moyise, *Old Testament*, 15.

47. In general see Aune, "Intertextuality," 233–34.

48. For Talbert's summary of the antiassimilationist interpretations see Talbert, *Apocalypse*, 11.

49. Accordingly, Isaiah (13–23), Jeremiah (46–51), and Ezekiel (25–32) all contain blocks of prophecy addressed to the nations.

50. Hiers, "Day of the Lord," 82; Scmitt, "Prophecy," 483.

By reliance upon these Jewish mentors, these prophecies of John are drenched with scriptural imagery and idiom[51] in order to galvanize believers in his congregations against external threats of idolatry, immorality, hostile Roman patriotism, and even internal apostasy that advocated assimilation to the surrounding culture.

B. Contour of Prophetic Ministry

The message of Revelation clearly recognizes the "prophets" as a distinct subgroup among the larger community of believers in Roman Asia. There are, for example, references to the eschatological reward for God's "servants, the prophets and saints" (11:18) and the shedding of "the blood of saints and prophets" (16:6; 18:24). The Jews who wrote the Dead Sea Scrolls likewise connected the two concepts of "servant" and "prophet" in statements such as, "The Teacher of Righteousness, to whom God has made known all the mysteries of the words of his servants, the prophets" (1QpHab 7.4–5). There is exultation and joy at the destruction of Babylon among the "saints and apostles and prophets" (18:20) who received their general commission from heaven to prophesy "about many peoples and nations and languages and kings" (10:11). It is to the circle of prophetic servants that God reveals the message of the impending doom of the Roman Empire (22:6, 10).

The paradigmatic portrait of the prophetic ministry given in Revelation chapters 10–11 likewise displays this perspective. The vision of "eating the scroll" (10:5–11) is informed by symbols from an Old Testament prophet (Ezek 2:9–3:3) who was concerned about the problem of assimilation to paganism among God's people. Furthermore, the graphic and dynamic images stemming from the ministries of the two figures Moses and Elijah were designed to correlate with the activities and destinies of the prophets of John's own day (11:5–6).

Since John's self perception of his ministry and words are focused through the lens of anti-assimilation, one should not view the seven letters

---

51. For an example of this, note the typological use of Babylon see Aune, *Revelation 6–16*, 829–32. For example, by using the term "Babylon" to represent the regime of Rome John highlights the sin of Rome in its active participation in promoting the assimilation of the elect people of God and thereby explains Rome's impending doom; similarly, the Qumran community interpreted the term "Chaldaeans" in its pesher on Habakkuk chapter 1 (1QpHab 2.6–VI.10) and its pesher on Nahum chapter 1 (4Q169=4QpNah 1.3–6) with the term "Kittim" to refer to Rome, see Lim, "Kittim," 469–71.

as solely consolation literature or a hagiographical portrayal of a martyr church. Certainly the seven churches of Asia were experiencing afflictions and deaths (2:13; 6:9–11), but the prophetic message of John is not designed only to comfort the afflicted. John's words were also clearly written to afflict those Christians who were guilty of assimilation to idolatry, immorality, and emperor worship, either in the present or future. Without doubt the letters destined for the seven churches of Asia contain the promise of blessings to the faithful, the overcomers, but with equal clarity they contain the assurance of divine punishment and retribution for those believers who surrendered themselves to the pressures of the surrounding culture and its mores.

These types of promised punitive actions and John's repeated demand for believers in these churches "to repent or perish" hardly support popular stereotypes that Revelation was solely written in order to give comfort and assurance of final victory to believers and suffering congregations. The promises to the overcomers in the seven letters are only for those who have successfully jettisoned attitudes of tolerance, pluralism, and the seductions of Graeco-Roman culture. The congregants of the seven churches, it should be remembered, sat and listened to sporadic threats that they too might receive the fearful wrath of God (18:4–6), or that the plagues that God promised to pour out upon the disbelievers could also fall upon them (22:18). Any Anatolian believer who recently heard through one of John's prophecies that he too could be vomited from the mouth of Jesus (3:16) would hardly have left church thinking that he had just experienced a word of consolation. This is the same Jesus who threatens violent warfare equally against believer (2:16) and nonbeliever (19:15–21).

The christophany of Rev 1:12–16, to explore another example of John's mentors, is taken primarily from Daniel chapters 7 and 10. This christophany contains powerful and horrific imagery and does not portray a Jesus into whose lap one can sit and be cuddled. This probably explains the meagerness of its representation in two thousand years of Christian ecclesiastical and devotional art. In light of the explicit use of this horrific christology in the seven letters, it is hard to maintain that its sole intended function was to assure believers that they would be victorious. Even though the first recipients of Revelation were to see themselves as "strangers in this world,"[52] alienated from Roman culture, this christophany portrays a militant Christ who is coming to punish equally both the oppressors of the church and those Christians who have ears, but refuse to

52. In general see Feldmeier, *Die Christen.*

hear the message of "strangers in this world." And for those believers who fail to hear and to embrace the divine warnings against assimilation, John's prophetic mentor Daniel[53] has a "prophetic word" about the physiognomy and nature of the Son of Man with whom they must deal.

C. John's Depictions of False Prophets

Since the Graeco-Roman setting of the seven churches of Asia was the crucible of assimilation, it makes sense that the adversaries of the Lamb would also be presented in an "anti-prophetic" or "pseudo-prophetic" paradigm. In fact, those who promote assimilation and inveigle the seven churches of Roman Asia are typecast in pejorative roles from the prophetic narratives of the Jewish Scriptures. Jewish literature of the Second Temple period is replete with references to the enemies of God mentioned in the Old Testament; this rhetorical style is also evident in Pauline (2 Tim 3:8) and other New Testament literature (Jude 11; 2 Pet 2:1, 15). These references were designed to highlight similarities between the enemies of faithfulness in ancient days and the enemies of faithfulness in the contemporary period. Interestingly there is a small document from the Dead Sea Scrolls that scholars have entitled "List of False Prophets." The document reads: "The false prophets who arose in Israel: Balaam son of Beor, the old man from Bethel, Zedekiah son of Kenaanah, Ahab son of Kolaiah, Zedekiah son of Maaseiah, Shemaiah the Nehelamite, Hananiah son of Azzur, the prophet from Gibeon" (4Q339).[54]

Accordingly, the apostate Christian woman at the church in Thyatira (Rev 2:18–29) is named Jezebel precisely because her namesake was an aggressive advocate of idolatry and immorality (1 Kgs 18–21). Both the historical woman Jezebel and her counter type at Thyatira were opponents of God's true prophet. Jezebel's sin was not only her own sin, but even more her leadership in drawing others into idolatry and immorality.

In a way similar to Jezebel, the association of the Balaam figure with heresy in the congregation at Pergamum (Rev 2:12–17) is built upon Balaam's anti-prophetic role in leading Israel into the polluting sins of idolatry and immorality (Num 25:1–5; 31:16).

---

53. Some Jews of the Second Temple period regarded Daniel as a prophet, "[It"it is [. . . a]s written in the book of Daniel, the prophet," 4Q174 (=4QFlorilegium) frag. 1, 2.3.

54. =4QList of False Prophets Aramaic.

Moreover, John's use of the phrase "the false prophet" to designate the second beast of Revelation 13 aligns this false prophet with John's anti-assimilation theology. This is clear since the activities of this beast were to make "the earth and its inhabitants worship the first beast" (13:12). By using such wording John is intentionally and explicitly pointing to the second beast that demands and coerces the assimilation of God's people. Concretely, the pagan cultic officials and civic magistrates who promoted the idolatry of the Emperor Cult and the persecution of dissident believers were transformed into a pseudo-prophetic role of the second beast. This transformation is clearly seen in the fact that the second beast, the beast from the earth (Rev 13:11–18), is later typecast as the false prophet (Rev 16:13; 19:20; 20:10). He will later be thrown into the lake of fire, to remain there forever. John's pastoral perspective coincided with that of the men and women of covenant loyalty mentioned in Jewish Scripture, all of whom believed that anyone who promoted spiritual adultery and tried to snare the elect of God deserved expectoration (Lev 18:27–29).

HISTORICAL SETTING AND HISTORICAL SOURCES

Just like Paul's and Peter's letters, John's prophetic revelation from God is addressed to congregations composed of believers who are spending the days and years of their lives in a specific region of the Roman world. These congregations stand at a specific point in the timeline of both Roman history and church history, and they are known to modern readers solely because of a specific cluster of problems and issues they faced that needed to be addressed. Although New Testament scholarship has typically shown a commitment to interpreting epistolary writings of the New Testament with a focus on the occasion of the epistles and a stated respect for authorial intention, such convictions have often been muted when Revelation is studied.

Notwithstanding this ambivalence toward the setting and matrix of Revelation, its occasion arises from specific pastoral issues and these stem from the interaction between congregations of Roman Asia and their surrounding Graeco-Roman culture. This contextual perspective in interpreting Revelation was well articulated almost one hundred years ago by Isbon T. Beckwith: "Like the other books of the New Testament the Apocalypse was written with the practical purpose of meeting a need of the particular readers addressed, in their existing condition and in the circumstances of their own time or of the time supposedly about to come. What is said of the other books is especially applicable to the Apocalypse; it is a 'Tract for the Times.'"[55]

This commitment to understanding the historical context of John and the occasional nature of Revelation places this present commentary purposefully in an interpretive paradigm that is historical. The term "historical" is used in the sense that John intended all the revelation given in this book to have a intelligibility to his first audience. That is, John's words made sense in their historical setting. There were parts of the narrative that needed explaining (e.g., 13:18; 17:9), but it was not because the words and concepts themselves were unintelligible. Moreover, this paradigm understands that the prophecies in Revelation were intended by John to be "occasional" in the broad context of congregational issues among the people of God. In this regard John's prophecies are very similar to those of his prophetic ancestors in the Jewish Scriptures whose prophecies were occasional to the setting and needs of their own generations. That is, they spoke to the near future, with an infrequent eye to the more remote future. Since virtually all other prophetic books of Scripture are historical, why should Revelation be the exception?

There is sometimes the accusation that paradigms similar to this historical approach are guilty of making Revelation irrelevant, particularly to the contemporary church. The assumption is that John's words have no message or relevance today unless they are a tract for the remote future as the Futurist paradigm advocates. This is an ill-founded accusation unless one believes that other prophetic books of Scripture such as Amos, Micah, Nahum, Habakkuk, Jeremiah, etc., are essentially irrelevant for the modern church. Indeed, the relevance of prophetic books lies in their specific connection with their own historical setting and not in their predictions about remote history and the end of humankind. It manifests an incorrect treatment of prophetic writings every time Christian interpreters put on their futuristic glasses and rob the prophetic books in the Jewish Scriptures of their historical relevance, meaning, and significance to those very people of God to whom they were written.

In order to reconstruct the context and occasion of Revelation, the modern reader must also enter the typically misrepresented world of the Graeco-Roman setting of Revelation. Too often students of the prophecies of John have little knowledge of this Graeco-Roman setting.[56] And the

---

55. Beckwith, *Apocalypse*, 208.
56. Lähnemann, "Die sieben Sendschreiben," 516–39.

knowledge they do have rarely goes beyond what has been preserved in the literature of the ancient Christian authors or in the generalizing and limited perspectives of some modern popular works on the world of the New Testament.

The abundant resources from the literature and the material culture of the Graeco-Roman world, especially pertaining to western Asia Minor, must come into play for the modern interpreter to properly and more fully understand the urban setting of those Christians who heard John's words. These same ancient resources will also open a window into the world of the emotions, beliefs, and prejudices of those who counted themselves as detractors and foes of the Christian gospel as well as those who chose to remain committed to the Christian faith.

Over forty years ago professor Robert Grant wrote harsh words for New Testament scholars who operated in ignorance of the important historical and archaeological resources for understanding the world of the early believers. He suggested that scholars desiring to advance New Testament scholarship needed to invest more time and energy in investigating the "concrete actuality of the ancient historians, of papyri, inscriptions, coins, and other archaeological remains,"[57] rather than imagining that they were advancing scholarship by merely reading each others' publications.

These harsh words still have meaning for the study of the book of Revelation. Thoughtful interpreters need to remain conversant with at least rudimentary literary and archaeological resources and methods that pertain to the setting of the seven cities of Revelation.[58] The increase in the number of relevant publications in the past generation mirrors the tremendous advances that have been made by the efforts of archaeologists focused upon Graeco-Roman remains in Asia Minor.

Nevertheless, many commentators and interpreters of Revelation still remain unaware or unimpressed and therefore uninfluenced by these changes.[59] An example of the neglect of archaeological data is Craig S.

---

57. Grant, "American New Testament," 48.

58. Friesen, "Revelation," 291–314 makes clear the problems in relying too heavily upon works by Ramsay or Hemer due either to their being outdated or to methodological problems.

59. Indices for noncanonical material within several commentaries show only the use of Dead Sea Scrolls materials from all of the myriad possible archaeological resources: Osborne, *Revelation,* 864–69; Prigent, *Apocalypse,* 698–711; Caird, *Revelation,* 314–16; while others contain no archaeological material: Thomas, *Revelation 8–22,* 665–66; Aune is a welcome exception to this trend (Aune, *Revelation 17–22,* 1352–54); Witherington reflects minimal usage of these sources (Witherington, *Revelation,* 296–300).

Keener, *The NIV Application Commentary*. The term "application" should not lead anyone to suppose that Keener is remiss to Graeco-Roman literary backgrounds. Keener's index entitled "Other Ancient Sources" includes approximately sixty-four columns of ancient citations.[60] Most of the sources are understandably Graeco-Roman literary and noncanonical Jewish materials. However, from the sixty-four columns, combined references to remains of material culture, (e.g., pagan papyri, epigraphy, and numismatics) represent no more than one column. This contrast, which is indicative of most commentaries, highlights the frequent academic neglect of the artifacts of Graeco-Roman material culture. Even the promising title *Religionsgeschichtliches Textbuch zum Neuen Testament* (*History of Religions Textbook for the New Testament*) by K. Berger and C. Colpe[61] employs only a few inscriptions and papyri in its nine page treatment of Revelation 1–3. The contemporary *Wettstein*, entitled *Neuer Wettstein: Texte zum Neuen Testament aus Griechentum und Hellenismus* (*The New Wettstein: Texts for the New Testament from Greek and Hellenistic Materials*) disappoints because there is nothing relevant, not to mention "new," in its treatment of Revelation from the perspective of Graeco-Roman archaeological remains.[62] Colin Hemer's work entitled *The Letters to the Seven Churches of Asia in their Local Setting* reflects a detailed familiarity with Graeco-Roman epigraphy, numismatic, and archaeological materials, but is very neglectful in its use of material from the Dead Sea Scrolls.

BACKGROUND STUDIES AND REVELATION

While it is crucial for a proper understanding of Revelation to appreciate the broad historical and cultural setting of these seven letters, sometimes too much has been claimed by scholars in their efforts to read these seven letters too narrowly in light of specific events in the history of these individual seven Asian cities.[63] In these instances interpreters rely too heavily

---

60. Keener, *Application Commentary*, 546–61. Osborne, *Revelation*, wrote an almost 800 page commentary, with indexes including Old Testament, New Testament, Old Testament Apocrypha, Old Testament Pseudepigrapha, New Testament Apocrypha, Rabbinic Writings, Qumran, Josephus, Philo, Classical Writers and Church Fathers; there is no index for Graeco-Roman archaeological materials.

61. Berger and Colpe, *Religionsgeschichtliches*, expanded in the English translation, Boring et al., *Hellenistic Commentary*, 548–86.

62. Strecker, *Neuer Wettstein*.

63. Friesen, "Revelation," 291–314.

upon local color and city history (sometimes centuries old) to provide a cipher for interpreting words and images from each individual letter. This overlooks, among other things, the fact that the denizens of each city are expected by John to fully understand the messages to the other six cities ("Let him hear what the Spirit says to the church*es*") even though they do not live in those other six cities. An intimate knowledge of centuries-old urban stories and legends cannot be a prerequisite for understanding the seven letters. As a result, it might be helpful to demonstrate the importance of proper interaction with Graeco-Roman sources so that interpreters and modern students can evaluate for themselves its importance and the price paid for ignoring it.

For purposes of illustration I want to focus on the literary phenomenon of globalism in Revelation. By globalism I mean the book's repeated reference to global occurrences. The following comment by Grant Osborne is typical of those interpreters who are aware of the globalism in Revelation: "The atmosphere of Revelation is global. . . . Throughout the book the action effects 'every tribe, people, language, and nation' (5:9; 7:9; 10:11; 13:7; 17:15) and 'all the inhabitants of the earth' (3:10; 6:10; 8:13; 11:10; 13:8, 14; 17:8)."[64] Writing from another perspective, one of the most influential modern interpreters of Revelation (Richard Bauckham) concurred that, "Revelation is full of universalistic language, referring to the whole world and its inhabitants."[65] Accordingly, it has seemed completely self-evident to many interpreters, especially futurists, that the various Johannine terms and phrases for "globalism" in Revelation should be taken as literal globalism. In fact, they argue that literal globalism is the only reasonable paradigm for the proper interpretation of Revelation.[66]

When one takes a step back, however, and explores the elements and use of globalism and its language in the broader historical and social world of Revelation, alternative understandings begin to emerge. When the light of ancient resources, e.g., coins, papyri, literature, inscriptions, and statuary remains, shines with its bright and distinctive light on this

---

64. Osborne, "Response," 239.

65. Bauckham, *Climax*, 239.

66. For example, see Thomas, *Revelation 8–22*, index for "World domination," "World population," and "Worldwide scope," 594–5; also Thomas writes, "The futurist approach to the book is the only one that grants sufficient recognition to the prophetic style of the book . . . The *literal interpretation* of Revelation is the one generally associated with the premillennial return of Christ and a view of inspiration that understands God to be the real author of every book of the Bible." Thomas, *Revelation 1–7*, 32, emphasis added.

topic, fresh and important alternatives become visible. Both visual and lexical evidence, long known outside the sphere of New Testament studies, creates new possibilities for understanding the kind of globalism intended by John and known to the members of those seven churches of Asia.

BIBLICAL EVIDENCE

It is best to begin with a review of biblical data, looking first at lexical features and then at rhetorical features.

Lexical Evidence

The seemingly simple Greek term often translated "earth" is *gē* (γῆ). When this Greek term is translated in a perfunctory way as "earth," then the globalism of a particular text is assumed rather than demonstrated. Although in a given text the term *gē* might be rendered "earth," in reality the translation "land" or "region" or "known world" might be more accurate. The Greek Old Testament usage of the term *gē* for "earth" in the phrase "kings of the earth" demonstrates this point, "All the kings of the earth (γῆ) would seek out the face of Solomon" (2 Chr 9:23). Or when the prophet Ezekiel (27:33) addresses the city of Tyre with the following words, he obviously has a very limited "globalism" in mind, "You satisfied nations from your abundance and from your sundries; you enriched all kings of the earth (γῆ)."

Many of the observations made about the limited globalism of the term "*gē*" could be made as easily about the term *oikoumenē* (οἰκουμένη), a term often rendered "world." In Acts 17:6 this term is used when Paul and his co-workers at Thessalonica are accused of fomenting trouble in other locations before they arrived at Thessalonica. The NRSV translates *oikoumenē* (οἰκουμένη) "turning the world upside down," while the NASB prefers "have upset the world," and the NIV employs the phrase "have caused trouble all over the world." The literal globalism implied in these three English translations is historically untenable. A "known world" globalism also seems highly improbable since it would suggest that Paul's prior trouble making exceeded the limitations of the Mediterranean Basin and stretched into places like India, China, Scotland, Ethiopia, Germany, etc. Even a "Roman Empire" globalism is unacceptable since Paul has surely not yet caused problems in Spain (cf. Rom 15:24–28).[67]

Rhetorical Evidence

In addition to the lexical issues above, biblical texts also employ the rhetorical device of hyperbole, and manifestations of globalism often reflect this hyperbole. One element in this hyperbole is the use of the word "all" (πᾶς). An example of this includes (cf. LXX Ps 117:10–11): "This is what Cyrus, king of the Persians says: The Lord, the god of the sky, has given me *all the kingdoms of the earth* (πάσας τὰς βασιλείας τῆς γῆς), and it is he who has commanded me to build him a house in Ierousalem, which is in Judea. Who of you is from all his people? His god shall be with him, and let him go up" (LXX 2 Chr 36:23; cf. Ezra 1:2).

As the previous evidence suggests, the language of globalism should not always be understood literally. There was also a fictive globalism and it was part of the conceptual *lingua franca* of authors of the biblical text. These authors would be shocked to learn of the hyper-literalistic globalism preferred or demanded by some interpreters of Revelation.

EVIDENCE OF THE EARLY ROMAN EMPIRE

Beyond the necessary overview of terminology of globalism in Scripture, it is crucial to analyze the use and function of "global" language in the contemporary resources of the late Roman Republic and Early Roman Empire. Those followers of the Lamb who walked the streets of Pergamum, Ephesus, and Smyrna and other urban centers saw Graeco-Roman statues, handled and used the prevalent coinage, knew of imperial inscriptions, and saw the iconography of monuments similar to these that were found on temples and in agoras. Although it may come as a surprise, there was a multifaceted globalism clearly revealed in many of these ancient urban resources.

An unknown fact to many modern readers, at least American readers, is that there was not a "flat earth" belief in the time of John and the early church, and there had not been one for generations. At least since the

---

67. A similar point can be made of English translations of *oikoumenē*, οἰκουμένη found in Acts 24:5 as well as in the text that mentions the Claudian famine (Acts 11:28).

Figure 5

third century BC, the globalism of the Graeco-Roman world was based on the fact that the earth was spherical in shape. Moreover, the correct size of the circumference of the earth had been calculated. A theory of lines of latitude and longitude was in place generations before the advent of the Christian faith.[68] In fact, artwork preceding and contemporary with John depicted the earth as a sphere,[69] and this iconography is attested throughout the Graeco-Roman world.

In order to delineate and substantiate the pervasiveness of fic-

Figure 6

tive globalism, we will first sketch the Roman self awareness of the spatial limitations of their empire and hegemony and then contrast that with concurrent statements and propaganda, both verbal and visual, that declared their unfettered mastery of the entire planet. It is this reality of the simultaneous use of the language of planetary domination and the use of

68. Tosi, "Eratosthenes," 18.

69. Zimmermann, "Cartography," 1142–44.

the language of territorial limitations that demonstrates fictive globalism. It happened with great frequency among the ancients that they would reason, plan, trade, make treaties, and write history with words of territorial limitations, but would fantasize, worship, write prophecy and poetry, and express honor with words of unfettered globalism.

Rome's sense of its own geographical and territorial limitedness was seen in several ways. First of all, Rome understood that there were regions

Figure 7

Figure 8

and provinces clearly in their control and then there were border regions that implicitly demonstrated the limitations of Roman control. Various series of *CAPTA* coins issued by the Romans during the early Empire and circulated throughout the Roman world sketched some of the general outline of the "captured" areas that constituted the boundaries of the Empire. These help in understanding the Roman view of their empire and the larger world.

Figure 9

Figure 10

Roman armies sometimes went beyond these borders, but their control of these regions beyond the *CAPTA* areas was tenuous. Four of these border areas are attested by numismatic evidence and represent Armenia, Egypt, Judaea, and Germany.[70] At times these border areas were even personified in statues.[71]

Figure 11   Figure 12

Early in his reign the Emperor Domitian sent the Twelfth Legion (*Legio XII Fulminata*) eastward to what is now the modern Republic of Azerbaijan, immediately west of the Caspian Sea.[72] At that location a certain Roman soldier, Lucius Julius Maximus, dedicated an inscription to "Imperator Domitian Caesar Augustus Germanicus." Lucius Julius Maximus knew very well that even though Domitian had sent this legion to northeastern extremities even beyond the *CAPTA* area of Armenia, there were still other peoples and kingdoms both north and east of his own location that were neither part of the Roman Empire nor even under the faintest influence of Rome. Thus this inscription attests to a mere foray into barbarian lands that were far, far beyond any serious Roman influence.

Similar circumstances existed to the south of the Roman Empire. The empire's control of the southern lower Nile between the first and second cataracts was firm. Permanent Augustan temples in Nubia seem to

Figure 13

70. For more information on *CAPTA* coins see primary source bibliography.

71. Beyond numismatic epigraphy and iconography, there are the visually effective monumental statues of "conquered nations" erected in early Roman Aphrodisias, an important city of Roman Asia not far removed from the cities addressed by John. Claudius's conquest of the remote region of Britain, for example, is clearly depicted as the vanquishing of a woman, as is also Nero's defeat of Armenia. Smith, "Imperial Reliefs," 115–17 [Plates XIV–XV]; Friesen, *Imperial Cults*, 77–95.

72. McCrumb and Woodhead, *Select Documents*, no. 369; also discussed in Keppie, *Understanding*, 89.

demonstrate this. However, Roman presence to the third and fourth cataracts was temporary, consisting of merely short lived forays that highlighted the limitations of their power in that direction.

Figure 14

These above mentioned numismatic, epigraphical, and monumental resources are not random testimony, but reinforce a Roman awareness of its own limitations

Figure 15

Figure 16

Figure 17

of hegemony and expansion. More than one Roman Emperor acknowledged that the size of the Empire had stretched Rome and her resources to her limit and that Rome simply could not administer any further regions. Hadrian was quick to surrender territory, especially the region of Mesopotamia and Armenia that Trajan had won.[73]

In addition, Rome was also aware of her commercial limitations. She did not produce all the products her people desired. Modern knowledge of this situation is gained from emporia, travelers, and traders of the early Roman Empire. One such emporium was Berenike, vibrant in the first century AD, and located on the eastern coast of Africa. The early Roman period at this site demonstrates significant commercial contact with the Persian Gulf, India, and Sri Lanka.[74] The first century AD Greek language navigation guide *Periplus Maris Erythraei*, indisputably demonstrates that the Roman Empire was not regarded as coterminous with the civilized world, much less with the entire planet.

Periplus reveals not only the vitality of trade and commerce between Rome and parts of sub-Saharan Africa as far south as Tanzania,[75] but it also documents the trade between Rome and the eastern coast of India near the Ganges River.[76] In addition, the ending chapters (64–66) state: "Beyond this country, now under the very north . . . lies a very great inland city called Thina, from which raw silk and silk yarn . . . and Chinese cloth . . . are brought overland. . . . Every year there comes to the boundary of Thina, a certain tribe, stunted of body and with very broad faces and completely flat noses. . . . The lands beyond these places, on account of excessive winters, hard frosts, and inaccessible country, are unexplored."[77]

---

73. According to Tacitus, in one of Augustus's last documents he judged that the Roman Empire should be confined to its present borders (*Ann.* 1.11.7).

74. Sidebotham and Wendrich, "Berenike," 23–50; the late Hellenistic–Early Roman document Pseudo-Aristotle, *On the Cosmos*," likewise mentions Sri Lanka (=Ceylon), 393B.

75. Chami, "Roman Beads," 237–241; also Chami, "Graeco-Roman," 205–15.

76. Casson, *Periplus Maris*; see also Begley and De Puma, *Rome and India*; the famous POxy no. 1380.226 credits Isis with providing the waters of the Ganges River in India.

77. Huntingford, *Periplus*, 56–7.

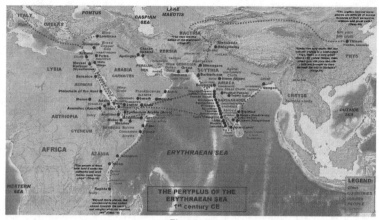

Figure 18

One should conclude, then, that notwithstanding the staggering size of the Roman Empire, even the Romans knew that the planet was a lot larger than the section they themselves dominated. Every time foreign goods reached the Mediterranean Basin from these eastern and sub-Saharan regions, their arrival constantly reinforced the awareness of Rome's spatial limitations.

The point of this overview is to demonstrate the Roman awareness of its own geopolitical and commercial limitation so that this can be set in stark relief with the following and oft repeated Roman assertions that Rome in fact held sway *over the entire planet*. If it can be shown that Rome proclaimed planetary domination, yet did not "really" mean it, then a new

Figure 19

Figure 20

possibility exists even beyond the lexical and rhetorical information of the LXX and the Greek New Testament for understanding the globalism of Revelation.

LATIN LITERATURE

Clear examples of the fictive use of global terminology to equate the "Roman Empire" with the total "inhabited world" and "planet earth" are preserved in Vergil's *Aeneid*. There Jupiter promises that he has put no limitations in regard to either time or space on Roman expansion and hegemony. Jupiter had given the Romans Imperium without limit.[78] In the *Res Gestae Divi Augusti*,[79] an autobiographical record of the accomplishments of Augustus preserved on the walls of imperial temples, the aging Emperor begins with a reference to his subjugation of the earth (*orbem terrarum*) and later mentions his military conquests throughout all the world (*toto in orbe terrarum*).[80]

Fictive language and imagery was repeatedly and consistently used to describe the "global atmosphere" and realities of the Roman Empire,

78. Vergil, *Aen.* 1.278–79 *His ego nec metas rerum nec tempora pono;imperium sine fine dedi.*

79. For summary see Purcell, "Res Gestae," 1309.

80. *Res Gestae.* In the bilingual text, the first example is found only in the Latin introduction. The second example is preserved in chapter 3 of the Latin and Greek texts. Similar evidence is available in Vergil, *Aen.* 3.95–99; 6.790–801.

Figure 21

even though the size of the Roman Empire and the earth were never imagined in reality to be the same, or even closely similar.

EPIGRAPHY

Just a few years after the beginnings of Christianity, the city of Assos, (cf. Acts 20:13–14) voted on the following resolution: "The rule of Gaius Caesar Germanicus Augustus, hoped and prayed for by all men (*pasin anthrōpois*, πᾶσιν ἀνθρώποις) has been proclaimed (*katēngeltai*, κατήγγελται) and the world (*ho kosmos*, ὁ κόσμος) has found unbounded joy and every city (*pasa polis*, πᾶσα πόλις) and every people (*pan ethnos*, πᾶν ἔθνος) has been eager for the sight of the god (*tou theou*, τοῦ θεοῦ) since the happiest age for mankind has now begun."[81] Later in the first century Augustus Imperator Galba, even though Emperor for barely seven months (June 68–Jan. 69), was described as bringing "light to us for the salvation of the whole human race" (*para tou epilampsantos hēmein epi sōtēria tou pantos anthrōpōn genous*, παρὰ τοῦ ἐπιλάμψαντος ἡμεῖν ἐπὶ σωτηρίᾳ τοῦ πάντος ἀνθρώπων γένους)

Figure 22

81. Merkelbach, *Inschriften von Assos*, no. 26, 51–59 (=*SIG* 797.5–9).

and with providing "the security of the inhabited world" (*tēn tēs oikoumenēs asphaleian*, τὴν τῆς οἰκουμένης ἀσφάλειαν).[82]

ICONOGRAPHY

Lest one imagine that all of these above examples were never intended by the Romans to depict the entire planet, one need only to investigate the numismatic, gem, and statuary evidence that also documents this fictive use of global imagery and propaganda.[83] Beginning already in the Roman Republic the visual depiction of the globe served to announce Rome's self-understanding of its fictive global mastery.[84] This continued in Augustan iconography and in the propaganda of later emperors and empresses.[85] It was an explicit visual expression of the conviction that the emperor was ruler "of land and sea."[86] This visual globalism was also frequently affirmed in the iconography on imperial gems.[87]

A different medium manifesting a splendid example of this fictive iconography is found in the statuary remains of the "Fountain of Trajan" located in Ephesus, with a globe at the feet of the colossal statue of the Emperor Trajan.[88] At other times artistic idiom put the globe of the world in the palm of the emperor's hand rather than at his feet,

Figure 23

Figure 24

Figure 25

82. Lewis and Reinhold, *Roman Civilization*, 2:295–96 (cf., Braund, *Augustus to Nero*, no. 600, 222).

83. Schlachter, *Globus*, 64–103, Plates 1–4.

84. Oster, "Numismatic," 204–8; also Zimmermann, "Cartography," 1144.

85. See "American Numismatic" in Primary Source Bibliography.

86. Augustus, for example, at Myra in southern Lycia, is referred to as "Ruler of land and sea (αὐτοκράτορα γῆς καὶ θαλάσσης) . . . savior of the entire world" (σωτῆρα τοῦ σύνπαντος κόσμου), Ehrenberg and Jones, *Documents*, no. 72; see also Momigliano, "Terra Marique," 53–64; Maximowa, "Un Camée," 64–69.

87. Oberleitner, *Geschnittene Steine*, 36 (plate 17), 41–42 (plates 22–23); and Kähler, *Alberti Rubeni*.

88. Oster, "Christianity and Emperor," 143–49; Scherrer, *Ephesus*, 116–17.

Figure 26

thereby proclaiming through fictive globalism that the Roman Emperor had the whole world in his hands.

It seems that further investigation of the semantic fields of geographical terminology employed by Revelation and by contemporary sources would advance the dialogue between the non futurist and the futurist interpreters of Revelation (see Appendix C).

Figure 27

Figure 28

GALACTIC UPHEAVAL AND THE TESTIMONY OF NATURE

Even when the fictive nature of globalism is granted, futurists would still appeal to the galactic and cosmic images of Revelation to support their views and conclusions about the pervasiveness of "end times" imagery throughout the book of Revelation. Scenes of cosmic upheaval and language of galactic catastrophe are essential ingredients in John's prophetic style. For example, a picture of a blackened sun juxtaposed to a blood red moon suspended above a planet with dislocated islands and a surface covered with fallen stars (6:12–14) certainly qualifies as a scene of galactic upheaval.

John's recurring use of cosmic language and galactic upheaval to portray divine punishment is not unique in the ancient world. Furthermore, it is certainly not the unique possession of Judeo-Christian authors. Although John's cataclysmic vocabulary clearly resonates with similar language and style preserved in Jewish Scriptures, this stylistic and linguistic feature was also part of the *lingua franca* of cosmic mythology in the surrounding Mediterranean world.

Figure 29

A Greek papyrus known as "Oracle of the Potter"[89] is an appropriate example of this phenomenon. One translator and commentator of this papyrus referred to it as "An Egyptian Apocalypse"[90] in light of its religio-socio-political setting as well as its use of dualistic, cosmic, and fictive language. This papyrus was written in response to foreign oppression and societal upheaval. In fact, it is noteworthy that the general occasion and time period of this papyrus corresponds with the assault against Judaism that engendered the Maccabean Revolt and inspired examples of Jewish apocalyptic literature. In addition to his attack upon Jewish culture,

Figure 30

89. In fact, it exists in more than one recension, see Koenen, "Die Prophezeiungen," 178–209.

90. Burstein, *Hellenistic Age,* 136.

Antiochus IV Epiphanes also attacked Egypt (170–168 BC), in response to a war begun by Egypt. This attempt to thoroughly Hellenize the culture of Egypt was only arrested by Roman intervention.[91]

In response to temporarily successful Seleucid military assaults and forceful attempts to Hellenize Egypt, an Egyptian oracle was given. According to this "apocalypse," unnatural weather will ruin the Nile River; the sun will darken; crops will fail; civil and familial strife will lead to mass killings; and gods will be forced from their native cities.

Divine control over nature was not only the tool of divine judgment and chaos, but also divine approval and blessing. This theme is well known in Scripture,[92] but also exists in Roman literature. The well-known *Fourth Eclogue* of Vergil,[93] written at the threshold of the Roman Empire, eloquently displays a world animated by the spiritual realities at the arrival of the Roman Golden Age. In this supernal new age the untilled earth will produce marvelous crops, livestock will no longer fear large lions, all the serpents and poisonous plants will die, and the latter will be replaced with exotic spice plants. The wool of sheep will naturally come in various colors, without human assistance and participation. The whole created order will exult as guilt from sin is removed and a new world order descends from heaven. All of this makes sense because of the fictive use of the language of the natural world under the control of the gods.

Regarding Jewish literature, it is not at all unusual for Jewish prophets to use cosmic terminology to communicate God's prophetic messages that warned of temporal earthly judgments finding fulfillment on the near horizon. Even when God's wrath was directed against only one earthly empire or region, representing only a fraction of the globe, this wrath was sometimes depicted in terms of the physical dissolution of the galaxy.

Isaiah 13 provides a helpful test case to show this fictive use of cosmic language. This prophecy explicitly states that it concerns God's judgment against the Babylonian Empire of the ancient Near East (Isa 13:1, 17, 19). Yet, if taken out of the context of the intended original audience and read with certain futuristic preconceptions, one might think that this prophecy foretold the cataclysmic end of the planet, and perhaps even the galaxy:

> The oracle concerning Babylon that Isaiah son of Amoz saw: . . .
> Listen, an uproar of kingdoms, of nations gathering together!
> The Lord of hosts is mustering an army for battle They come

91. In general Habicht, "Seleucids," 341–50.
92. See Ps 98:7–9; Isa 11:6–8; 55:12–13; 65:25; Amos 9:13–15.
93. Clausen, "Theocritus and Virgil," 315–17.

from a distant land, from the end of the heavens, the Lord and the weapons of his indignation, to destroy the whole earth. . . . For the stars of the heavens and their constellations will not give their light; the sun will be dark at its rising, and the moon will not shed its light. . . . Therefore I will make the heavens tremble, and the earth will be shaken out of its place, at the wrath of the Lord of hosts on the day of his fierce anger. . . . See, I am stirring up the Medes against them, who have no regard for silver and do not delight in gold. (Isa 13:1–17).

Texts about the Babylonians and Medes certainly were not penned to forecast the end of the universe. The above text of Isaiah 13 is not an isolated example of this rhetorical phenomenon (cf. Amos 8:9–10).

Similar hyperbole was used against the rather small nation state of Judea in the mid-seventh century BC by the prophet Zephaniah (1:2–4) when describing the Babylonian destruction of Jerusalem and the captivity of the elect in Jerusalem. A glance at a Bible atlas reveals that behind the grandiose fictive galactic language of Zephaniah's prophecy lies a very, very small piece of land. When interpreting the language of John's Revelation, it is just as inappropriate to force a cosmic literalism on John the prophet as it would be on the prophets Isaiah or Zephaniah.

This means, then, that when John describes activities related specifically to the Roman Empire of his own time, the modern interpreter should not immediately globalize these statements with an unwarranted literalism. Seen from the perspective of fictive language, God's judgment against Roman oppression of believers in John's time need not automatically be taken to refer to all humankind.

EMPEROR CULT

For the student of the Revelation of John the availability of ancient resources for the study of the Emperor Cult has never been better than at the present time. Not only does each decade bring forth many additional resources, but the research methods used in the investigation of these resources continue to be refined and sharpened, and with more enthusiasm than ever before. These pronounced developments and the general

Figure 31

enthusiasm for the study of the Emperor Cult, however, have not always been matched by a commitment on the part of commentators of Revelation to incorporate these findings or to share this enthusiasm. Fortunately for the study of Revelation, the Cult of the Emperor located in Roman Asia Minor is one of the best documented regions of the Roman Empire.[94] Admittedly a commentary is not the place for specialized study and discussion of the phenomenon of the Emperor Cult, but many commentaries are remiss in their interaction with the ancient materials and methodological advances related to this important topic.

One reality that has become increasingly evident is that the Roman Emperor Cult, in both its nature and its development, was extremely variegated and complex. The brevity of this overview will require that generalizations be stated in lieu of detailed analyses and that the plethora of ancient documents can regrettably only be viewed like the proverbial tip of the iceberg.

The mid-first century BC saw the deterioration of the Roman Republic and the exacerbation of conditions that led to the origin of the Roman Empire. This is often associated with the decision of Julius Caesar to commit a capital offense by entering Republican Italy illegally with a standing army (his army *Legio XIII*) when he crossed the Rubicon River in northern Italy (approximately 210 miles north of the city of Rome). Julius Caesar's crossing of the Rubicon eventuated the beginning of the Roman Empire a generation later when Augustus conquered Mark Antony and Cleopatra in a sea battle at Actium in 31 BC. It is clear to historians that during this approximate two decade period between the crossing of the Rubicon and the Battle of Actium the notions and practices associated with later Emperor Worship already existed in embryonic form.

There had been generations of worship of Hellenistic monarchs and their families in the kingdoms that were left by the death of Alexander the Great. There had been, moreover, not only a readiness, but even a proclivity for the worship of political rulers as gods in the region that was to become Roman Asia. The broad outline of this story of the worship of rulers as gods has been well sketched by Hans-Josef Klauck.[95] With generations of tradition, religious ceremonies, and political theology in place, it did not take a lot of time following the military defeat of Cleopatra and Mark Antony for those in Roman Asia to switch their loyalty and religious devotion from Antony and Cleopatra to the new conqueror, Octavian.

94. Price, *Rituals and Power*.
95. Klauck, *Religious Context*, 252–88.

Many of these pieces of information will be given at various places in the commentary. One convenient rubric for presenting this material given by Philip A. Harland is fourfold: (1) official worship of dead and divinized emperors, (2) provincial imperial temples, (3) imperial cults sponsored by cities,[96] and (4) emperor worship stemming from small groups and families.[97] One of Harland's categories that deserves mention at this point is the issue of provincial imperial temples. For our purposes these should be kept separate from urban temples, since the provincial ones reflect a wider span of participation in the veneration of the emperor.

Roman provinces possessed an organization known as the *Koinon* (=Federation) of important cities. Thus, the *Koinon* of Macedonia, for example, was made up of important cities from Macedonia. These provincial *Koina* were an important part of the interface between Rome and its various provinces. The *Koina* became the institutions that, among other things, petitioned Rome for the privilege of having an officially sanctioned Roman temple in their province, a temple in which various emperors and their family members, the Roman Senate, and the goddess Roma were worshiped and venerated.[98]

Since the location of a provincial temple in a specific city was a beneficial as well as sacred honor, these cities were eventually referred to by the Greek term "*neokoros*."[99] In the beginning *neokoros* referred to individuals who helped with or attended to the needs of a deity and a temple. Later it was corporately applied to the role of a city in its divine obligation to attend to and to protect a deity's temple and the general welfare of the cult.[100] Thus, it was a small step to transfer this term from its use in describing a city's special relationship to a traditional deity, as in the instance of Ephesus being the "guardian of the temple" of the Ephesian Artemis in Acts 19:35, to a city's special protection and care for an imperial provincial temple.[101]

In 29 BC the *Koinon* of Asia requested the permission of Augustus to build a provincial temple for him in Pergamum (Tacitus, *Ann.* 4.37; Dio, *Rom Hist.* 51.20.6). Similarly during the reign of Tiberius (AD 14–37) the city of Smyrna in AD 26, after competition with several other Roman

---

96. An excellent treatment of urban imperial cults in Roman Asia is given by Friesen, *Imperial Cults*, 56–103.

97. Harland, *Associations*, 121–3.

98. Friesen, *Imperial Cults*, 28–29, 34–35, 105–7.

99. Burrell, *Neokoros*.

100. Oster, "Ephesian Artemis," 24–44.

101. Friesen, *Twice Neokoros*, 56–59; much of the following material can be found in Friesen, *Twice Neokoros*.

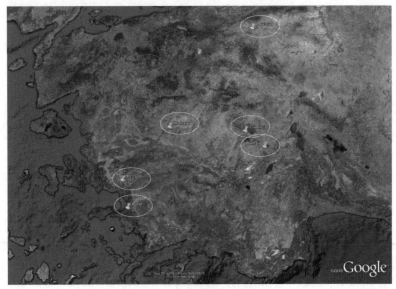

Figure 32

Asian cities, was awarded permission to have the second provincial temple of Roman Asia, this one dedicated to Tiberius, to Livia, and to the Roman Senate (Tacitus, *Ann.* 4.15; 4.55–56). Due to the megalomania and divine pretensions of the Emperor Gaius (Caligula) there was a short lived interest in a provincial temple in Miletus where he would be worshiped as a god in an "exceedingly beautiful temple which the Milesians were building for Apollo."[102] This attempt at the usurpation of the temple of Apollo took place contemporary with Caligula's attempt at the usurpation of the Temple of YHWH in Jerusalem when he "ordered a colossal statue [of himself] gilt all over . . . by way of insult to be set up in the temple of the metropolis" of the Jews (Philo, *Legat.* 30. 203). The next year (AD 41) the nefarious Emperor Caligula was assassinated by the members of the Praetorian Guard, a unit ironically charged with the protection of the Roman Emperor (Suetonius, *Cal.* 4.58).

Of more interest to the study of Revelation is the provincial temple awarded to the city of Ephesus by the Emperor Domitian "in the early to mid-eighties of the first century."[103] Of all of the provincial temples allowed by the various emperors and the Roman Senate, this fourth provincial temple at Ephesus was the first to use the term "neokoros," probably based

102. Dio Cassius, *Rom Hist.* 59.28.1; cf. also Friesen, *Imperial Cults*, 39–41.

103. Friesen, *Twice Neokoros,* 49.

upon its previous use of the term for the Ephesian Artemis (Acts 19:35).[104] Stated well on an Ephesian coin, Ephesus was now "twice *neocorate*," once for the goddess Artemis and now for her second god Domitian (and his divine predecessors Vespasian and Titus). The remains of this temple have been excavated at Ephesus and is "generally associated [with] inscriptions referring to a common temple of the emperors in Ephesus and was originally erected in honour of Domitian and his deified predecessors."[105] This provincial temple at Ephesus dominated the landscape of the upper forum much as the large bath-gymnasium complex built by Domitian[106] dominated the landscape near the harbor not far from the lower forum.

The imperial temple was the epicenter of the imperial cult in cities of Roman Asia, the place where priests and sacrifices were found. Based upon evidence from the early imperial era and not far from Roman Asia one learns that these imperial temples were the focal point of public devotion to the emperor where also pledges of allegiance were taken; for those not near the imperial temple, then the oath of loyalty was taken in the presence of an imperial altar.

This devotion to the emperor was not some mere ceremonial formality or perfunctory religion, as has been asserted so often in the past. A set of documents were published and distributed by the *Koinon* of Asia in 9 BC and they highlight the pious devotion felt by many Roman Asians toward the emperor.

It seemed good to the Greeks of Asia, in the opinion of the high priest Apollonius of Menophilus Azanitus:

> "Since Providence, which has ordered all things and is deeply interested in our life, has set in most perfect order by giving us Augustus, whom she filled with virtue that he might benefit humankind, sending him as a savior [σωτῆρ], both for us and for our descendants, that he might end war and arrange all things, and since he, Caesar, by his appearance [ἐπιφανεῖς] (excelled even our anticipations), surpassing all previous benefactors, and not even leaving to posterity any hope of surpassing what he has done, and since the birthday of the god Augustus was the beginning of the good tidings for the world that came by reason of him [ἦρξεν δὲ τῶι κόσμωι τῶν δι' αὐτὸν εὐαγγελίων ἡ γενέθλιος ἡμέρα τοῦ θεοῦ]."[107]

---

104. Ibid., 50–57.
105. Scherrer, *Ephesus*, 92.
106. Yegül, *Bathing*, 160–61.
107. See Evans for translation.

The significance of the Imperial Cult radiated far beyond the mere location of the temple and statues of the emperor god located there. In addition to the more cultic activities that occurred at the temple like sacrifices and hymns, there were public banquets in city squares, city wide parades and festivals, imperial birthday celebrations and the like that were associated with the imperial cult. Any one or all of these provided sufficient opportunity for followers of the Lamb to decide to which Lord and to which God one would give devotion.

2

John the Prophet on Patmos

Rev 1:1 The revelation of Jesus Christ, which God gave him to show his servants what must soon take place; he made it known by sending his angel to his servant John, 2 who testified to the word of God and to the testimony of Jesus Christ, even to all that he saw. 3 Blessed is the one who reads aloud the words of the prophecy, and blessed are those who hear and who keep what is written in it; for the time is near.

MUCH LIKE THE APOSTLE Paul before him, John knew that his desire and hopes to guide the communities of believers in Roman Asia could not rest solely on his own authority. Similar to that of Moses (Exod 3:1–15), Isaiah (6:1–10), Jesus (Mark 1:9–13) and Paul (Gal 1:1–5, 16–17; Acts 9:1–16), John's authority rested upon the foundation of a direct revelation from God himself. Revelation begins with a prologue in 1:1–3, indicating the divine origin of the message, with Christ and his angel as agents of revelation. The prophet John and the hearers are designated as "servants."[1] Reflecting a theocentrism well known in the Fourth Gospel,[2] John designates God as the source of this revelation that he gave to Christ. The concept and experience of divine revelation would be familiar among the believers in these

---

1. This metaphorical use of the term "slave" is found in Jewish, pagan and Christian religious sources, see BDAG, 259–60.

2. Osborne, *Revelation*, 31–32 correctly begins his treatment of the theology of Revelation with the "Doctrine of God." See also John 5:19; 8:28.

seven churches. The civilizations and cultures of John's time were replete with oracles and prophetic messengers—pagan,[3] Jewish,[4] and Christian.[5]

John does not indicate specifically how God "gave him" this revelation. In this prophetic work John uses terminology such as, "by sending his angel" (1:1),[6] "in the Spirit" (1:10)[7] and an "open door into heaven" (4:1),[8] all of which clearly locate him in a metaphysical world where he both "sees"[9] and "hears"[10] heavenly realities. The phrase "by sending his angel" anticipates the regular appearance of angels in this work. Throughout the Jewish Scriptures as well as the New Testament, angels play a regular role in bringing messages from God to humans.[11]

Since the author of Revelation identifies himself only as John, the reader is left to question, "which John." Whether this John is to be identified with the "beloved disciple," the author of the Fourth Gospel, is not as significant as some have thought for an interpretation of Revelation. The setting and occasion of the Gospel and epistles of John are far removed from the issues and occasion of Revelation. The evidence of the second century is exceedingly strong for the identification of the author of Revelation with the beloved disciple, but the author's own silence about his "apostolic" identity might justify the modern reader's caution in being too

3. Lucian, *Syr d.* 36: μαντήϊα . . . καὶ ἐν τῇ δέ Ἀσίῃ πολλά ἐστιν; Lucian, *Alex.* passim.; Aune, *Prophecy,* 23–79.

4. For Jewish individuals and literature see Aune, *Prophecy,* 103–52; Brooke, "Prophecy," 694–700.

5. Aune, *Prophecy,* 189–231; 247–90; for primary sources from the Apostolic Fathers see Ign. *Smyrn.* 7.2.; Ign. *Phld.* 5.2; *Did.* 11.3, 7–12; *Barn.*1.7; Herm. *Mand.* 11.

6. Revelation far exceeds every other book in the New Testament in its use of the term "angel." On the angelology of Revelation see Aune, *Revelation 1–5,* 108–12.

7. This wording associates John with early Christian prophecy, e.g., 1 Cor 12–14 and also Old Testament prophetic ministries such as Ezekiel's, e.g., 2:2; 3:12; 8:3; 11:5; 43:5.

8. Viewing the portal of heaven as an access point for divine revelation is seen as early as the patriarchal narratives (Gen 28:17); the association with "open heaven" and revelation is known in both pagan and Jewish sources.

9. Rev 1:2, 17; 5:1, 2, 6; 6:1, 9; 7:1, 2; 8:2; 9:1, 17; 10:1, 5; 13:1, 2, 11; 14:6; 15:1, 2; 16:13; 17:3, 6 (2x); 18:1; 19:11, 17, 19; 20:1, 4, 11, 12; 21:1, 2, 22.

10. Rev 1:10; 5:11, 13; 6:1, 3, 5, 6, 7; 7:4; 8:13; 9:13, 16; 10:4, 8; 12:10; 14:2, 13; 16:1, 5, 7; 18:4; 19:1, 6; 21:3; 22:8.

11. See notes on Rev 1:20; LXX examples Gen 16:7–16; Gen 22:11–14; Gen 31:11–13; Gen 19:12–13; Judg 13:3; Num 22: 31–35; 1 Kgs 13:18; Tob 12:6–22; New Testament examples Luke 1:11–20; Matt 1:20; 28:2–7; Acts 8:26; 27:23–24; Gal 1:8; Davidson, "Angel," 148–55.

dogmatic about the issue.[12] Later opinion was divided in the patristic era about which John this was.[13] Furthermore, the debate regarding the identity of the author draws not only upon patristic convictions, but also upon the similarities and differences between this work and other "Johannine" works in the New Testament.[14] Notwithstanding the issue of the identity of John, we do know, nevertheless, that Revelation was one of the most often cited New Testament books in the second century.

Wording such as things that "must soon take place" (1:1) and "the time is near" (1:3) has understandably drawn interpreters into discussions about the nature and extent of the prophet's eschatological convictions. Similar discussions have occurred that look to the issue of the "apparent" failure of these prophecies to take place on a perceived schedule.[15] Whatever else one may think of John's sense of *imminency* seen in this work (e.g., 2:16; 3:11; 22:6, 7, 12, 20), he certainly reflects the spiritual outlook and priorities of other New Testament authors such as Paul, Peter, and James in terms of this doctrinal issue of eschatological *imminency*.[16]

John pronounces a benediction ("blessed is he") upon both the reader and the audience of these prophecies. This is the first of several occurrences of the phrase "blessed is/are" (Rev 14:13; 16:15; 19:9; 20:6; 22:7, 14). Since there are seven of these, this phrase provides an example of an implicit heptad, a phenomenon also known in literature from the Dead Sea Scrolls.[17] The blessing of God mentioned here is bestowed not only upon the faithful hearers of his message, but also upon the faithful doers of the message of Revelation. This correlation of receiving God's blessing with "keeping what is written," seen classically in the blessing and curse theology of Deut 28–30, is thematic to Revelation and found throughout Scripture.[18] This theme resonates with the words of the earthly Jesus, who described the reward given to the one who "who hears these words of mine and acts on them" (Matt 7:24–25; cf. Rom 2:13 and Jas 1:22–25).

12. Evidence available in Carson and Moo, *Introduction,* 700–707.

13. Wikenhauser, *New Testament,* 548–49.

14. Smalley, *Revelation,* 4–5.

15. My own perspectives on this issue are set forth in Appendix B.

16. E.g., Rom 13:11; 1 Cor 16:22; Jas 5:8; 1 Pet 4:17.

17. 4Q403 7–9 (=Songs of the Sabbath Sacrifice) gives a list of seven items of seven each.

18. Christensen, *Deuteronomy,* 673–74; also Osborne, *Revelation,* 58.

Grant Osborne quite helpfully observes, "In fact, the Hebrew word for 'hear' also means to 'obey'; the two concepts are inseparable biblically."[19]

We learn that the content of this book is characterized as "words of prophecy." Elsewhere in Revelation John reveals that this document is to be understood as prophecy (Rev 10:11, 19:9–10; 22:6, 7, 9, 10, 18, 19). Osborne rightly underscores the significance of this when he writes, "This tells us that John does not conceive of this writing purely as Jewish apocalyptic . . . but as linked with OT prophetic works,"[20] thereby manifesting both John's focus on ethical issues and also his focus on God's impending judgment in history.[21] The longstanding debate[22] about the dichotomy between prophecy (concerned with history) and apocalyptic (concerned only about the end of time and history) is quite complex,[23] as are the different terms that characterize each genre and message. For example, some apocalyptic authors regarded themselves as prophets (4 Ezra 12:42). Stated briefly, it seems to me that John's message is fundamentally focused on God's acts in history in dealing with Satan, the false prophet, and beast, identified with the political-historical phenomena of Rome, realities of time and space in Roman Asia. After the false beast and prophet are permanently removed from the prophetic narrative (Rev 19:20–21), this leaves Rev 20 for the eschatological removal of Satan (Rev 20:10) and for the eschatological judgment of humankind (Rev 20:11–15).

The announcement that "the time is near" reminds us that most biblical prophecy is intended for events that will occur within the lifetime or near future of the original readers. For example, the teaching of Deut 18:20–22 for discerning true and false prophecy makes most sense if the prophecy can be fulfilled within the lifetime of its original audience,[24] a feature that is also true of the discernment of Christian prophecy (1 Cor 14:29; 1 Thess 5:20). It would be a peculiar form of encouragement for suffering believers in Roman Asia to listen to prophecies focused upon events at least two millennia in the future. The wording of the phrase "the time is near" is repeated in 22:10 and underscores the conviction of

---

19. Osborne, *Revelation*, 58.

20. Ibid.

21. Typically the Jewish books that most influenced Revelation were themselves focused upon God's judgment in history, not God's termination of history.

22. An earlier attempt to mediate this dichotomy is given by Fiorenza, "Apokalypsis," 105–28.

23. von Rad, *Old Testament*, 2:301–8 gives a classic presentation of this distinction.

24. Merrill, *Deuteronomy*, 274.

eschatological fulfillment that filled the hearts of the early believers (cf., 1 Cor 16:22; 1 Thess 4:15–17).

Rev 1:4 John to the seven churches that are in Asia: Grace to you and peace from him who is and who was and who is to come, and from the seven spirits who are before his throne, 5 and from Jesus Christ, the enduring witness, the firstborn of the dead, and the ruler of the kings of the earth. To him who loves us and freed us from our sins by his blood, 6 and made us to be a kingdom, priests serving his God and Father, to him be glory and dominion forever and ever. Amen. 7 Look! He is coming with the clouds; every eye will see him, even those who pierced him; and on his account all the tribes of the earth will wail. So it is to be. Amen. 8 "I am the Alpha and the Omega," says the Lord God, who is and who was and who is to come, the Almighty.

Rev 1:4 includes the initial evidence concerning the recipients of John's prophecies, namely seven congregations in the province of Roman Asia, one of the most significant provinces of the entire Roman Empire.[25]

Since John employs the number seven in reference to these congregations, this is an appropriate place to introduce the symbolism of the number seven in Revelation. First of all, numerical symbolism was well known in antiquity,[26] and its use in Revelation was not an effort by John to use arcane language or furtive symbols. On the contrary, John's use of numerical symbolism reflects its widespread acceptance within the cultures of the Mediterranean Basin. At least since the time of the Greek philosopher and mathematician Pythagoras, it was common to believe in the symbolic value of numbers.[27] The use of the number seven is seen in art work as well as literature of antiquity. The Roman-era Latin novel written by Apuleius entitled *Metamorphoses* contains the narrative of a man named Lucius who undergoes a religious conversion to the great Egyptian goddess Isis. Early in the process of conversion, Lucius writes: "Anxious to purify myself, I went to bathe in the sea. Seven times I plunged my head under the waves, since the divine Pythagoras pronounced that number to be very especially suitable in sacred rites. Then with a tear-stained face I prayed to the all-powerful goddess."[28]

25. General studies on Roman Asia Minor include the older work by Magie, *Roman Rule*; Mitchell, *Anatolia*; for studies on the worship of the Roman Emperor in Asia Minor see Price, *Rituals and Power*; for early Christianity in Asia Minor see Oster, "Christianity in Asia Minor," 938–54.

26. Potter, "Numbers," 1053–54; Staehle, "Zahlenmystik," 1147–49.

27. Kahn, "Pythagoras," 1283–84.

28. Griffiths, *Apuleius* 11.1, 71 and notes on 113; cf. 2 Kgs 5:10, "Elisha sent a messenger to him, saying, 'Go, wash in the Jordan seven times, and your flesh shall be

The use of the number seven is particularly well documented among literary, philosophical, and religious authors of antiquity. One can eavesdrop in Rome on Cicero's comments about the "music of spheres" and the "seven different sounds—a number which is the key of almost everything" (*The Republic* 6.18.18). Or in first century AD city of Alexandria one learns of the Jewish author and philosopher Philo[29] who states that: "I doubt whether any one could adequately celebrate the properties of the number 7, for they are beyond all words. Yet the fact that it is more wondrous than all that is said about it is no reason for maintaining silence regarding it. Nay, we must make a brave attempt—to bring out at least all that is within the compass of our understandings, even if it be impossible to bring out all or even the most essential points."[30]

Leaving the Hellenized culture of Alexandria Egypt and moving northeasterly to the Judean desert, one reads the sectarian Jewish document "Songs of the Sabbath Sacrifice" with its heptads within heptads. The copy of the "Songs of the Sabbath Sacrifice"[31] found at Masada proclaims,

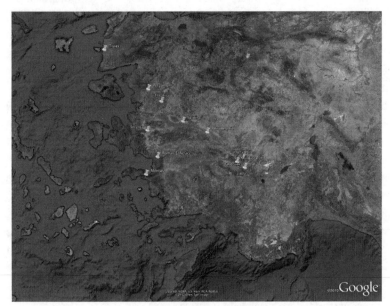

Figure 33

restored and you shall be clean.'"

29. General guides to Philo include Schenck, *Guide to Philo*; Williamson, *Jews*.

30. Philo, *Opif.* 30 [par. 89]; see also 31 [par. 96], 43 [par. 128]; in general see Staehle, *Zahlenmystik*, 34–50.

31. Ması̄k 2.18–22 (4Q403 1.7–9); Newsom, "Songs," 887–89.

He will sing to the King of holiness seven times, with seven words of wonderful songs.

1. Seven psalms of his blessings.

2. Seven psalms of magnification of his justice.

3. Seven psalms of exaltation of his kingdom.

4. Seven psalms of praise of his glory.

5. Seven psalms of thanksgiving for his wonders.

6. Seven psalms of exultation in his strength.

7. Seven psalms of songs of his holiness.

It is difficult not to notice the ubiquity of numerological convictions about the number seven that were similar to John's. John's outlook would have been easily understood and appreciated by his original audiences.

It is also important to notice that the use of the number seven does not represent the total number of churches in the province of Asia. We know, for example, that there were also churches in Asia at Troas (Acts 20:6–12), Colossae, and Hierapolis; perhaps there were congregations at Miletus (Acts 20:17; 2 Tim 4:20). Within less than two decades of the writing of Revelation, Ignatius of Antioch also wrote letters to Asian congregations at Magnesia and Tralles.[32] Not all scholars, however, concur about the symbolism of the number seven when used of the congregations. Prigent,[33] among others, strips away any numerical symbolism in this instance by asserting that these seven churches were mentioned because they were the only ones "experiencing in a concrete way the seductions of heresy [and would listen to John]."

Rev 1:4b–5 contains a salutation of "grace and peace"[34] from the tri-fold Father, Spirit, and Jesus Christ. God the Father is described as "who is, and who was, and who is to come," a description found also in 1:8 and in the Trisagion of Rev 4:8. Scholars debate the origin and exact meaning of this threefold temporal designation.[35] There are obvious Jewish elements

---

32. Oster, "Christianity in Asia," 938–54.

33. Prigent, *Apocalypse*, 132.

34. "Grace to you and peace" is a ubiquitous epistolary salutation in the New Testament (Rom 1:7; 1 Cor 1:3; 2 Cor 1:2; Gal 1:3; Eph 1:2; Phil 1:2; 1 Thess 1:1; 2 Thess 1:2; 1 Tim 1:2; 2 Tim 1:2; Titus 1:4; Phlm 1:3; 1 Pet 1:2; 2 Pet 1:2). For the distinctiveness of this wording see Arzt-Grabner, *Philemon*, 115–23.

35. Thomas, *Revelation 1–7*, 73; Mounce, *Revelation*, 45–46; Witherington, *Revelation*, 75; Beale, *Revelation*, 188–89; Aune, *Revelation 1–5*, 30–33.

Figure 34

in this terminology,[36] e.g., the use of *ho ōn* (ὁ ὤν; the one who is) as the personal name of God (Exod 3:14, LXX; Philo *Mos.* 1.75; *Abr.* 121). Moreover, the prophet's distinctive wording seen in his use of the phrase "to come" rather than the phrase "shall be" manifests the impact of the Jewish concept of eschatology and of the "coming one" (Mark 1:7; Luke 3:16; John 4:25; Acts 7:52; 13:25).[37]

John's threefold temporal phrase (is, was, is to come) highlights the eternality of God and in so doing manifests similarities to the threefold temporal phrase also known in pagan descriptions of their gods and goddesses. At the oracular site of Dodona, women prophets chanted the religious stanza, "Zeus was, Zeus is, Zeus shall be; O mighty Zeus."[38] There was a statue of Athena-Isis in Egypt that carried the inscription, "I am all that has been, and is, and shall be."[39] Equally important is an Augustan era

36. McDonough, *YHWH*.

37. See Osborne, *Revelation*, 61.

38. Pausanias, *Descr.* 10.12.10: Ζεὺς ἦν, Ζεὺς ἐστίν, Ζεὺς ἔσσεται, ὦ μεγάλε Ζεῦ.

39. Plutarch, *Is. Os.* 354C: ἐγώ εἰμι πᾶν τὸ γεγονὸς καὶ ὂν καὶ ἐσόμενον.

monument from Eleusis that mentions a statue of Eternity (=Aion), the deity who remains forever and "who is and was and shall be, not having beginning, middle or end."[40]

Geographically closer to the cities of the seven churches was the Augustan era statue of the god Aion uncovered at Aphrodisias. As at Eleusis,[41] the Aphrodisias[42] testimony of the god Eternity was a clarion testimony to Roman propaganda concerning the endlessness of the Roman golden age inaugurated by Augustus. The Roman golden age ideology, however, was a conviction patently antithetical to the theology of the book of Revelation (e.g., 11:15; 12:10; 14:8; 16:10; 18:21). John's theology allowed only one golden age (Rev 21–22), and it certainly would not be the same one imagined, to use John's concept, by that idol-propagating mother of all whores (Rev 17:1–6)—the Empire of Rome.

In the conflicting ideologies regarding eternity, the Roman State certainly had a more sophisticated marketing and multimedia department than the church had. Astral symbolism, for example, was powerfully employed by numismatic iconography through state mints to promote the veneration of the Emperor. Dating from the reign of Trajan (AD 98–117) there exists a coin with Trajan's bust on the obverse and the symbolism of eternity on the reverse.[43] The image of eternity (*Aeternitas*) uses the symbolism of the sun and moon to proclaim the eternity of the reign and influence of Trajan. Whatever the followers of the Lamb lacked in marketing resources, they made up for with an audacity that imagined that their beliefs and mores could topple an Empire whose stability and influence would purportedly last forever and ever.

It is the Holy Spirit, in the judgment of many interpreters,[44] who is described as "the seven Spirits who are before his throne." This use of the term "seven" is rooted not only in the significance of seven, but also clearly

40. *SIG* 1125; consult also Clinton, "Eleusinian Mysteries," 1509–13. Plato's argument in *Tim.* (37E–38A) that gods should not be described with "was" and "shall be" but only with "is" indicates that this threefold temporal designation was well known in his own era, even though this trifold paradigm displeased him.

41. *SIG* 1125.5: εἰς κράτος Ῥώμης.

42. Thus argued by Zuntz, *Aion.* and Zuntz, *Aion im Römerreich*; Smith, *Monument*, 45–48 undervalues, in my judgment, the Eleusinian inscriptional evidence for a Roman political interpretation of this contemporary iconography of Aion from Aphrodisias.

43. *ERIC II*, Trajan, Type:*Aeternitas*, no. 9; Plate, image 9, p. 144. Forum Ancient Coins, "Denarius of Trajan."

44. Beckwith, *Apocalypse*, 425; Lupieri, *Apocalypse*, 102–3; Beale, *Revelation*, 189; Thomas, *Revelation 1–7*, 67; Osborne, *Revelation*, 61; cf. Witherington, *Revelation*, 75.

in the Old Testament notion of the presence of God in Zech 4:1–10.[45] This particular identification would also be supported by the use of the phrase "the seven Spirits of God" as it is associated with the throne of God in Rev 4:5 and 5:6.

The reader should not move too quickly over the phrase "Spirits who are before his throne" (1:4; 4:5). The prepositional phrase "before his throne" is associated with the "sea of glass" (4:6), the twenty-four elders (4:10), their "crowns," (4:10), the "great multitude" (7:9), angels, elders, and four living creatures (7:11), those in "white robes" (7:15), the "golden altar" (8:3), the "144,000" (14:3), and all "the dead" (20:12). It is noteworthy that unlike the Father and Son, the Holy Spirit is never depicted as enthroned, either here or in other New Testament texts where enthronement is central. The closest the Holy Spirit gets to the throne is when he is subsumed under the enthroned Lamb and

Figure 35

Figure 36

is depicted as the "seven eyes" of the Lamb (Rev 5:6). Stuckenbruck is certainly correct when he notes that "Interpreters should be wary of reading later trinitarianism into the phrase"[46] of Rev 1:4b–5a.

Jesus Christ is given a very important trifold description as a "the faithful witness, the firstborn of the dead, and the ruler of the kings of the earth." From a pastoral perspective it is significant that the three ways Jesus Christ is described here would be particularly meaningful in light of the occasion of the seven letters and the circumstances of the readership of John's book. That is, all three of these christological emphases relate specifically to the conditions of the churches of Western Asia Minor. This follows the typical pattern of the New Testament, where christology is

45. Sweeney, *Twelve Prophets*, 2:612–13; Meyers, *Haggai*, 236; Jauhiainen, *Zechariah,* believes about Zechariah 4 that "the seven continually burning lamps on the lampstand, together with the light it provided, were a symbol of Yahweh's presence with his people" (46), although the "relationship between Zech 4 and the seven spirits . . . is not via a direct allusion" (88).

46. Stuckenbruck, "Revelation," 1537.

formulated in terms and phrases appropriate to the context and occasion of the readership. As Collins perceptively observed, "The theology and christology . . . are shaped by these elements of crisis and trauma."[47]

The term "witness" (*martus*, μάρτυς), which occurs in Revelation more than in the rest of the New Testament, except Acts, has overtones of martyrdom in this particular book and in this particular historical setting.[48] What better foundation on which to call for the faithfulness of believers (2:10, 13) than by highlighting the faithfulness of Jesus's own character and testimony (3:14; 19:11), even to the point of death. The only other instance of the phrase "faithful witness" in Revelation is in reference to the martyr Antipas (2:13).

The use of the term "firstborn from the dead" here brings to mind Paul's use of this same word in his letter to the congregation at Colossae (Col 1:15, 18), which also made its way to Laodicea (Col 4:16), one of John's seven congregations (3:14–22) decades later. The phrase "firstborn from the dead" does not mean that Jesus was the first person to ever be raised from the dead, but rather that he was the first to rise from the dead and remain alive forever (cf. Acts 26:23). The phrase "firstborn from the dead"[49] underscores the Christian conviction that the future resurrection of Christians was grounded in God's raising Jesus from the dead (Rev 1:18).

This claim of the gospel that Jesus is the "firstborn from the dead" stands in sharp contrast to the message about death found in the iconography of so many Graeco-Roman sarcophagi. Time and again the outside of these stone coffins contain faces of Medusa, designed to scare away evil sprits or circumstances in the afterlife, rather than proclaiming a victory over death in the resurrection.

There was hardly a more audacious claim (viewed from a Roman worldview) than that the Messiah Jesus was the ruler over all the rulers of all the human empires known to man. The early vignette seen in Acts 17:6–7 documents the disturbing reality of the idea that Jesus might be regarded as a usurper king competing for the throne of the Roman Empire.[50] It comes as no surprise in light of the widespread practice of swearing the "pledge

47. Collins, "Revelation," 706.

48. The debate about the nuances of the term "witness" is longstanding. The history of the debate with accompanying arguments and evidence is given recently in Peters, *Mandate*, 77–118; cf. Prigent, *Apocalypse*, 110–11.

49. Also known in the theology of other New Testament authors, e.g., Rom 8:29; Col 1:18; Heb 11:28.

50. Cuss, *Imperial Cult*, 23; also Rowe, *World Upside*.

Figure 37

of allegiance" to the Roman Emperor and his family that there would be
a profound conflict between Christian believers and patriotic Greeks and
Romans. These oaths were frequent, ubiquitous, and represented a solemn
event. Typical of these oaths are the following words taken from a Greek
inscription dated March, 3 BC, and found in the political capital of the
Paphlagonian region in north central Galatia. This oath was taken by the
indigenous peoples as well as the Romans living there.

> I swear by Zeus, Earth, Sun, all the gods and goddesses and Au-
> gustus himself that I will be favorably disposed toward Caesar
> Augustus and his children and descendants all the time of my
> life in word and deed and thought, considering as friends those
> whom they may consider friends and holding as enemies those
> whom they may judge to be enemies and for things that are of
> interest to them I will spare neither my body nor my soul nor
> my life nor my children, but in every way for the things that
> affect them I will undergo every danger; and whatever I might
> perceive or hear against them being said or plotted or done, I
> will report it and I will be an enemy to the person saying or
> plotting or doing any of these things; and whomever they may
> judge to be their enemies, these, on land and sea, with arms and
> steel will I pursue and ward off. If I do anything contrary to this
> oath or anything not in agreement with what I have sworn, I
> pray that there may come upon myself, my body and soul and
> life, my children and all my family and whatever is of use to us
> destruction, total destruction till the end of all my line and of
> all my descendants, and may neither the bodies of my family or
> of my descendants by earth or sea be received, nor may earth or

sea bear fruit for them. In the same words was this oath sworn by all the inhabitants of the land in the temples of Augustus throughout the districts of the province by the altars of Augustus. And likewise the Phazimonians living in what is now called Neapolis swore the oath, all of them, in the temple of Augustus by the altar of Augustus.[51]

Furthermore, the ascription of titles and prerogatives for Christ were often in potential conflict with the emperors of Rome, who were repeatedly acclaimed, in both words and iconography, as lord, ruler, god, son of god, and master over all "land and sea."[52] This audacious Johannine belief about the hegemony of Jesus over all earthly governments and monarchs forms part of the foundation for the subversive prophecies against the kings and their nations that are spoken by John and other prophets (10:11).[53]

Even though the trifold imagery of Rev 1:5 is shaped in response to the ministerial needs of the congregations in Roman Asia, this does not mean that John had no textual foundation for this in mind. It is repeatedly seen in Revelation that the Royal Davidic covenant of the Hebrew Scriptures exerted a profound influence on John and his presentation of God's revelation through Christ to him.

Psalm 89 is especially focused on the Davidic covenant (begun in 2 Sam 7) and it contains themes found in John's text.

- a faithful witness: Ps 89:37b—"enduring witness"

- firstborn: Ps 89: 27a—"I will make him the firstborn"

- ruler of the kings: Ps 89:27b—"the highest of the kings of the earth"

Even though these seven epistles will reveal that Christ's expectations for accountability and authenticity among believers is high, indeed very high, it is no accident that John's statement gives first place to *agapē* (ἀγάπη) in this important doxology. But this is not a North American style agape, synonymous with permissiveness toward sin or assimilation to the broader culture in the name of "tolerance." As we proceed, the spiritual integrity demanded by the theology and discipleship of these letters will seem draconian, perhaps non-Christian. This is probably because of the

51. Translation taken from Sherk, *Rome*, no. 105, 135–36.

52. See Cuss, *Imperial Cult*, 50–74; epigraphical testimony is still available in Deissmann, *Light*, 346–47. Likewise the symbolism of an Augustan gem portrays the Emperor's control over all "land and sea," Oberleitner, *Geschnittene Steine*, 35–36.

53. Similar christology is affirmed by Christ himself (Matt 27:11; John 18:33–37); divine leadership over the mighty empires of the world is frequently expressed in the Old Testament, e.g., Isa 40.

"cheap grace" fostered by many churches and denominations in the Christian West. John would have seen in Bonhoeffer a kindred spirit on the dangers of "cheap grace:"

> Cheap grace is the deadly enemy of our Church. We are fighting today for costly grace. . . . Cheap grace is the preaching of forgiveness without requiring repentance, baptism without church discipline, Communion without confession, absolution without personal confession. Cheap grace is grace without discipleship. . . . To put it quite simply, we must undertake this task because we are now ready to admit that we no longer stand in the path of true discipleship. We confess that, although our Church is orthodox as far as her doctrine of grace is concerned, we are no longer sure that we are members of a Church which follows its Lord. We must therefore attempt to recover a true understanding of the mutual relation between grace and discipleship. The issue can no longer be evaded.[54]

If the modern church dared embrace John's new reality where Christ was honored as the appointed King of the universe, then the shocking consequences would include that church members must view themselves as a unique fellowship consisting of followers loyal to the King. In John's days discipleship meant eschewing all values and propaganda of Rome that stood against the values of the one true God revealed in Jesus. With an utter simplicity that shows no regard for wealth, education, or culture, the values of this new reality could provide a compass for the modern followers of God who long for the eradication of the evils of economic discrimination, educational injustice, classism, and the toxic values of the entertainment and fashion industries within American culture.

Slogans and mantras of these slavelike (1:1 2x) followers of this "King of kings and Lord of lords" would not highlight "look how imperfect and needy we are," but rather "even though harassed and wounded, where can I stand duty?" Even if there were a time and place for the church to posture itself solely as a hospital for the weak, the time and place of Revelation was not to be it. There were Graeco-Roman religious cults that specialized in the hospital self-understanding, including pagan healing cults such as Asclepius, with its spas, theaters, and hospitals. John is looking for believers who will follow Jesus wherever he leads (Rev 14:4).

---

54. Bonhoeffer, *Cost*, 45, 47, 60.

Even though the vocabulary of "love" (*agape*, ἀγάπη) is missing from the Lukan account of the apostolic preaching to nonbelievers in the book of Acts, *agape* (ἀγάπη) does exert a major role in the epistolary sections of the New Testament.[55] Accordingly, when *agape* (ἀγάπη) is found only half a dozen times in Revelation (1:5; 2:4, 19; 3:9; 12:11; 20:9), this reveals a frequency noticeably lower than the epistles and Gospel of John.

The doctrine of the vicarious atonement through Jesus's blood anticipates the later emphasis upon Jesus as the slain Lamb (5:6, 9, 12, 13:8)[56] as well as the book's emphasis upon the shedding of blood by believers (6:10, 16:6, 17:6, 18:24, 19:2). John's idea of salvation from sin through the blood of Jesus rests upon a theological bedrock in the New Testament. C. M. Tuckett's statement about the centrality of the blood of Jesus stands in agreement with this when he writes: "The claim that Jesus's death on the cross should be seen as a sacrifice has exerted enormous influence on subsequent Christian theology and piety. It is quite clear that such language has deep roots in the NT itself. It is probably reflected in references to Jesus's death as "blood" . . . and in many of the references to Jesus's death being "for many/our sins/us/others."[57] The blood of Jesus is undoubtedly part of the Pauline gospel (Rom 3:25; 8:3; Eph 1:7); it is prominent in Jesus's words at the Last Supper (Matt 26:28); it is evident in the christology of the Fourth Gospel (John 1:29, 36), and letters of John (1 John 1:7); it is foundational to the apostolic parenesis of Peter (1 Pet 2:24; 3:18; cf. 1:18–19) and to the author of Hebrews (9–10 passim; 13:10–12). These facts cast doubt on the attempts by some recent interpreters to understand the atonement language of Revelation as only a metaphor or illustration of God's love, but having no literal and intrinsic reality.[58]

John's use of "kingdom" (*basileia*, βασιλεία) is very significant in the context and occasion of this book (cf. the new song of Rev 5:9–10), especially since it anticipates the climactic seventh trumpet of the seventh seal that declares that the "the kingdom of the world has become the kingdom

55. The Greek words ἀγάπη and ἀγαπῶ never occur in the Acts of the Apostles or Pauline summaries of his preaching to pagan audiences, e.g., 1 Thess 1:8–10, though the epistolary materials written for believers of the New Testament are replete with these two Greek words.

56. Keener, "Lamb," 641–42.

57. Tuckett, "Atonement" 518.

58. Reddish, *Revelation*, 157–58, for example, writes that "blood imagery, along with other sacrificial terminology, is only one way in which New Testament writers attempted to understand the redemptive significance of the life and death of Jesus. . . . All of these images need to be understood, not as objective realities, but as metaphors."

of our Lord and of his Messiah" (11:15). Stated clearly, John is telling these believers that they comprise the kingdom by means of which someday the Lord God will dominate and extinguish the kingdom of this world, including Rome. The designation of God's elect as priests has an important history in the Old Testament (Exod 19:6 and Isa 61:6). Exod 19:6 (LXX) reads "royal priesthood" (cf. 1 Pet 2:9) while the Hebrew text reads "kingdom of priests." In either case the two notions of royal/kingdom and priest are in Exod 19:6 and provide the background to 1:6.

It is not surprising that these are "priests serving his God and Father" since the God and Father of Jesus Christ is repeatedly pointed to in Revelation as the primary object of worship. Excluding the references to worship (*proskuneō*, προσκυνέω) of beasts, dragons, and angels, the worship of God the Father is mentioned ten times (4:10; 5:14; 7:11; 11:1, 16; 14:7; 15:4; 19:4, 10; 22:9) while the worship of Christ is mentioned only one time in Revelation and that in conjunction with the Father (5:14). In my judgment the christocentrism of so much modern hymnody would shock John, e.g., "Jesus, Lover of My Soul" and its praise to Jesus that "you alone are God."[59] The phrase "glory and power" is used both of God (Rev 1:6) and of God and the Lamb (5:13). This doxology ends with the frequent pattern of "Amen."[60]

Although it might initially sound strange to some futurists, this mention of Jesus's "coming with the clouds" is one of the few references to Christ's Second Coming in the entire book of Revelation.[61] Most of the references to impending punishment in Revelation are either against the seven churches or are plagues, bowls of wrath, and the like, against the Roman Empire. Rarely in Revelation is the wrath of God and the Lamb directed against the entire planet with all its inhabitants. Reference to "coming with the clouds" is derived from Dan 7:13 while the phrases "shall see him," "pierced him" and "will mourn" are derived from Zech 12:10. This conflation of these two Old Testament texts is seen elsewhere and earlier in Matt 24:30.[62]

Alpha and Omega are the first and last letters of the Greek alphabet (also see notes on Rev 1:17) and here refer to God the Father. The phrase Lord God Almighty (*pantokratōr*, παντοκράτωρ) is a favorite term of

59. Oakley, "Jesus, Lover."

60. Wu, "Liturgical Elements," 661–62.

61. Beale, *Revelation*, 196–99 discusses this verse in light of "already-and-not-yet" eschatological interpretations.

62. Beale, *Revelation*, 196–99; Prigent, *Apocalypse*, 121–22; Aune, *Revelation 1–5*, 50–56.

John, and he uses it only for God the Father (1:8; 4:8; 11:17; 15:3; 16:7, 14; 19:6, 15; 21:22). The term "Almighty" (*pantokratōr*, παντοκράτωρ) occurs only one other time in the New Testament (2 Cor 6:18), though it is also found in pagan and Jewish Greek literature.[63]

The background to the Greek term *pantokratōr* in the LXX is noteworthy. The Hebrew term "Shaddai" is normally translated *pantokratōr* in the LXX, though one time it is only transliterated as Shaddai in the Greek text of Ezek 10:5. When one looks at the LXX, including the Deuterocanonical works, it becomes evident that there is a noticeable clustering of this term *pantokratōr* in the exilic and postexilic literature, and many times *pantokratōr* is also a translation of the Hebrew (YHWH) Sabaoth (Lord of hosts). The Hebrew phrase "Lord of hosts" often bespeaks militaristic themes. Militarism would naturally be a part of the description of the God whom the Christians worship since this is the same God that will come and destroy Rome, unless she repents.

Rev 1:9 I, John, your brother who share with you in Jesus the persecution and the kingdom and the patient endurance, was on the island called Patmos because of the word of God and the testimony of Jesus. 10 I was in the spirit on the Lord's day, and I heard behind me a loud voice like a trumpet 11 saying, "Write in a book what you see and send it to the seven churches, to Ephesus, to Smyrna, to Pergamum, to Thyatira, to Sardis, to Philadelphia, and to Laodicea."

In 1:9 John begins by informing the readers of his own situation. He is on the island of Patmos, "because of the word of God and the testimony of Jesus." Some interpreters take this to mean that John went there voluntarily to spread the word through Christian preaching.[64] Leonard Thompson, for example, argues that since John uses the same Greek verb and preposition (*egenomēn en*, ἐγενόμην ἐν) in the phrases "I was on the island" (Rev 1:9, *egenomēn en tē vēsō*, ἐγενόμην ἐν τῇ νήσῳ) and "I was in the Spirit" (Rev 1:10, *egenomēn en pneumati*, ἐγενόμην ἐν πνεύματι) he "draws Patmos into a sacral, spatial homologue with the sacred state of being 'in the Spirit' and the sacred time of the Lord's Day."[65]

Perhaps John had fled voluntarily to the island of Patmos to escape persecution in Roman Asia, acting upon Jesus's commandment in Matt 10:23 ("When you are persecuted in one place, flee to another"). Others argue, more cogently, that John was confined because of official hostility

---

63. BDAG, 755.

64. Thompson, *Revelation* (1998), 56.

65. Thompson, *Revelation* (1990), 173.

toward his Christian message and leadership as well as the lifestyle practiced among his followers in the congregations of Roman Asia (Irenaeus, *Haer.* 5.30.3). While issues associated with Christian doctrines often brought ridicule from outsiders in the days of primitive Christianity, it was the issues of lifestyle that so often brought animosity and alienation, as it had for Judaism also. In so many instances modern Western Christianity would seem to be an anomaly to John, since lifestyle is rarely any longer the point of contrast between Christians and non-Christians.

It is easy to imagine why local officials could have viewed John as a threat. In some instances religious leaders and astrologers were expelled from Rome for composing books of prophecies that contained acrimonious messages against certain contemporary Roman administrators and their policies. Both Jewish (4Q318 frag. 2, 2.6–8) and pagan writings were known to have predicted the demise of a particular politician or ruler based upon heavenly signs. At an earlier period these prophetic books and horoscopes became so suspect that Augustus, as Pontifex Maximus: "collected whatever prophetic writings of Greek or Latin origin were in circulation anonymously or under the names of authors of little repute, and burned more than two thousand of them."[66] Under the reign of Tiberius (AD 17) there was senatorial legislation that exiled Roman astrologers and prophets who predicted the vicissitudes of the political and military fortunes of Rome and its leaders; foreigners who did such were executed.[67] Archaeologists have discovered an official government papyrus written within approximately a century of John's ministry that sheds light on the issue of seditious prophecy such as John's. It states:

> Encountering many who believed themselves to be deceived by the practices of divination I quickly considered it necessary, in order that no danger should ensue upon their foolishness, clearly herein to enjoin all people to abstain from this hazardous inquisitiveness. Therefore, let no man through oracles, that is, by means of written documents supposedly granted under divine influence . . . pretend to know things beyond human ken and profess (to know) the obscurity of things to come, neither let any man put himself at the disposal of those who enquire about this or answer in any way whatsoever.[68]

---

66. Suetonius, *Aug.* 31.1; cf. Tacitus, *Ann.* 6.12; Dio, *Rom. Hist.* 56.25.4–6

67. Beard et al., *Religions of Rome*, 271, citing Ulpian, *Duties of the Proconsul* 7.

68. Rea, "New Version," 153.

This papyrus ends with a threat of capital punishment for violators as well as government officials who are derelict in enforcement of this edict. Based upon the seditious messages of Revelation (e.g., 17–18), John would have certainly been viewed as an "enemy of the Roman order."[69]

Being exiled in the Roman Empire was not a uniform legal proceeding.[70] For example, individuals could be punished by confining them to a certain location; or they could be banished from their homes (Acts 18:2), but allowed to live or wander wherever they wished.[71] Patmos was probably one such example from several small islands in the Aegean Sea that served as destinations for confinement, although Patmos itself is never mentioned by name in such lists.[72]

Since confinement to an island like Patmos for antigovernment sentiment was well known in John's day, modern readers should not imagine that John's situation was unique or even necessarily dramatic. Roman rulers and administrators were naturally suspicious of and hostile toward anti-Roman thinkers. Under the reign of Vespasian, for example, the Emperor: "expelled from Rome all the philosophers except Musonius [Rufus]; Demetrius and Hostilianus he even deported to islands. . . . It became strikingly clear that Vespasian hated Helvidius Priscus . . . because he was a turbulent fellow who cultivated the favour of the rabble and was for ever denouncing royalty and praising democracy. Helvidius's behavior, moreover, was consistent with this opinion of him; for he banded various men together, as if it were the function of philosophy to insult those in power, to stir up the multitudes, to overthrow the established order of things, and to bring about a revolution."[73] The Roman satirist Juvenal, writing within fifty years following Revelation, complained about philosophic and political dissidents who sought notoriety by being arrested for their anti-Roman and countercultural leanings. Individuals of this ilk, according to Juvenal,[74] fit a recognizable social pattern and profile. Often they gained credibility among the *hoi polloi* by various high visibility actions such as being sent off to some remote prison, being shackled hand and foot, having close calls with death, and receiving a term of confinement to

69. MacMullen, *Enemies* is still a very valuable source for this issue generally. Druid prophecies were naturally anti-Roman (MacMullen, *Enemies*, 142).

70. Details are summarized by Aune, *Revelation 1–5*, 77–80.

71. This was apparently the case with the Druids expelled under Tiberius. See Pliny, *Nat.* 30.4.1.

72. Thompson, *Revelation* (1990), 173; Pliny, *Nat.* 4.12.23.

73. Dio, *Rom. Hist. Epitome* 65.13.2, 65.12.2–3; cf. Tacitus, *Ann.* 12.52.

74. Juvenal, *Sat.* 6.560–64.

the islands. Accordingly, John's relegation to a small island because of his antigovernment preaching (Rev 10:11; 17–18) fits comfortably into the social fabric of the contemporary Roman political culture as we know it.[75]

If John was confined to the island of Patmos for political reasons, the question naturally arises, "Why didn't the officials instead just summarily execute him?" Light is perhaps shed on this question from well-known rulings of Roman law. Seditious individuals, according to Roman law, were not treated uniformly. "According to the nature of their rank, [they are] either crucified, thrown to wild beasts, or deported to an island. . . . Persons who administer abortion potions . . . are, if humble, deported to the mines; if of superior rank, deprived of part of their property and relegated to an island" (Paulus, *Opinions* 5.22–24).[76] Thus, John may have been spared death because of some perceived significance he held, or perhaps because of a temporary moment of compassion by a Roman official. We know of an official who offered to spare the Christian leader Polycarp from martyrdom: "What harm is there in saying, 'Caesar is Lord,' and offering incense . . . and thereby saving yourself?" (*Mart. Pol.* 8:2).

There is no trustworthy information about the conditions under which John lived on Patmos or even how long he was there. Accordingly, all the theories and suggestions about it are mere speculation, whether Tertullian's tale (*Praescr.* 36) that "the apostle John, after he had been immersed in boiling oil without harm, was banished to an island" or Victorinus's statement (*Comm. In Apoc.* 10:3 [or 10:11]) that John was "condemned to the mines" on Patmos, or Craig Keener's view[77] that John's "conditions would be harsh for someone of his age." John's circumstance on Patmos seems to be better than many others who were relegated to an island. The description given by the pagan Greek author Dio Chrysostom, a contemporary of John, noted that "unfortunate human beings are banished to sundry uninhabited isles" (Dio Chrysostom, *Dei cogn.* 37).[78] In the case of Patmos, however, the island was clearly inhabited during the time period when John was there.[79]

Much ink has been spilled in the discussion of the origin, etymology and meaning of the phrase "On the Lord's day" in Rev 1:10 and whether

---

75. Balsdon, *Romans*, 113–15 has an important "Appendix: Known Places of Exile" that follows a chapter on "Expulsion from Rome, Italy, and Your Homeland," 97–113.

76. From Lewis and Reinhold, *Roman Civilization*, 2:510–11.

77. Keener, *Revelation*, 83.

78. Presented by Dio in AD 97.

79. The decisive inscriptional evidence is presented by Aune, *Revelation 1–5*, 77.

John coined this idiom to compete, as Deissmann argues, with the religious days devoted to emperor veneration.[80] Epigraphical evidence beyond that given by Deissmann does indeed point to the establishment of a day named after Octavian's divine epithet "Augustus."[81] Whether John's use of the terminology "Lord's day" was patterned on Augustan precedent is more difficult to establish.

Regarding the meaning of the phrase "Lord's day" itself, the weight of the evidence favors viewing this as a reference to "Sunday." The contemporary Christian author Ignatius of Antioch wrote these words to a congregation in the Roman Asian city of Magnesia less than two decades after Revelation: "If, then, those who had lived according to ancient practices came to the newness of hope, no longer keeping the sabbath but living in accordance with the Lord's day (*kata kuriakēn*, κατὰ κυριακὴν), on which our life also arose through him and his death (which some deny)" (Ign. *Magn.* 9.1). If the longstanding identification of the "Lord's day" with Sunday (an identification held by Protestant, Roman Catholic, and Orthodox churches alike) is correct, then believers and Christian leaders from the apostolic and post-apostolic eras would possibly be perplexed to see the encroachment of convenience-driven, Saturday night worship in lieu of the Lord's day celebration of the resurrection of the Messiah on Sunday.

Before leaving this topic it should be pointed out that Ben Witherington is mistaken in asserting as fact that: "We have confirmation of worship on Sunday in this vicinity from the early second century when Pliny writes to Trajan about Christians meeting in early morning on the first day of the week to sing and worship (see *Ep. Tra.* 10.96.8ff)."[82] In reality, neither Pliny nor Trajan mentions the "first day of the week." Pliny passes on hearsay testimony that includes a reference to a "predetermined day" (*stato die*) when Christians in that region met,[83] but nowhere mentions explicitly the "first day of the week."

80. Deissmann's argument is given in *Light*, 359. Prigent, *Apocalypse*, 129 is dismissive of this suggestion; Aune, *Revelation 1–5*, 84 regards Deissmann's reconstruction as "highly unlikely" while Bauckham, "Lord's Day," 244, acknowledges the possibility that Deissmann's argument is correct.

81. Latin text in *Res Gestae* 11 reads *et diem Augustalia ex cognomine nostro appellavit*; see Freyburger, "Augustalia," 354, and esp. commentary by Cooley, *Res Gestae*, 152.

82. Witherington, *Revelation*, 80.

83. Pliny, *Ep. Tra.* 10.96.7; Pliny's summary, coming from lapsed believers, may imply Sunday, but that is certainly not stated. Early Christian sources are clear on this issue, e.g., the contemporary letter of Ign. *Magn.* (9:1) and the report from Justin Martyr in the mid-second century, *1 Apol.* 67.

The command to John to "write down" the content of the revelation he received resonates with stories in both Jewish[84] and pagan[85] literature about the reception of oracles from the deities. The following wording in a Greek inscription from eastern Asia Minor reveals a typical pagan perspective on the reception of divine revelation and the subsequent recording of it.

> I have, in obedience to the inspiration of the gods, ordered to be inscribed upon sacred, inviolable stelae a holy law, which shall be binding upon all generations of mankind who . . . shall successively be destined to dwell in this land [of Commagene]; they must observe it without violation, knowing that the stern penalty of the deified royal ancestors will pursue equally the impiety occasioned by neglect as that occasioned by folly, and that disregard of the law decreed for the honor of the heroes brings with it inexorable penalties. For the pious it is all a simple matter, but godlessness is followed by backbreaking burdens. This law my voice has proclaimed, but it is the mind of the gods that has given it authority.[86]

John hears this particular revelation (*kai ēkousa*, καὶ ἤκουσα), although at other times revelations are seen by him (Rev 1:12, 17; 4:1; 5:1; 6:1; 7:1, etc.), in ways perhaps similar to examples from Jewish Scriptures, e.g., Isa 13:1; Nah 1:1; Hab 1:1. John's phrase "I was in the Spirit" (*en pneumati*, ἐν πνεύματι) reminds the reader of other texts in Revelation (e.g., 4:2; 17:3; 21:10) as well as numerous prophetic experiences mentioned in the Old Testament, e.g., Ezek 2:2; 3:12, 14, 24; 8:3; 11:1; 37:1. John's words "in the Spirit" point clearly to the Spirit of God and are meant to guarantee that the revelation occurs under divine hegemony. Beale[87] suggests that the phrase "loud voice like the sound of a trumpet" (*phōnēn megalēn hōs salpingos*, φωνὴν μεγάλην ὡς σάλπιγγος) should be understood in light of Exod 19:16 with its correlation of the Horeb theophany and a "very loud trumpet sound" (LXX *phōnē tēs salpingos ēchei mega*, φωνὴ τῆς σαλπιγγος ἤχει μέγα).

---

84. Exod 17:14; Jer 30:2; Isa 30:8 LXX; Tob 12:20.

85. Note also Aelius Aristides speech where he remembers, "Dream visions compel us to bring these things somehow to light. Still I can say this much that straight from the beginning the god ordered me to write down these things," Aelius Aristides 48:2. Other examples are mentioned by Aune, *Revelation 1-5*, 86-7.

86. Dörner and Young, "Nomos Inscriptions," 215.

87. Beale, *Revelation*, 204-5.

In Rev 1:11 John specifies which seven churches he was commanded to address. He also makes it clear that the words and visions recorded in the book of Revelation were destined for these particular seven churches. This means that all theories of interpretation of Revelation must take quite seriously the intended literary and thematic connection between the geographical setting of the seven churches and the rest of John's prophecies recorded in Revelation. It is totally inappropriate, for example, to read Rev 4:1–19:21 in light of church conditions in Judaea, either before or after the fall of Jerusalem, since this would inexcusably fragment the literary unity of the book of Revelation. It would also render the book incomprehensible since there is little connection between the political, social, and religious realities of western Roman Asia and far away Judaea. Even though some interpreters have suggested this, it is blatant fantasy to identify these seven congregations with seven distinct periods of later ecclesiastical history. There is simply no justification for this type of allegorization of John's first-century communication with these seven congregations of western Anatolia.

There have been questions about the sequence in which John mentions the seven cities. More important than their sequence, however, is their significance. These seven cities[88] were politically significant and were active participants, indeed leaders, in the *Koinon* of Asia.[89] This *Koinon*, or league, was a political and civic institution heavily involved in the local practices of the imperial cult, emperor veneration, and patriotic enthusiasm.[90] Cities in this *Koinon* of Asia were naturally competitive for the right to have an imperial temple in their city. According to the Roman historian Tacitus, the cities of Laodicea, Pergamum, Ephesus, Sardis, and Smyrna

---

88. Boxall proposes a simplified version of the older view, i.e., Ramsay's, and states that the sequence "reflects the natural route followed by the deliverer of Revelation," *Revelation*, 41.

89. Mitchell, *Anatolia*, 1:100–117; Mellor, Θεὰ ʿΡώμη, 79–82; a pre-Christian Greek inscription from Roman Asia lists, similarly to Pliny's *Nat.* 5.105–126, Ephesus, Smyrna, Pergamum, and Sardis, among others, as member cities of the *Koinon* (=Sherk, *Roman Documents*, no. 52, 272–76) and Magie, *Roman Rule* (see index "Commonalty of Asia").

90. Tacitus reports an incident when the cities of Asia voted a temple, in gratitude, to Tiberius, his mother and the Roman Senate (*Ann.* 4.15.4). Those eleven Asian cities which petitioned to have this imperial temple in their own city included Laodicea, Pergamum, Ephesus, Sardis, and Smyrna (4.55.3–7); also Merkelbach, "Der Rangstreit," 287–96.

Figure 38

were in such competition; and the cities of Pergamum, Smyrna, and Ephesus each had an imperial temple before the end of the first century.[91]

Rev 1:12 Then I turned to see whose voice it was that spoke to me, and on turning I saw seven golden lampstands, 13 and in the midst of the lampstands I saw one like the Son of Man, clothed with a long robe and with a golden sash across his chest. 14 His head and his hair were white as white wool, white as snow; his eyes were like a flame of fire, 15 his feet were like burnished bronze, refined as in a furnace, and his voice was like the sound of many waters. 16 In his right hand he held seven stars, and from his mouth came a sharp, two-edged sword, and his face was like the sun shining with full force. 17 When I saw him, I fell at his feet as though dead. But he placed his right hand on me, saying, "Do not be afraid; I am the first and the last, 18 and the living one. I was dead, and see, I am alive forever and ever; and I have the keys of Death and of Hades.

Ancient artists, authors, and philosophers struggled with the idea of communicating their original visual experiences to others, regardless of the object of their original visual experience. For example, how does the great Greek sculptor Phidias depict in three dimensional art what Zeus looks like? Moreover, if one has seen this achievement of Phidias in the Temple of Zeus at Olympia, regarded as one of the Seven Wonders of the Ancient World, how can words communicate the description so powerfully that a reader can experience the Phidian Zeus through another's words?

John's description of Christ brings the reader of Revelation into the rhetorical world of *ekphrasis* that was so popular and widespread in the ancient Graeco-Roman world. This technique's goal was to give "a description which tries to bring its object clearly in front of the reader' eyes: persons, things, situations, cities, seasons, celebrations, etc."[92] This means that Revelation's early christophany is not ornamental, but is placed strategically to cast a prominent shadow over the letters to the seven congregations. Broadly conceived, this particular *ekphrasis* of John's christophany is presented to give a detailed description of Christ (the longest in the New Testament) that is intended both to help the audience experience

91. Burrell, *Neokoroi*, 17–85.
92. Fantuzzi, "Ekphrasis," 872.

the original vision and to exert an impact on the surrounding epistolary materials in chapters two and three. In some instances, "Images of gods, for example, are attributed special sacredness through enormous size and weight, exalted dignity, and old age."[93] The picture of Christ recorded by John in this opening chapter certainly employs notable and distinctive features reminiscent of *ekphrasis*.

Initially John does not know who speaks to him while he is in the Spirit. Quite naturally, though, he turns in the direction of the voice. Commentators have often inquired about the nature of this voice that is ostensibly visible. The best interpretation seems to be that of James Charlesworth, who argues that John's use of the term "voice" is a hypostatization, which means John conceives of "'the Voice' as a divine being."[94]

The meaning of the vision of the Son of Man in Rev 1:16 has been much more opaque and problematic for later interpreters than it would have been for the men and women in John's first audience. The scriptural antecedents of this depiction of Christ are of great importance in its proper interpretation. In particular, most of the imagery comes into greater clarity when viewed through the lens of Dan 7:9–15, 10:5–6; Isa 11:4, 49:2, and Zech 4:2, 11.

Theme	Revelation	Old Testament
Seven lampstands	Rev 1:12b–1:13a	Zech 4:2, 11
Son of Man	Rev 1:13b	Dan 7:13
Robe and golden sash	Rev 1:13c	Dan 10:5
White hair	Rev 1:14a	Dan 7:9
Fiery eyes	Rev 1:14b	Dan 10:6
Bronze feet	Rev 1:15a	Dan 10:6
Roaring voice	Rev 1:15b	Dan 10:6
Seven stars in hand	Rev 1:16a	cultural symbols
Sword from mouth	Rev 1:16b	Isa 11:4; 49:2
Radiate face	Rev 1:16c	Dan 10:6

Quite naturally, however, the Old Testament components of the image have been adapted to varying degrees in their presentation of Christ in order to respond to the needs of the context of John's ministry to these seven congregations. This context of ministry explains why this description of

93. Ibid., 878.
94. Charlesworth, "Voice and Early," 130.

Christ is later distributed among the letters to the seven congregations (see notes on Rev 1:18).

For both historical and theological purposes it is important to comment briefly on the christophany John records here in his efforts to minister to believers. When gazing, or perhaps gasping, at this visionary image described as "one like the Son of Man," the grotesqueness of the christophany in this vision should not be overlooked. A believer at Sardis, Pergamum, or Ephesus, for example, could not avoid being struck by the stark contrast between the essential beauty of the classical gods and goddesses his eyes had seen in the past day's walk through the markets, plazas, and streets of these urban centers[95] and the grotesque picture that John puts before him.

In the countless dreams, visions, and oracles left us by pious pagans of Graeco-Roman antiquity, the deities was often displayed in his or her beauty, compassion, splendor, and majesty. It is often unknown, or forgotten, that in their original setting the statues of gods and goddesses in the Graeco-Roman were not the white, colorless forms that greet the usual tourist or museum visitor today. Ancient statues of deities were colorful, ornate, beautifully clothed, visually charming, and seductive to the sight. They were typically designed to be aesthetically pleasing. The same cannot be said of John's vision of Christ. John's inability to reveal something like the "attractive Christ"[96] that has continued for two thousand years of Christian history reveals an iconographic strategy of Revelation 1. This countercultural strategy is not one that should be a total surprise to students of Scripture. While the contrast between John's iconography of divinity and that of his contemporaries is sharp-edged, the edge between John's iconography and that of the later church's is serrated.

John certainly knows from experience and his spiritual heritage that when God's people are confronted with the beautiful allurement and benefits of paganism (see esp. Jer 44:15–19), there will always be a Balaam or Jezebel who chooses to craft the proverbial Trojan Horse of assimilation. Even though the Christian advocates of assimilation often genuinely believe that partial imitation of paganism is the best way forward and

95. Paganism did have a handful of scruffy-looking minor deities, but these certainly were regarded as marginal or were participants in the apotropaic and occult dimensions of ancient religion.

96. Even the unattractiveness of Isa 53:2 has assumed a redemptive attractiveness. Certainly the "friend of children," "pale Galilean," "robust carpenter," "Marxist liberator," "peasant martyr," Michelangelo's Pietà, etc., have all projected a facet of attractiveness.

necessary for ultimate success, the very bridges that the assimilationists build toward their surrounding culture typically become the same pathway for the intrusion of paganism.[97] The visual beauty of *golden gods* at Horeb was patently more scintillating to the eyes and more attractive to the people than an unassimilated and invisible depiction of YHWH (Exod 32:1–5).

The prophet first sees seven lampstands, apparently not the seven-branch menorah described in Exod 37:18 and attested to in Jewish iconography of the early Roman Empire. John sees seven individual lampstands, each with a single flame, which was commonplace in the Roman world

John's statement that he saw someone "like a Son of Man," is best interpreted from the setting of Dan 7:13.[98] The phrase "Son of Man" clearly refers to Jesus Christ in this instance (notwithstanding the absence of the usual article in Greek; cf. 14:14)[99] as it also does in the gospels.[100] It is important to note the adaptation of Dan 7 that is apparent in the prophet's vision. Whereas in Dan 7 the Son of Man and the Ancient of Days are two distinct figures, here the Son of Man is identified with the Ancient of Days based upon the imagery in Rev

Figure 39

1:14 (Dan 7:9). According to evidence presented by Aune,[101] this identification may have already occurred in the pre-Christian era.

In the judgment of some interpreters the mention of robe and golden sash is thought to refer to either a person of great significance or to the Jewish high priest (Exod 28:4).[102] It is probably more accurate to see these

97. MacMullen's book documents this for the patristic era, *Christianity and Paganism*, esp. chap. 4, "Assimilation," 103–49. Viola and Barna, *Pagan Christianity?* makes similar points on a more popular level.

98. Osborne, *Revelation*, 87–88.

99. See Thomas, *Revelation 1–7*, 97–98 for a discussion of this issue.

100. Marshall, "Son of Man," 775–81.

101. Aune, *Revelation 1–5*, 90–92.

102. Osborne, *Revelation*, 89.

Figure 40

images in terms of angelic imagery from Dan 10:5–6 and Ezek 9:2.[103] The image of white hair stems from the description of the Ancient of Days in Dan 7:9, "the head of his hair were as white as white wool." The references to blazing eyes and bronze feet derive from Daniel, but in this instance from 10:6, "his eyes like were like a flame of fire, his feet were like burnished bronze." Unlike Daniel 7, which describes the Ancient of Days and the Son of Man, this imagery in Daniel 10 describes an angelic being.[104] What we have then is a composite christophany that brings together imagery from the Ancient of Days and Son of Man in Dan 7 and combines it with angelic imagery from Dan 10:5–6.[105]

The Revelation of John is a book that strongly appeals to the senses, and this mention of the loud voice is only the first of many such examples. Jesus Christ (Rev 1:10), various angels (Rev 5:2; 7:2; 14:9, 15, 18; 19:17), the martyrs (Rev 6:10; 7:10), midair eagles (Rev 8:13; 14:7), and a divine voice (Rev 16:1, 17; 21:3) all speak with what John calls "a loud voice." Indeed, in the description portrayed by John, the throne of God seems to be eternally surrounded by the ambient sound of a loud thunderstorm (Rev 4:5; 11:19; cf. 10:3–4). Many of God's earthly punishments also include a component of noise, often a trumpet sound (Rev 8:6, 7, 8, 10, 12; 9:1, 13; 11:15). The roaring voice of the Messiah, like many waters, may likewise derive from the "sound of the multitude" of Dan 10:6, assuming that the point of comparison to "many waters" is the loudness of the voice (cf. Ezek 1:24; 43:2). One can only imagine the decibel level of the Messiah's authoritative roaring voice, but clearly it sounds more like loudly thundering waves than like the noise of a trickling fountain in a meditation garden.

103. Stuckenbruck, "Revelation," 1539.

104. Beale (*Revelation*, 210) writes, "For a similar portrayal of heavenly beings based on Dan 10:5–6 see also Apocalypse of Abraham 11; Apocalypse of Zephaniah 6:11–13; 2 En. 1:5"; Aune, *Revelation 1–5*, 95 cites examples of "fiery eyes" in Jewish as well as Graeco-Roman literature.

105. Stuckenbruck, *Angel Veneration*, 205–18; Aune, *Revelation 1–5*, 90–91.

This powerful celestial image of Christ steps beyond the standard pool of images in Scripture when it mentions the seven stars Christ holds in his right hand (Rev 1:16a). Astral imagery was part of the religious *lingua franca* of John's day, and Revelation does not shy away from employing it, as seen in the book's multiple references to the stars and moon (Rev 1:16, 20; 2:1, 28; 3:1; 6:13; 8:10; 9:1; 12:1, 4; 22:16). Interpreters sometimes ask about John's use of astral imagery in light of the prohibitions against astrology that are well known in ancient Judaism (Deut 4:19; cf. the reform of Josiah, 2 Kgs 22–23): "And when you look up to the heavens and see the sun, the moon, and the stars, all the host of heaven, do not be led astray and bow down to them and serve them, things that the Lord your God has allotted to all the peoples everywhere under heaven." The later Hellenistic–early Roman Jewish writing Wisdom of Solomon (13:1–2) contains convictions similar to those associated with Moses centuries earlier. "For all people who were ignorant of God were foolish by nature; and they were unable from the good things that are seen to know the one who exists, nor did they recognize the artisan while paying heed to his works; but they supposed that either fire or wind or swift air, or the circle of the stars, or turbulent water, or the luminaries of heaven were the gods that rule the world." Notwithstanding these stern warnings, even hyper-orthodox groups like the sect of the Dead Sea Scrolls used horoscopes.[106] In this regard it is also noteworthy that the Gospel of Matthew (2:1–16) depicts eastern astrologers (Matt 2:1–2, *idou magoi apo anatolōn paregeneto eis Ierosoluma*, ἰδοὺ μάγοι ἀπὸ ἀνατολῶν παρεγένετο εἰς Ἱεροσόλυμα) using their astrological training to locate Jesus, the King of the Jews.

A visual commentary on John's astral imagery is provided by the numismatic iconography of a gold coin (and also silver denarii) that uses the seven star symbolism to depict ideas about the divinity of the emperor's family.[107] Ironically, this obvious piece of historical evidence has been neglected by some scholars. The following negative assessment by Prigent[108] about the lack of numismatic testimony to the "seven star" imagery in imperial iconography certainly seems inappropriate: "As for the imperial coins on which seven stars, which are seen as the symbolic expression of and pretension to universal domination, it must be pointed out that they are rare coins and, in any case, are dated well after the period of time in

---

106. 4Q186 (4QHoroscope). Albani, "Horoscopes," 370–73.

107. This coin can be found in Sutherland, *Roman Coins*, 191, plate 347. On this particular coin, the "seven star" theme is associated with one who became fully divine in his immortal state following death.

108. Prigent, *Apocalypse*, 140.

question!" This particular golden coin, as well as silver ones like it, was struck during the reign of Domitian. The divinized infant (the dead son of Domitian) is surrounded by seven stars, while he himself has hands that have become stars, perhaps indicating that he was holding multiple stars in each of his hands.

The symbolism of the term "sword" in this text stems from texts such as Isa 11:4, "And he will strike the earth with the rod of his mouth,"

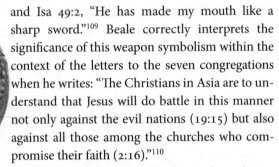

and Isa 49:2, "He has made my mouth like a sharp sword."[109] Beale correctly interprets the significance of this weapon symbolism within the context of the letters to the seven congregations when he writes: "The Christians in Asia are to understand that Jesus will do battle in this manner not only against the evil nations (19:15) but also against all those among the churches who compromise their faith (2:16)."[110]

Figure 41

This militaristic and bellicose face of Jesus is bothersome to some interpreters (see notes on Rev 2:26–27). This warrior theme is cut from the same cloth as John's heavy reliance upon a Royal Davidic christology. Indeed, one of the textual backgrounds to this image (Isa 11:4) is an explicit Royal Davidic text that mentions the offspring of Jesse (Isa 11:1).

With the realities of the post-Constantinian church, bastardized in regard to its relationship with the Roman State, most of Christian history has been characterized by a sordid abuse and exploitation of sword imagery from Scripture, starting at least as early as Julius Firmicus Maternus in the fourth century.[111] When a religion is content to make an internecine "law imposing the death penalty for celebrating Easter on the wrong day of the year," it comes as no surprise that deadly force against other religions could flow very naturally when they interpreted literally metaphors

---

109. Compare Wis 18:15–16, "Your all-powerful word leaped from heaven, from the royal throne, into the midst of the land that was doomed, a stern warrior, carrying the sharp sword of your authentic command, and stood and filled all things with death, and touched heaven while standing on the earth."

110. Beale, *Revelation*, 212; Caird, *Revelation*, however, does not even mention this significant imagery.

111. Julius Firmicus Maternus was a mid-fourth century Christian author, perhaps the first, who suggested the use of force and threat of death in the conversion of pagans to the Christian faith; Potter, "Julius Firmicus Maternus," 598.

Figure 42

Figure 43

about swords in Scripture.[112] Accordingly, it needs to be pointed out that in both Isa 11:4 and 49:2 as well as in Rev 1:16 the bellicose imagery is already understood metaphorically. That is, already with Judaism these verses were based upon a metaphorical and nonliteral use of the term "sword." The reason that both verses have the term "mouth" is to highlight the fact that this is real, but metaphorical, militarism (Isa 49:2; cf. Eph 6:10–17).

The solar and luminous face of Jesus Christ ("like the sun shining") described here is reminiscent of the description of Jesus on the Mount of Transfiguration (Matt 17:2; cf. Mark 9:3) and subtly anticipates the solar references later mentioned in the New Jerusalem (Rev 21:23; 22:5). Some interpreters suggest for this image the verbal background provided by Judges 5:31 ("So perish all your enemies, O Lord! But may your friends be like the sun as it rises in its might"),[113] while others argue for "The Face like a Sun as an Angelomorphic Feature of Christ."[114]

When seen in the pastoral context of Roman Asia, one must ask whether this iconic image of a face shining like the sun was known and in vogue outside of Christian circles of thought. It would be remiss not to also consider Roman imperial sources that visually depict the luminous face of deities and Rome's divine emperors. This sun-like description of the face of the Son of Man is similar to an iconic depiction in the Graeco-Roman world of nascent Christianity known as radiate.[115] It is naturally

112. MacMullen, *Christianizing*, 93.

113. Beale, *Revelation*, 212.

114. Hoffmann, *Destroyer*, 230–34.

115. Stevenson et al., "Radiata Corona," 679; also Forum Ancient Coins, "Radiata Corona."

found with portraits of the sun god Helios.[116] In its basic form the icon had sunrays coming from the head of the sun god. When adapted to divinized rulers, there would be a regal crown that had rays of the sun emanating upward from the crown.[117] This iconic theme is found early in the Hellenistic era. This visual language likewise appears on artifacts pertaining to the first Roman Emperor Augustus. This radiate theme is preserved in both numismatic and other visual works of art from the Roman era and certainly would have been known to John and his audience.[118]

Figure 44

By displaying this iconic symbol John is not only placing the risen Christ in competition with many of the gods and certainly the Roman emperors, but also arguing for the splendor and terrifying solar brilliance of Christ. As a point of contrast one should consider what often happened in Greek mystery religions when the emphasis of initiation was not so much on what one learned but what one experienced.[119] At the site of the great Eleusinian Mysteries, for example, there was a relief of the goddess Demeter that showed the rays of sunlight streaming from the face of the goddess.[120] According to Plato these initiation experiences of the deities were beautiful and were "simple and calm and happy apparitions" (Plato, *Phaed.* 250B–C).

By rather sharp contrast John's prophecy might be suggesting that it is not always pleasant to look at Christ. At times it might be just as painful, intolerable, and dangerous to stare at the unfiltered glory of Christ as it is to stare at the sun. After all John was almost killed by the experience (Rev 1:17).

John's response to this christophany resonates with biblical themes. Being in the presence of God's revelation clearly highlights the concept of awe and reverence. In addition, the connection between "seeing" and

---

116. Rapp, "Helios," 1993–2026.

117. Bergmann, *Die Strahlen* is replete with examples of this preserved in various media from the Graeco-Roman world. While part of Bergmann's thesis is to show that much of this imagery was metaphorical, this does not detract from its value for this study.

118. Bergmann, *Die Strahlen*, e.g., plates 1–7, 22.

119. Klauck, *Religious Context*, 87.

120. Clinton, *Myth and Cult*, 89–90; fig. 78.

"dying" stems from the biblical conviction about seeing holy things and dying (Num 4:20). This connection is also powerfully presented in a story found in the book of Exodus. (33:18–23; cf. Exod 3:6; 20:19; Deut 18:16): "Moses said, 'Show me your glory, I pray.' And he said, 'I will make all my goodness pass before you, and will proclaim before you the name, "The Lord"; and I will be gracious to whom I will be gracious, and will show mercy on whom I will show mercy. But,' he said, 'you cannot see my face; for no one shall see me and live.' And the Lord continued, 'See, there is a place by me where you shall stand on the rock; and while my glory passes by I will put you in a cleft of the rock, and I will cover you with my hand until I have passed by; then I will take away my hand, and you shall see my back; but my face shall not be seen.'" John's fear is understandable, primarily because of the holiness associated with the frightful "Son of Man," but also because he stands in the presence of one who had returned from the dreaded underworld.

The terms "the First" and "the Last" are certainly divine epithets here, in the Old Testament (Isa 41:4; 44:6; 48:12),[121] and in non-Christian religions.[122] Here the terms are designed to associate Christ with the Alpha and Omega mentioned earlier in the chapter (1:8), an association made clearer in Rev 22:13, "I am the Alpha and the Omega, the first and the last, the beginning and the end."

Jesus's resurrection from the dead was certainly in the cluster of bedrock convictions of the early church (1 Cor 15:1–5). This conviction held even more significance for a suffering church that was warned to expect additional martyrdoms in the future (6:11). In embryonic form the Old Testament already revealed a belief in the resurrection of the dead. One thinks of Isa 26:19 LXX (cf. Dan 12:1–2 and perhaps Isa 66:24): "The dead shall rise, and those who are in the tombs shall be raised (*anastēsontai hoi vekroi kai egerthēsontai hoi en tois mnēmeiois*, ἀναστήσονται οἱ νεκροί καὶ ἐγερθήσονται οἱ ἐν τοῖς μνημείοις), and those who are in the earth shall rejoice; for the dew from you is healing to them, but the land of the impious shall fall." It is noteworthy, though, that the Old Testament testimony

---

121. The LXX of all three of these texts contain the term "first," but lack the term "last," preferring instead different prepositional phrases pointing to the future, respectively *eis ta eperchomena*, "for the things that are coming"; *kai egō meta tauta*, "and I am after these things"; *kai egō eimi eis ton aiōna*, "and I am forever" (εἰς τὰ ἐπερχόμενα; καὶ ἐγὼ μετὰ ταῦτα; καὶ ἐγώ εἰμι εἰς τὸν αἰῶνα).

122. Surprisingly BDAG and Spicq, *Theological Lexicon* are devoid of any Graeco-Roman references to these terms in pagan religions; see Aelius Aristides, *Oration* 43.8, "Zeus is the First" (πρῶτος); likewise Koenen and Kramer, "Ein Hymnus," 19–21.

is only embryonic. Notwithstanding the centrality of the resurrection to New Testament theology, it is one of several important New Testament doctrines that has only faint testimony in the Old Testament. "The [Hebrew] Bible mostly denies or at least ignores the possibility of a future life," N. T. Wright correctly says, "with only a few texts coming out strongly for a different view; but in the second-Temple period the position is more or less reversed."[123]

The term "key(s)" is found four times in Revelation (1:18; 3:7; 9:1; 20:1). Three of these occurrences are associated with confinement in the underworld, a world full of dreadful chthonian horrors and beings associated with demonic forces. The fourth reference is to the "key of David" and this stems from Isa 22:22 (see commentary 3:7).

The term Hades (ᾅδης) occurs more often in Revelation than in any other book in the New Testament, and in Revelation it is always coupled with the term death (1:18; 6:8; 20:13, 14). In the Old Testament Hades was typically regarded as the resting place of the dead, but on occasion could be personified (Hos 13:14).[124]

Hades was considered a deity in the Graeco-Roman world and was personified in art and poetry.[125] With the abundant number of sarcophagi preserved from the world of Greece and Rome it is not unusual to see a sarcophagus adorned with closed doors to represent the entrance to Hades. In one such instance the god Hermes is even stationed at the doorway to Hades to escort souls to the underworld.[126] Since noxious and deadly gases came from some cave entrances around Greece and Asia Minor, it was widely held by Graeco-Roman individuals that these were literal doorways into the underworld of sulfur and fire (cf., Rev 9:17–18; 14:10; 19:20; 20:10; 21:8). There were only a few sites in the Roman world that contained a *Plutonium*, a sacred cave and sanctuary to the god Pluto (=Hades) that led directly to the underworld. The remains of one of these is still at the archaeological site of Hierapolis in Roman Asia.[127]

While many in the Graeco-Roman world of early Christianity had a robust belief in the immortality of the soul, the Christian hope of the

---

123. Wright, *Resurrection*, 129.

124. Wächter, "*sheol*," 239–48.

125. Bremmer, "Hades," 1076–77; Scherer, "V. Hades," 1793–813.

126. Bremmer, "Hades," 1076–77; Scherer, "V. Hades," 1793–813.

127. D'Andria, *Hierapolis of Phrygia*, 142–44. Ancient sources about the Plutonium at Hierapolis include Strabo, *Geogr.* 12.8.17; 13.4.14; Dio Cassius, *Rom. Hist.* 68.27.3; and Pliny, *Nat.* 2.208. Bremmer, "Hades," 1076–77; Scherer, "V. Hades," 1793–813.

Figure 45

resurrection of the body was absolute superstition to them.[128] Midway through the administration of the Roman Emperor Nero, the emperor sent a Roman Procurator named Porcius Festus to administer Judaea (AD 59–62).[129] In the course of his administration of the Jews he had the opportunity to hear an apologetic speech from the Apostle Paul. When Porcius Festus heard Paul's statement about the resurrection of Jesus and that Jesus was the "first to rise from the dead" (Acts 26:23, *ei pathētos ho christos ei prōtos ex anastaseōs nekrōn,* εἰ παθητὸς ὁ χριστός εἰ πρῶτος ἐξ ἀναστάσεως νεκρῶν) he could only respond by screaming "you are out of your mind, Paul!" (Acts 26:24, *ho Phēstos megalē tē phōnē phēsin mainē Paule,* ὁ Φῆστος μεγάλῃ τῇ φωνῇ φησιν μαίνῃ, Παῦλε). Like so

128. An often forgotten source for Graeco-Roman notions about postmortem reality is Vergil's *Aen.* 6.

129. Rajak, "Porcius Festus," 1226.

83

Figure 46   **Figure 47**

many of his pagan contemporaries (cf. Acts 17:32a) Porcius Festus could
not imagine a new religion where Hermes was gone, where the face of
Medusa no longer had any apotropaic strength on sarcophagi, and where
all the doors to Hades would ultimately be knocked from their hinges by
the resurrection of Jesus. The epitaph of the Lamb, "I was dead, and see,
I am alive forever and ever" (1:18) would certainly have caught the eye of
a pagan observer who was accustomed to reading epitaphs that expressed
exactly the opposite. One such Greek epitaph reads, "After having died, no
one comes back to life from here" (*enteuthen outheis apothanōn egeiretai,*
ἐντεῦθεν οὐθεὶς ἀποθανὼν ἐγείρεται),[130] or the well known Latin abbre-
viation on tombstones N F F N S N C (*Non Fui Fui Non Sum Non Curo*; I
was not; I was; I am not; I do not care).[131]

Figure 48

It would be hard to overestimate the
role of this christophany in the structure
of the first three chapters. This revelation
of the Son of Man sets the stage for the
seven letters and plays a critical role in
their later interpretation. It is noteworthy, for example, that many of the components

---

130. Peek, *Griechische Grabgedichte*, no. 480 (= *IG* XIV.2130).

131. Lattimore, *Themes*, 84–85.

of the description of Christ will appear in the opening verses of each of the seven letters,[132] thereby making a proper study of the seven letters impossible without an interpretation of the prior christophany. This use and adaptation of the christophany in the subsequent letters to the seven churches reveals to the reader, among other things, that John's prophecies have a structured character.

Furthermore, this tight literary and theological connection between the Christ of chapter 1 and the message of chapters 2 and 3 demonstrates that John's visions of Christ undergirds the instructions to the seven congregations. It would be inappropriate for the hearer of the seven letters, for example, to view the materials from Christ through the lens of the "slain Lamb of God" (Rev 5:6, 8, 12, 13; 6:1, 7, 9, 16; 7:9, 14, 17; 8:1; 12:11, etc.) christology revealed only later in the book.

The seven congregations of Roman Asia are about to be offered both sublime rewards and victories and also trenchant warnings and threats, both from the same divine source, the terrifying Son of Man. Accordingly, John wants both the threats and the assurances to the congregations to come from the same divine presence and spiritual reality manifested in the Messiah.

Christophany		*Letters to Churches*	
1:12	Seven golden lampstands	2:1, 5	Ephesus
1:14	Eyes like flame of fire	2:18	Thyatira
1:15	Feet like burnished bronze	2:18	Thyatira
1:16	Seven stars	2:1; 3:1	Ephesus, Sardis
1:16	Sharp two–edged sword	2:12, 16	Pergamum
1:17	First & last; died & now alive	2:8	Smyrna
1:18	Possession of keys (?)	3:7	Philadelphia (?)

The original recipients of John's prophecies needed more than merely a scintillating vision of the Christ, even if grounded in Scripture. They had a dire need for a transcendent vision that would challenge their movement toward assimilation as well as support them in their time of trial and growing alienation from most of their prior cultural moorings. Thus, the pastoral directives to these seven congregations are linked to the preceding christological visions that John has presented in dramatic detail and with pregnant iconography. In this way the promise and hope of the

---

132. Prigent, *Apocalypse,* 149–50; Hoffmann, *Destroyer,* 213–15.

congregations, either of reward or of punishment, can be traced back to God's Messiah depicted in stark images and themes.

It would be remiss toward John's prophetic christophany as well as the anemic condition of "popular" christology not to point out this irony, that even though this christophany of Rev 1 is the most detailed depiction of Christ in the New Testament it is simultaneously the most avoided and neglected portrait of Christ in Christian art, ecclesiastical iconography, and Christian preaching.

Rev 1:19 Now write what you have seen, what is, and what is to take place after this. 20 As for the mystery of the seven stars that you saw in my right hand, and the seven golden lampstands: the seven stars are the angels of the seven churches, and the seven lampstands are the seven churches.

The specific meaning and interpretive significance of the threefold temporal reference in 1:19 (i.e., "have seen," "is now," and "take place later") has generated much discussion. Some suggest that this threefold paradigm comes from the very nature of a divine voice who is described as, "who is," "who was," and "who is to come" (1:4). Of course this verse reflects a different sequence. Rev 1:4 uses present, past, and future, while 1:19 employs the different sequence of past, present, and future.

Others see the instructions of 1:19 as an expanded restatement of Rev 1:11--"Write in a book what you see," though its form was probably influenced by contemporary religious literary forms. These particular literary forms have been labeled as "tripartite prophetic formulas." What this means is that in Greek and later Latin literature stretching for almost a millennium (from the early Greek author Homer, *Il.* 1.70, to the early Augustan Latin author Ovid, *Metam.* 1.517–518)—authors frequently formulated divine revelation in the three categories of "what was," "what is," and "what will be."[133] To give only one of several examples, in Plato's *Resp.* the goddess Necessity had three daughters; one revealed the things that were, another the things that are, and the third the things that will be (*Resp.* 10.617c).

This tripartite temporal division also anticipates aspects of the narrative of Revelation, since there are clearly some things that John has already experienced (Rev 1); there are obviously matters and conditions that currently exist (Rev 2–3); and there are events that are prophesied to occur in the future (4–22). To be sure, in the case of Revelation these temporal boundaries between the three periods are porous at times. This is demonstrated by the presence of future promises and future tenses in the "what

133. van Unnik, "Formula," 86–94; also Aune, *Revelation 1–5*, 112–14.

is now" section (chapters 2–3) and past events in the "what will take place later" section (chapters 4–22).[134]

Christ's epiphany ends with an interpretation of two parts of the visual symbolism of Rev 1:12–13, 16. It is noteworthy that with all the robust iconography employed in the christophany the term "mystery" (*to mustērion*, τὸ μυστήριον) is used only two times and both of these are associated with the number seven. The first are the seven stars located in the right hand of the Son of Man that are identified with the seven angels (*angeloi*, ἄγγελοι) assigned to these seven congregations. Understandably there has been much debate about the meaning and significance of congregational angels.[135] The most probable source for this concept is Jewish Scripture and Jewish writings from the period of the later Second Temple. In these writings one finds the concept of God's assignment of intermediary spiritual beings. Coming from the Second Temple period, the LXX version of Deuteronomy 32:8 reads that when God divided the nations, he did so according to the number of the angels of God (*hote diemerizen ho hupsistos ethnē hōs diespeiren huious Adam estēsen horia ethnōn kata arithmon angelōn theou*, ὅτε διεμέριζεν ὁ ὕψιστος ἔθνη ὡς διέσπειρεν υἱοὺς Αδαμ ἔστησεν ὅρια ἐθνῶν κατὰ ἀριθμὸν ἀγγέλων θεοῦ). In the Hebrew version of Deuteronomy found among the Dead Sea Scrolls it states that this division of nations was based upon the number of supernatural or

Figure 49

134. Compare Thomas, *Revelation 1–7*, 113–16 with Aune, *Revelation 1–5*, 105–6.
135. Aune, *Revelation 1–5*, 108–12.

divine beings called children of God.[136] From the Old Testament, nations such as Israel, Persia, and Greece have their own individual angels (Dan 10:13, 20) who serve as intermediaries and advocates.

Turning to the literature beyond Scripture, it is noteworthy among the Dead Sea Scrolls that the "Songs of the Sabbath Sacrifice" is replete not only with references to the number seven, but also with references of numerous angels and other divine beings who serve and worship in the vicinity of the One seated on the throne. In that context there is reference to seven assemblies or congregations (4Q404 frag. 2 + 3AB), presumably congregations of divine or angelic beings. Another relevant writing from the community at Qumran is known as 1QRule of the Congregation (1Q28a 2.8–9). In a section that is clearly referring to the assembly and congregation of the people of Qumran it states that defiled individuals "shall not en[ter] to take their place [a]mong the congregation of the men of renown, for the angels of holiness are among their [congre]gation." Similarly, in the Qumran War Scroll it is clear that God has assigned "holy angels" to individual armies of the Lord (1QM (=1QWarScroll) 7.6–7). Although fragmentary there is a document from Cave 4 from Qumran that states, "There will be no pestilence in your land. For God is with you and his holy angels are in the midst of your Community."[137]

It seems, then, that the angelology evident in the seven letters where each of these seven congregations is served and overseen by a divinely appointed angel makes abundant sense in the context of the complex Jewish angelology existing at that time (see notes on Rev 2:1).[138]

The second aspect of John's concept of mystery focuses on the seven lampstands mentioned earlier; they are now identified as congregations. Thus, the destination of this grand revelation with all its literary and thematic sophistication is specifically congregations (1:11). The stage for this epiphany of the Son of Man is not like the lofty clouds of heaven in Daniel and the synoptic gospels (Matt 24:30; Mark 13:26, 14:62; Luke 21:27), but rather the congregational lampstands of Western Asia Minor (1:12–13, 20). Even the potent astral iconography of the stars (1:16)[139] is brought under the perspective of congregational existence (Rev 1:20).

136. Abegg et al., *Scrolls Bible*, 191.

137. 4Q285 (=4QSefer ha-Milhamah) frag. 1.9.

138. Most commentators rightly reject attempts to turn these angelic beings into mere human messengers to the churches or, even less acceptable, into bishops of the churches.

139. See entries in *Brill's New Pauly* "Astrology" and "Astronomy," 196–210 and the older but still helpful work by Cramer, *Astrology*.

From first to last the Christ of Revelation is an ecclesiastical Jesus, a Jesus for the congregations of God. Whether seen under the rubric of the 144,000 sealed on their foreheads, or the Bride of the Lamb, or the city he loves, or the great multitude that no one can count, or the saints, or the witnesses of Jesus, or the New Jerusalem, the Jesus Christ that John knows and proclaims is one for the collective people of God, the congregations of Roman Asia. The prophet John's identity is inseparably linked with congregations (*ekklēsiai*, ἐκκλησίαι, 1:4); the identity of Jesus is inseparably linked with seven congregations (*epta ekklēsiai*, ἑπτὰ ἐκκλησίαι, 1:11); and the significance of the book of Revelation is inseparably linked with congregations, "It is I, Jesus, who sent my angel to you with this testimony for the churches" (*epi tais ekklēsiais*, ἐπὶ ταῖς ἐκκλησίαις, 22:16). Christianity outside the 10/40 Window would do well to abandon some of its individualism, perhaps repent, and confess that Jesus is not a parachurch Messiah. We see then that John has adapted lampstand imagery from Zech 4 for his own ecclesiology in order to emphasize the Messiah's presence[140] among the congregations of western Anatolia.

---

140. Jauhiainen, *Use of Zechariah*, 46–47.

3

Introduction to the Seven Letters

Overview of 2:1–3:22

EVEN THOUGH CHAPTERS 2 and 3 of Revelation are typically identified as the "letters to the seven churches," John himself actually never uses the term "letter" (*epistolē*, ἐπιστολή) in this prophetic work. The term "book" (*biblion*, βιβλίον) instead is used for the entire document (1:11; 22:7, 9, 10, 18, 19), including chapters 2 and 3, even though they stylistically conform to the epistolary genre. Divine letters as well as divine books[1] were well known in the broader contexts of John and his first audience. This includes both Jewish and pagan religious culture.

A Thessalonian Greek inscription, for example, dated mid-to-late first century AD, focuses on a divine epistle sent by the Egyptian deity Sarapis to a certain man named Xenainetos. This man was from the town of Opus south of Thessalonica and was visiting in the city of Thessalonica. This epistolary revelation was sent to him both to spread the popular religion of the Egyptian deities Sarapis and Isis and to promote personal reconciliation between Xenainetos and a political opponent back in his home city of Opus.[2]

---

1. Aune, *Revelation 1–5*, 124.

2. Totti, *Ausgewählte Texte*, 34–35; for a discussion of this important inscription see Horsley, "A 'Letter from Heaven,'" 29–32. In this inscription the term ἐπιστολή is used in lines 6, 10, 11, 13 and 16.

Like the book of Revelation, the Jewish Scriptures contains examples of prophetic letters (2 Chr 21:12–15; Jer 29) as does also the LXX (Ep Jer 1). The Qumran document 4QMMT may also represent a prophetic letter.[3] These Jewish documents share with chapters 2 and 3 of Revelation the deep concern to highlight and to resist the threat of assimilation, whether from lapsed insiders or from surrounding paganism.

Figure 50

The content and tenor of these seven prophetic letters of John are not identical in every instance. Four of the letters contain both praise and judgment against their recipients: Ephesus (no. 1), Pergamum (no. 3), Thyatira (no. 4), and Sardis (no. 5). The letters to the churches of Smyrna (no. 2) and Philadelphia (no. 6) contain only praise. Only the letter to the church of Laodicea solely records displeasure with a congregation (no. 7).[4]

Notwithstanding the diversity in their content, two broad stylistic phenomena characterize the letters. They generally allude to the iconography of the christophany of Rev 1 and each of them follows a distinctive and recurring epistolary pattern.[5] All seven of these letters manifest seven recurring stylistic elements in the following pattern:

1. "To the angel of the church" (2:1; 2:8; 2:12; 2:18; 3:1; 3:7; 3:14)

2. The command to "write" (2:1; 2:8; 2:12; 2:18; 3:1; 3:7; 3:14)

3. For a general discussion of epistolary remains at Qumran and consideration of 4QMMT as a separatist and anti-assimilationist document see Lindenberger, "Letters," 480–85; see also Schiffman, "Miqtsat Ma'asei," 558–60. "And you know that we have segregated ourselves from the multitude of the people and from mingling in these affairs, and from associating with them in these things. . . . And also we have written to you some of the works of the Torah which we think are good for you and for your people. . . . Reflect on all these matters and seek from him that he may support your counsel and keep far from you the evil scheming and the counsel of Belial, so that at the end of time . . . it shall be reckoned to you as justice when you do what is upright and good before him," 4QMMT.

4. Osborne, *Revelation*, 106; Beckwith, *Apocalypse*, 487; Caird, *Revelation*, 27.

5. Aune, *Revelation 1–5*, 119–24; Mounce, *Revelation*, 65; Witherington, *Revelation*, 91; cf. Charles, *Revelation*, 1:xxii–xxiv, 8, who considers the entire book an epistle.

3. Some association with the previous christophany (2:1; 2:8; 2:12; 2:18; 3:1; 3:7(?))

4. The acknowledgement "I know" (2:2; 2:9; 2:13; 2:19; 3:1; 3:8; 3:15)

5. Warnings and commandments appropriate to the situation of each congregation (2:2–6; 2:9–10; 2:13–16; 2:19–25; 3:1–4; 3:8–11; 3:15–20)

6. Promise of divine reward to "Him who overcomes" (2:7; 2:11; 2:17; 2:26; 3:5; 3:12; 3:21)

7. Admonition for receptivity "He who has an ear, let him hear" (2:7; 2:11; 2:17; 2:29; 3:6; 3:13; 3:22)

The recurring phrase in the seven letters, "Let anyone who has an ear listen to what the Spirit is saying to the churches (ἐκκλησίαι, plural)" supports the idea that John expected each congregation to respond appropriately to everything written to the other six churches.[6]

It has often been observed that there are themes and phrases broached in the seven letters that seem to vanish in Revelation 4–20, only to be reintroduced in the final two chapters. There they reappear and are treated in the context of the new heavens, new earth, and the New Jerusalem.[7] In commenting on these themes that reappear later in the book, Richard C. Trench observed generations ago: "Especially these seven epistles, which at first sight might seem . . . to be but slightly attached to the other parts of the Book, do yet on nearer examination prove to be bound to them by the closest possible bands."[8]

The following comparison shows the intertextuality that exists between imagery in chapters 2 and 3 in the beginning of Revelation and chapters 21 and 22 at the end.

Seven Letters	New Heaven and Earth
Explicit	
I come quickly	I come quickly
He who overcomes	He who overcomes
Tree of Life	Tree of Life
Book of Life	Book of Life

6. Beale, *Revelation*, 226; Osborne, *Revelation*, 105; Thomas, *Revelation 1–7*, 126.

7. Minear, *New Earth*, 59–61; Prigent, *Apocalypse*, 150; Beale, *Revelation*, 134–35, 1057–58.

8. Trench, *Epistles*, 103.

Second Death	Second Death
Morning Star	Morning Star
City of God	City of God
New Jerusalem	New Jerusalem
Implicit	
According to Works	According to Works
Name	Name
Idolatry	Idolatry
Sexual immorality	Sexual immorality
Destiny of nations	Destiny of nations
Temple of God	Temple of God
Throne of God	Throne of God

This commentary assumes a holistic approach to the entire Revelation of John and to the seven letters and their integration with the remainder of the book of Revelation.[9] As a literary unit, then, these seven prophetic messages will not be easily fractured from their larger whole just in order to satisfy a theological, millenarian, or literary idea imposed anachronistically upon them. This holistic paradigm requires, furthermore, that the issues broached in these letters must not only stem from the same historical soil as the rest of the book (Rev 4–22), but that they also reflect an outlook and purpose compatible with, what the author calls, "the words of this prophecy" (Rev 1:3).

---

9. Unlike Aune's commentary, this work does not interpret Revelation on the basis of a putative multistage editorial process, *Revelation 1–5*, cxviii–cxxxiv.

4

The Prophecy to Ephesus

Rev 2:1 "To the angel of the church in Ephesus write: These are the words of him who holds the seven stars in his right hand, who walks among the seven golden lampstands: 2 "I know your works, your toil and your patient endurance. I know that you cannot tolerate evildoers; you have tested those who claim to be apostles but are not, and have found them to be false. 3 I also know that you are enduring patiently and bearing up for the sake of my name, and that you have not grown weary. 4 But I have this against you, that you have abandoned the love you had at first. 5 Remember then from what you have fallen; repent, and do the works you did at first. If not, I will come to you and remove your lampstand from its place, unless you repent. 6 Yet this is to your credit: you hate the works of the Nicolaitans, which I also hate. 7 Let anyone who has an ear listen to what the Spirit is saying to the churches. To everyone who conquers, I will give permission to eat from the tree of life that is in the paradise of God.

THE OPENING PHRASE "to the angel" (*tō angelō*, τῷ ἀγγέλῳ), given at the beginning of each letter, has engendered much debate on at least two points: the nature of the angel and the extent of the angel's apparent culpability for the sins of the congregation. It seems best to translate the Greek term *angelos* (ἄγγελος) as "angel," even though some interpreters still favor the term (human) "messenger."[1]

---

1. The identification of the *angelos* (ἄγγελος) of each congregation with a human messenger is strongly argued by Kraft, *Die Offenbarung*, 50–52.

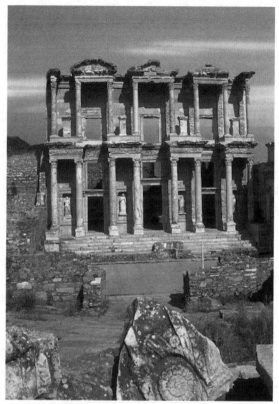

Figure 51

The issue of the angel's participation in the activities (see notes on Rev 1:20b) and guilt of the respective congregations is a complex issue, obscured for some by lack of clarity in English language pronouns and verbs. The evidence of the seven letters reveals a heavy reliance upon second person singular verbs and pronouns, referring to the respective angel of each congregation. This fact, however, must be balanced with the significance of the repetition of the phrase in all the letters, "What the Spirit says to the churches." This double address to both the angels and the congregations seems to suggest "equivalency of churches and angels."[2]

A type of correlation between a particular angel and the members of his congregation is more apparent in verses such as Rev 2:13: "I know where you are living [*second person singular*], where Satan's throne is. Yet you [*second person singular*] are holding fast to my name, and you [*second person singular*] did not deny your faith in me even in the days of Antipas my witness, my faithful one, who was killed among you [*second person*

2. Aune, *Revelation 1–5*, 109; for a survey of views see 108–12.

plural], where Satan lives." Similarly, in 2:16 one reads, "Repent [*second person singular*] then. If not, I will come to you soon and make war against them [*third person plural*] with the sword of my mouth."[3] The tenor of the seven letters seems to suggest that while all the churches are being addressed by the Spirit, both to comfort and to castigate, the style of this address is both individual and corporate. Thus, each angel represents the particular church over which he has been placed by God (cf. notes on Rev 1:20b).

The place of Ephesus as the first of the seven churches to be mentioned has been explained on the basis of its proximity to Patmos and Ephesus's good harbor.[4] Others have suggested that its priority was because of the city's leadership in the imperial cult and provincial government.[5] The city's designation as "The first and greatest metropolis of Asia,"[6] clearly portrays what the Ephesians thought about their own provincial status. William Ramsay suggested a correlation between the fact that Ephesus (2:1–7), Smyrna (2:8–11), and Pergamum (2:12–17) are named first and the fact that these three were "the greatest and outstanding cities of the Province."[7] Since chapters 2 and 3 of Revelation assume the delivery of these letters Stephen Mitchell's assessment of Ephesus and Roman communication routes should not go unmentioned. He noted that: "The Romans, as one would predict, devised an elaborate series of [communication] networks. In Asia the headquarters was Ephesus, where a college of tabellarii [i.e., letter carriers, couriers] was based, and from which routes must have radiated to all the administrative centres of the province."[8]

This letter to the Ephesians follows John's technique of incorporating attributes taken from the christophany, in this instance both seven stars and seven lampstands (see notes 1:12–20). The idea of "walking among" certainly brings to mind important episodes where such imagery is used to underscore the presence of the Lord. "[Adam and Eve] heard the sound

---

3. Cf. also Rev 2:10 begins with second person singular and moves into second person plural.

4. Beale, *Revelation*, 229; Boxall, *Revelation*, 47.

5. For governmental importance see Aune, *Revelation 1–5*, 136–37; Mounce, *Revelation*, 66; for imperial cult see Witherington, *Revelation*, 95.

6. *Hē prōtē kai megistē metropolis tēs Asias* (ἡ πρώτη καὶ μεγίστη μητρόπολις τῆς Ἀσίας): this phrase is attested in many inscriptions, e.g., *Inschriften von Ephesos*, vol. 1, no. 24b, 1–2; vol. 2, nos. 282d, 5–6; 300, 4–5.

7. Ramsay, *Letters*, 181.

8. Mitchell, *Anatolia*, 1:129; *Inschriften von Ephesos*, 2200 A. In general see *New-Docs* 7:1–57 (Conveyance of Letters); and Weeber, "Post."

of The Lord God walking in the garden at the time of the evening breeze" (Gen 3:8) and: "And I will walk about among you (*emperipatēsō en humin,* ἐμπεριπατήσω ἐν ὑμῖν) and will be your God, and you shall be for me a nation. It is I who am the Lord your God who brought you out of the land of Egypt since you were slaves, and I have shattered the bond of your yoke and led you with boldness" (Lev 26:12–13).

Christ's assurances and threats to the angel of the church in Ephesus are based upon its deeds or works (*ta erga sou,* τὰ ἔργα σου).[9] In light of John's contextual use of the theme of works (*ta erga,* τὰ ἔργα) in this letter (2:2, 5, 6) and elsewhere in chapters 2 and 3 (2:19, 22, 23, 26; 3:1, 2, 8, 15), it is clear that concepts like "works righteousness" or "popular Pelagianism" are far removed from John's mind. This message of the risen Christ plainly teaches the same theology as expressed by the historical Jesus, "'For the Son of Man is to come with his angels in the glory of his Father, and then he will repay everyone for what has been done." (Matt 16:27, *hekastō kata tēn praksin autou,* ἑκάστῳ κατὰ τὴν πρᾶξιν αὐτοῦ = Ps 61:13b [LXX] *hekastō kata ta erga autou,* ἑκάστῳ κατὰ τὰ ἔργα αὐτοῦ [=Ps 62:12b NRSV]).

Throughout the book of Revelation deeds are tantamount to required behavior, indeed messianic behavior (2:26), similar to Peter's words, "Therefore, brothers and sisters, be all the more eager to confirm your call and election, for if you do this (*tauta gar poiountes,* ταῦτα γὰρ ποιοῦντες), you will never stumble. For in this way, entry into the eternal kingdom of our Lord and Saviour Jesus Christ will be richly provided for you" (2 Pet 1:10–11). These deeds are the basis for divine judgment (2:23), especially eschatological judgment (20:12–13; 22:12), and they follow the faithful believer into eternity (14:13). John's emphasis upon using behavior as a litmus test for covenant faithfulness certainly places him within the camp of other Biblical prophets such as:

- Micah (6:8): "He has told you, O mortal, what is good; and what does the Lord require of you but to do justice, and to love kindness, and to walk humbly with your God?"

---

9. This particular concept of "deeds" or "works" can be associated with both Paul's and Jesus's emphasis upon deeds and fruit bearing. The recurring phrase that believers as well as nonbelievers will be rewarded "according to their deeds" (Rev 2:23; 18:4–6; 20:12–13; 22:12) certainly resonates with the Pauline view that God will repay according to each one's deeds (Rom 2:5–8; cf. Gal 6:7–9); more detailed presentations can be found in Kim, *God Will Judge,* 220–61 and Stylianopoulos, "Know Your Works," 17–32.

- Amos (5:22–24): "Even though you offer me your burnt-offerings and grain-offerings, I will not accept them; and the offerings of well-being of your fatted animals I will not look upon. Take away from me the noise of your songs; I will not listen to the melody of your harps. But let justice roll down like waters, and righteousness like an ever-flowing stream."

- Jeremiah (7:22–23): "For on the day that I brought your ancestors out of the land of Egypt, I did not speak to them or command them concerning burnt-offerings and sacrifices. But this command I gave them, 'Obey my voice, and I will be your God, and you shall be my people; and walk only in the way that I command you, so that it may be well with you.'"

Moreover, in Revelation none of this emphasis upon deeds undermines the necessity of the atoning blood of the Lamb and eternal life, *freely given* (*dōrean*, δωρεάν, 21:6; 22:17). In fact, focus upon works magnifies the significance of the Lamb's death, since the Lamb's death requires that followers follow him wherever he leads (14:4).

Although coming from a different author, 1 Thess 1:3 contains a combination of the terms *ergon* (ἔργον) (deed/work), *kopos* (κόπος) (hard work/toil) and *hupomonē* (ὑπομονή) (perseverance) used here by John, We remember "before our God and Father your work (*ergon*, ἔργον) of faith and labor (*kopos*, κόπος) of love and steadfastness (*hupomonē*, ὑπομονή) of hope in our Lord Jesus Christ."

It seems that the noteworthy deeds of the Ephesian angel consist of its hard work and perseverance in tenaciously upholding the cause and name of Christ within a stressful and, indeed, hostile urban setting. This means concretely that this angel has valiantly resisted assimilation. The admirable deeds of the Ephesian congregation encompasses, however, not only toil and endurance, but also its intolerance (*ou dunē bastasai*, οὐ δύνῃ βαστάσαι) of other Christians described as "evil men." As troubling as it sounds to the ears of many comtemporary believers, it is evident that in this particular Ephesian setting spiritual intolerance was a virtue in the judgment of the risen Christ. As the reader is soon to learn, while this congregation cannot carry the burden (*bastazō*, βαστάζω) of toleration of evil individuals, it must carry the burden (*bastazō*, βαστάζω) of "hardships" for the sake of Christ (2:3).[10]

The visible manifestation of the evilness of these believers is their impersonation of apostles. In Revelation the term "apostle" (*apostolos*,

10. Hort, *Apocalypse*, 21.

ἀπόστολος) possesses some of the same ambiguity that it has in other New Testament writings. Like other New Testament writers John uses it to refer to the twelve apostles (21:14) as well as here to an ecclesiastical office broader than the Twelve (cf. 18:20).[11] Both Jewish and Graeco-Roman documents contain examples of this term referring to individuals sent on journeys, often of a secular nature and less frequently of a religious journey.[12] It is worth mentioning, nevertheless, that the verbal form (*apostellō*, ἀποστέλλω) of this term "apostle" is used in an earlier Ephesian inscription to describe the journey of special religious envoys sent from Ephesus to the Temple of Artemis located in Sardis.[13] This neglected epigraphical testimony reads "The special envoys were sent (*apostalentōn*, ἀποσταλέντων) by the city [of Ephesus] according to ancestral law . . . to Sardis and to the temple of Artemis established by the Ephesians."

What the prophet meant by "testing" must be determined in conjunction with a decision about the nature of the false apostleship that the Ephesians rejected. It is highly unlikely that these impersonators were attempting to present themselves as part of the twelve apostles. Due to the late date of Revelation, it is unlikely that these false apostles were claiming to have seen the Risen Lord (1 Cor 9:1–2; cf. Acts 1:22; 10:41–42). The phrase false apostles here focuses on the two characteristics of this evil. These individuals were commissioned and sent like apostles to proclaim a competing message (cf. false apostles in 2 Cor 11:13), and secondly the falseness was probably associated with the pluralistic and assimilationist theology of the Nicolaitans. The Ephesian congregation is applauded by Christ for its ability to discern, to hate, and to decisively reject these efforts by a competing group of followers of Christ whom John labels as Nicolaitans (2:6).[14]

In the context of this letter to Ephesus, having to endure "hardships for my name" points in all likelihood to the church's perseverance in the face of false Christians. One is reminded of the letter of bishop Ignatius written to believers in the same city less than two decades later: "For there

---

11. Aune, *Revelation 1–5*, 144–45; Rengstort, "ἀπόστολος," 420–24; Müller, "Apostle," 128–35.

12. Spicq, *Theological Lexicon*, 1:186–94.

13. ὅτι θεωρῶν ἀποσταλέντων . . . εἰς Σάρδεις καὶ τὸ ἱερὸν τῆς Ἀρτέμιδος τὸ ἱδρυμένον ὑπὸ Ἐφεσίων, *Inschriften von Ephesos*, vol. 1, no. 2.3–9.

14. Within two decades Ignatius writes concerning the congregation at Ephesus, "But I have learned that certain people from there have passed your way with evil doctrine, but you did not allow them to sow it among you. You covered up your ears in order to avoid receiving the things being sown by them," Ign. *Eph.* 9.1a.

are some who are accustomed to carrying about the Name maliciously and deceitfully while doing other things unworthy of God. You must avoid them as wild beasts. For they are mad dogs that bite by stealth; you must be on your guard against them, for their bite is hard to heal" (Ign. *Eph.* 7.1). False faith is rarely overcome easily and simply, and prophetic leaders like John knew that there was a temptation for believers to grow weary in this particular kind of struggle. The recognition of this weariness in combating false teaching and lifestyles may lie behind the reason that Jesus (Matt 7:15; Mark 13:22; Luke 6:26), Acts (20:28–31) and Paul (2 Cor 11:3–4, 13; Gal 2:4) both encouraged followers to be on the alert to false teachings and behavior from those within the community of faith.

The Ephesian community of believers had started a dangerous fall that (cf. Gal 5:4) can only be rectified by repentance[15] and works. Though there is ambiguity in the text regarding the meaning of the phrase "your first love" (*tēn agapēn sou tēn prōtēn*, τὴν ἀγάπην σου τὴν πρώτην), I do not see any clear textual reason to identify first love with enthusiasm and then to identify its later abandonment with a "harsh zeal for orthodoxy."[16] While orthodoxy bashing finds fertile soil in contemporary postmodern settings and apparently works well homiletically, finding it in this particular letter is difficult in my judgment.[17]

Due to the presence of the inferential particle "therefore" (*oun*, οὖν) and the repetition of the term "first" (*prōtos*, πρῶτος) in "first love" and "first deeds," it seems to be the (mis)behavior of the Ephesians that demands repentance. All that can be said exegetically is that these issues demanding repentance exceed the virtue of their orthodoxy (seen in opposing false apostles) and their commendable toil and patience.

The goal of this criticism coming from Jesus is to recall the Ephesians to their original devotion at the time of their conversion. It is a common theme in Scripture to call God's elect back to their roots (cf. Deut 4:9, 23; 6:10–12; 8:10–14; 32:18; Isa 51:12–3; Jer 2:1–5, 32; Ezek 16; Hos 13:6), and John's message is designed to galvanize the obedience of these Ephesian believers through rededication.

Jesus's threat is that he will "come" and that he will "remove your lampstand from its place." Jesus's warning "I will come to you" (2:5)

15. Eight of the twelve references to repentance in Revelation are directed to Christians, while the remaining four are directed to non-Christians.

16. Osborne, *Revelation*, 116.

17. Witherington's view that the particular problem is that the Ephesian believers "have lost their ability to distinguish between hating the sin and loving the sinner" seems speculative (*Revelation*, 96).

naturally raises the issue of timing and chronology. Is this promise to be fulfilled at the Second Coming of Christ or at some time prior to that? Jesus's wording, "I am coming" (*erchomai*, ἔρχομαι), occurs seven times (another heptad) in Revelation (2:5, 16; 3:11; 16:15; 22:7, 12, 20) and five of these (2:16; 3:11; 22:7, 12, 20) are conjoined with the term "soon" (*tachu*, ταχύ). In each instance the meaning of this phrase must be determined on the basis of congregational context and exegesis. While it is clear that some of these seven examples refer to the Second Coming of Christ, this particular example in the letter to Ephesus refers to a coming of Christ prior to his final return depicted in Rev 20.[18]

The specific threat addressed to the angel is to remove the Ephesian congregation (= lampstand, 1:20). It is very important to distinguish Jesus's threat toward the congregation from the distinctly different suggestion that Jesus's threat was to remove or act adversely toward the city of Ephesus itself. It is a serious case of mistaken identity to think that the lampstands are cities rather than congregations. It is easy to imagine the origin of this widespread, but mistaken, idea. Approximately two hundred

Figure 52

years ago it was not unusual for early explorers of western Turkey to observe the extremely desolate conditions on the site of ancient Ephesus and conclude that Jesus threatened both city and congregation: "Ancient Ephesus is now in ruins,—that the candlestick is utterly removed, and that the

---

18. Osborne, *Revelation*, 118; Aune, *Revelation 1–5*, 147; Thomas, *Revelation 1–7*, 195; Reddish, *Revelation*, 54.

very place where Christ's Apostles preached, and where the brightest stars were shining, is at present without a church,—without a minister,—without a solitary Christian."[19] Many interpreters have embraced this popular misconception even though there is no evidence in this text of Revelation, in the historical sources, or in the archaeological record from the early Roman Empire to suggest that the city of Ephesus was headed for extinction in the generations following John's prophecies.

Some have even suggested that the demise of Ephesus came from the decline and disuse of Ephesus's harbor. One commentator imagines the city "fighting for its life against the silting of the harbor."[20] Certainly there were necessary dredging activities in the harbor, but these, in fact, were successful, and during the early Roman period the Ephesians never seemed to have been in the kind of panic suggested by the words "fighting for its life."[21] Furthermore, all evidence for decades to come after John's ministry points to busy harbors, a vigorous economy, and a regional hegemony for Ephesus. As the Greek author Aelius Aristides (ca. AD 120–190) observed:

> I think that all men who live between the Pillars of Hercules and the River Phasis (idiom for "far west to far east") would rightly regard Ephesus as having a connection with them both through the accessibility of its harbors [NB. plural] and through all its other means of reception. All men journey to it, as if their own country, and no one is so foolish, or so flies in the face of reality, that he would not concede that the city is the common treasury of Asia and a refuge in time of need. Nor is there anyone so fond of finding fault that he would criticize the boundaries of that city. It is extensive for whoever journeys into the interior; it is even extensive on the seacoast; it is everywhere capable of providing all that a city needs and of satisfying every way of life that men can live and choose to live (Aelius Aristides, *Oration* 23.24).

Figure 53

19. Wallace, *Seven Churches,* 41–42.

20. Osborne, *Revelation,* 118–19.

21. The governor of Roman Asia in the early 60s, Marcius Barea Soranus, had "industriously cleared the harbor of Ephesus" (Tacitus, *Ann.* 16.23).

Equally as important as the literary record is the archaeological record. Fortunately there is a noteworthy official decree during the proconsulship of Lucius Antonius Albus (AD 146–47) specifically discussing the criminality of contributing to the impassability of the Ephesian harbor. Based upon this large Greek inscription from Ephesus, we learn that certain merchants and labor unions were not particularly "green" in their outlook and conduct. Through their recurring criminal behavior, they were disturbing the ecology and maintenance of the harbor, thereby creating a situation that was unacceptable to Ephesus (this greatest metropolis of Asia), to the Emperor himself (who had repeatedly sent letters about the problem), and to "practically the whole world."[22] There is no question that an open harbor was always considered essential to Ephesus's welfare, but through laws and

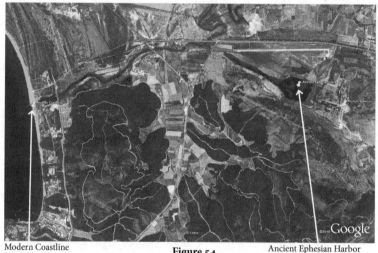

Modern Coastline   **Figure 54**   Ancient Ephesian Harbor

contemporary technology the harbor's future was not in serious question during or following the time of John's writing from Patmos.

In order to balance any words of condemnation to the Ephesian congregation, John next records words of praise for the angel in the congregation there. In particular, the Ephesian angel is commended because he too shares Jesus's own divine hatred[23] for the works and lifestyle of a group

---

22. The inscription, with translation in German, is given in *Inschriften von Ephesos*, vol. 1, no. 23, 140–43 (= Lewis and Reinhold, *Roman Civilization*, 2:107–8 for translation alone). Discovered only in the mid-twentieth century, the original text can also be found in *SEG* XIX (1963), no. 684.

23. Reddish, *Apocalypse*, 86–87 regrettably attacks the message of parts of the seven letters as "even sub-Christian" and sinful. While some of the language of the

labeled the Nicolaitans. Historians and interpreters have been perplexed since there is confusion in the early Christian sources regarding the origin and nature of this group. When investigating various questions and speculations about the origins of this group and its name, it is important to keep in mind the observation made by the historian Arnaldo Momigliano when he noted: "We have to learn to live with a disproportion between the intelligent questions we can ask and the plausible answers we can give. . . . The most dangerous type of researcher in any historical field is the man who, because he is intelligent enough to ask a good question, believes that he is good enough to give a satisfactory answer."[24]

With this in mind, there are three possible solutions offered in regard to the origin of the name. The earliest suggestion comes from a patristic discussion (Irenaeus, *Haer.* 1.26.3) that traces this heretical Gnostic sect back to the Christian named Nicolaus in Acts 6:5. Others have proposed, at least as far back as the eighteenth century,[25] a portmanteau which derives the name Nicolaitans from the two Greek terms *nikaō* + *laos* (νικάω and λαός) which means "conquer the people." Accordingly, the term Nicolaitans would be viewed as an epithet for a sect within the congregation at Ephesus set on destroying God's people through assimilation, just as Balaam (cf. 2:14) had. Another proposal for the name[26] suggests that it derived from the transliteration of a Semitic term that meant "let us eat," thereby pointing to the sect's violation of John's position not to eat food associated with idolatry (2:14, 20).

In light of the brief reference to this group in the church at Pergamum (2:15) and its association with assimilation in the Pergamene congregation, scholars usually regard the Ephesian Nicolaitans as a faction promoting unapproved participation in the surrounding urban culture, especially in eating foods devoted to idols.[27] John and his readers certainly knew exactly what specific practices and participation in the culture lay behind

---

seven letters is vitriolic, against both fellow believers and nonbelievers, John's rhetoric at this point is certainly not outside the bounds of the rhetoric of Scripture in other places. It is interesting that Reddish has the insight and skills that allow him to read through the seven letters and discern which verses *really and truly* come from Christ and which verses come only from John's "sub-Christian" mentality.

24. Momigliano, "Biblical Studies," 225.

25. Evidence is set forth in Prigent, *Apocalypse*, 160, fn. 16.

26. Aune, *Revelation 1–5*, 149.

27. Osborne, *Revelation*, 120–21; Lupieri, *Apocalypse*, 116; Thomas, *Revelation 1–7*, 147–50.

this epithet. John was not the only first-century monotheist fighting the good fight against the intrusion of polytheism.

Insight, perhaps, can be derived from the writings of Philo of Alexandria since he too was fighting assimilation in his own monotheistic

Figure 55

Figure 56

Jewish community earlier in the first century AD.[28] Philo characterizes the assimilationists in his own setting as "exhorting one to be cheerful among

Figure 57

the multitude, and to approach the same temples and to adopt the same sacrifices" (Philo, *Spec.* 1.316). Beyond the question of visiting these ubiquitous pagan temples, theaters, stadiums, public baths and gymnasiums, there was the issue of whether one could belong to the professions that constructed them. All of these were likely flash points for assimilation.

Once again Philo provides a monotheistic countercultural perspective when he contrasts the cultural elevation of gymnasium education as a necessity for social mobility and cultural acceptance in contrast to the Jewish commitment to divine education in synagogues. "But we who are the followers and disciples of the prophet Moses, will never abandon our investigation into the nature of the true God; looking upon the knowledge of him as the true end of happiness; and thinking that the true everlasting life, as the law says, is to live in obedience to and worship of God" (Philo, *Spec.* 1.345).

This first of seven references to "hearing ears" among the seven churches (cf. 13:9) fits appropriately within the prophetic message of John. As Beale has noted, these words are "based on virtually the same wording in the Synoptic Gospels, which itself alludes to Isa 6:9-10." Isa. 6:9-10: "And he said, 'Go and say to this people: "Keep listening, but do not comprehend; keep looking, but do not understand."' Make the mind of this people dull, and stop their ears, and shut their eyes, so that they may not look with their eyes, and listen with their ears, and comprehend with

28. Very helpful in regard to Philo and this topic is Sandelin, "Danger," 109-50; also Schimanowski, "Die jüdische Intergration," 111-35.

their minds, and turn and be healed.'"[29] Consequently, this locates John's prophetic idiom in a well known setting where some of God's elect will both hear and repent, while others will stand condemned because they only listen.[30]

Significantly, these pertinent words find their home in a setting even earlier than Isaiah when Moses (Deut 29:4) uses this spiritual idiom to confront Israelites disloyal to God's covenant. He confronts members of the covenant who listen to the words of God as members of the covenant, but in reality do not manifest loyalty because they do not obey God's voice.

The following two Old Testament prophetic texts poignantly show the people of God caught in the snare of assimilation. These two stories provide spiritual idiom[31] for John since he too wishes to confront similar assimilation in his own context. Jer 5:19–21: "And when your people say, 'Why has the Lord our God done all these things to us?' you shall say to them, 'As you have forsaken me and served foreign gods in your land, so you shall serve strangers in a land that is not yours.' Declare this in the house of Jacob, proclaim it in Judah: Hear this, O foolish and senseless people, who have eyes, but do not see, who have ears, but do not hear." Ezek 12:1–2: "The word of the Lord came to me: Mortal, you are living in the midst of a rebellious house, who have eyes to see but do not see, who have ears to hear but do not hear."

Jesus's offer to reward those in the congregations (*tais ekklēsiais*, ταῖς ἐκκλησίαις) is manifestly conditional. G. B. Caird correctly observed, "Yet the predestination in which John believes is a conditional predestination. A man cannot earn the right to have his name on the citizen roll, but he can forfeit it."[32] It is only "unconditional" for those who overcome (*tō vikōnti*, τῷ νικῶντι). Each of the seven angels of the seven congregations receives this admonition regarding the "overcomer." In its broadest terms,

---

29. Beale, *Revelation*, 234.

30. Unfortunately Vos's treatment of this issue focuses primarily upon technical issues regarding the use of these logia of Jesus, with no interest in their rhetorical and spiritual function within (*Revelation*, 71–75).

31. Isa 42:17–20, "They shall be turned back and utterly put to shame—those who trust in carved images, who say to cast images, 'You are our gods.' Listen, you that are deaf; and you that are blind, look up and see! Who is blind but my servant, or deaf like my messenger whom I send? Who is blind like my dedicated one, or blind like the servant of the Lord? He sees many things, but does not observe them; his ears are open, but he does not hear."

32. Caird, *Revelation*, 49, while three decades later Harrington, *Revelation*, 68 writes very similar words, "Election is conditional: while one cannot earn the right to have one's name in this book [of life], one can forfeit it."

this teaching on God's reward to all faithful believers is given in Rev 21:7, "Those who conquer will inherit these things, and I will be their God and they will be my children." In specific letters, however, the presentation of the reward to the overcomer is contextualized to the setting and conditions of the particular congregation. This explains why at times it appears that the overcomer is any faithful believer (2:7),[33] while at other times it appears that the term "overcomer" refers only to martyrs (2:10–11).[34]

Commentators rightly acknowledge the significance of the theme "overcomer" (*ho nikōn*, ὁ νικῶν) for John and an understanding of these seven letters, but often unnecessarily limit the conceptual and cultural backgrounds of this concept. Osborne, for example, sees it as "an athletic and military metaphor,"[35] while Craig Keener[36] believes this victory relates to "God's end-time army." Stephen Smalley, noting the use of the idea "overcome" in the Johannine letters (1 John 2:13, 14; 4:4; 5:4, 5), believes it points in Revelation to spiritual and moral conquest.[37] However, the social and conceptual framework for this theme is far more profound than Bauckham imagines when he suggests that the offer of blessing to each "overcomer" is: "to invite the readers to participate in the eschatological war which is described in the central part of the book, where the vocabulary of conquest (*nikan*, νικᾶν) is frequent, and so gain their place in the new Jerusalem."[38]

The usage of the theme "overcoming" in the latter part of the LXX (NRSV) is suggestive in helping our understanding of overcoming, especially ideas in 4 Macc, since "the suffering of the Jewish people is the major topic of 4 Maccabees."[39] Prior to 4 Macc one reads about victory in the context of Jewish military struggle against the godless. One sees already in 1 Macc 3:19, "It is not on the size of the army that victory in battle depends, but strength comes from Heaven," while it states elsewhere that the Jewish "victory [came] not only [from] their valor but also their reliance on the Lord" (2 Macc 10:28, cf. 10:38). This outlook is not surprising for an army whose leader was Judas Maccabeus and who "gave his troops the watchword, 'God's victory'" (2 Macc 13:15).

---

33. Wilson, *Victor Sayings*, 88–91.

34. Kiddle, *Revelation*, 61–65.

35. Osborne, *Revelation*, 122.

36. *NIV Application*, 108.

37. Smalley, *Revelation*, 64.

38. Bauckham, *Climax*, 213.

39. Harrington, *Apocrypha*, 216; consult likewise DeSilva, *Apocrypha*, 352–79.

John's concerns and situation seems closer to those in 4 Macc than to those in 1 and 2 Macc for he writes about individual sufferers and potential martyrs. In 4 Macc the focus on victory is seen in the context of the harassment, suffering, and deaths of martyrs. One can see a partial correspondence between the plight of John's audience and those Jewish martyrs in 4 Macc. These brief quotations demonstrate this theme: "All people, even their torturers, marveled at their courage and endurance, and they became the cause of the downfall of tyranny, over their nation. By their endurance they conquered the tyrant (*turannida vikēsantes ton turannon tē hupomonē*, τυραννίδα νικήσαντες τὸν τύραννον τῇ ὑπομονῇ), and thus their native land was purified through them (4 Macc 1:11). "O mother, soldier of God in the cause of religion, elder and woman! By steadfastness you have conquered even a tyrant (*dia karterian kai turannon enikēsas*, διὰ καρτερίαν καὶ τύραννον ἐνίκησας), and in word and deed you have proved more powerful than a man" (4 Macc 16:14). Notwithstanding the important similarities between the experiences of some in John's audience and the Maccabean literature, the cultural and religious matrix of John's message is not limited to that of Judean martyrs. To put it in other words, the essential understanding of God and the divine victory he offered had to compete with ideas in the religious marketplace of the Graeco-Roman world where there existed a robust spirituality about victory.

Accordingly, it seems unwise to neglect other prominent uses of this concept in the religious cultures and iconography of that period, if for no other reason than its importance in shedding light on the concept of divine overcoming in the Graeco-Roman world of John's audience. After all, a major goddess revered in the minds and hearts of Graeco-Roman worshipers was named "Victory" (*Nikē*).

For example, there is an instance of religious victory of a pagan community in a setting of its overcoming harassment. In this particular case the aretology of the Sarapis cult on the Greek island of Delos is instructive. From a Greek inscription one learns of the legal harassment of the Egyptian deity Sarapis and his priest on Delos by those who opposed this god's presence there.[40] However, by means of a punitive miracle, the god Sarapis silences the voice of those who oppose his followers and worshipers and reassures his priest Apollonios with this divine promise, "The victory will be ours" (*nikēsomen*, νικήσομεν).[41] Reflecting upon this religio-political

---

40. Engelmann, *Delian Aretology*, 44; also in Totti, *Ausgewählte Texte*, no. 11, lines 25–28; Nock, *Conversion*, 49–56.

41. Engelmann, *Delian Aretology*, 7, line 26.

victory, the priest of Sarapis responds, "And now, since we have emerged as victors in the struggle in a manner worthy of God (*kai nikēsantōn hēmōn axiōs tou theou*, καὶ νικησάντων ἡμῶν ἀξίως τοῦ θεοῦ), we offer appropriate thanks in our praise to the gods" (*epainoumen tous theous*, ἐπαινοῦμεν τοὺς θεούς).[42]

The Greek goddess *Nikē* (Νίκη cf. Latin *Victoria*) was well known and the depiction of "victory" or "overcoming" permeated the life and thought of the Graeco-Roman world.[43] One would anticipate *prima facie* that worshipers of pagan gods and goddesses both experienced and spoke of religious victories in their own lives. They experienced this "overcoming" in the perceived prosperity, health, and successes of their families, their cities, their regions, and their nations.

Figure 58

Figure 59

Figure 61

Figure 60

42. Ibid., lines 27–28; Totti, *Ausgewählte Texte*, 26, no. 11, lines 23–28.

43. Scherf, "Nike I Mythology," 754–55; Bäbler, "Nike II Iconography," 755–56; likewise helpful is Hölscher, *Victoria Romana*; Lippold, "Nike," cols. 285–307; consult Weinstock, "Victoria," cols. 2501–42.

Figure 62

Figure 63

Even a cursory look at the extant evidence from Graeco-Roman sacred texts, votive offerings, altars, sacred architecture, and religious iconography, which were both ubiquitous and profound, seems to leave no other interpretation about the general feeling of spiritual success and victory. In addition, the Greek religious epithet "bringer of victory" (*Nikēphoros*, νικηφόρος) provides additional evidence for this outlook in the Hellenistic and Roman cultures of the ancient world.[44]

Two prominent religious examples regarding *Nikē* especially highlight this religious component of pagan "overcoming." The close association of the goddess *Nikē* with the two important deities

Figure 64

44. Examples in LSJ, 1176.

Athena (in the Parthenon of Athens) and Zeus (in his famous temple in Olympia) is instructive. By her close association with these two very deities, Nike's significance and influence were guaranteed in the world of Greece and Rome. This association likewise demonstrates the goddess Nike's influence far beyond mere military, imperial, and athletic realms. Further proof of the pervasive presence of this theme of "overcoming" is manifested in the numerous coins, pieces of jewelry, lamps, and decorations that depict this goddess in diverse contexts.

Figure 65

This goddess of "overcoming" was very personally associated with the piety of many pagan worshipers. This is portrayed in the iconography seen in the numerous monuments that show this winged goddess Victory facilitating the successful worship of pagan devotees. Sometimes this worship could be associated either with a liquid offering or with leading an animal to sacrifice. The point of this cultic symbolism was to depict the invisible and heavenly goddess Nikē bringing a particular sacrifice from the visible and earthly worshiper to the invisible heavenly deity, thereby facilitating worship. The task of these winged celestial *Nikai* was to bring sacrifices, petitions, libations, etc. to the deities. Accordingly, on the Acropolis in Athens: "Swift-winged Nikai quickly come and go, clad in swirling garments. They lead animals to the altar or arrange trophies or offer something to the goddess who is herself present. . . . This relief of a Nike mounting a stair originally stood above the right side of the stairway by means of which people approaching the Propylaia could enter the precinct of Athena Nike. Thus worshipers at the temple of Athena Nike were accompanied up the steps

Figure 66

Figure 67

Figure 68

Figure 69

by Nike."[45] These types of scenes resonate with those worshipers whose petition for divine assistance and personal victory was associated and connected with the response of sacrifice to Zeus, Athena, or some other god or goddess.[46]

For those with repentance and acceptable deeds at Ephesus their reward is access to the eschatological tree of life. This reward is part of the new heaven and new earth and is located specifically in the heavenly Jerusalem (22:2, 14, 19). The combination of the phrases "tree of life" and "paradise of God" demonstrate the reliance of this image on scenes from Genesis chapters 2 and 3. Pre-Christian Jewish literature, both canonical[47] and non canonical,[48] anticipate John's adaptation of this symbolism.[49] The tree of life imagery had already attained proverbial status in the Jewish Scriptures (Prov 3:18; 11:30; 13:12; 15:4).

Figure 70

Using allegory and typology, patristic writers initiated a trajectory, continued by many modern advocates, that connects the "tree" closely with the cross of Christ.[50] The roots, however, of this Johannine image of the tree of life should not be traced primarily back to the cross of Jesus, but

45. Brouskari, *Acropolis Museum*, 157, 162.

46. The older European dissertation by Kunisch, *Die stiertötende*.

47. Instructive is the LXX reading at Isa 65:22 (τοῦ ξύλου τῆς ζωῆς) in the context of the "new heavens and new earth" text of Isa 65; see Wallace, "Garden of God," 906–7.

48. Aune, *Revelation 1–5*, 151–54 gives a well balanced presentation. Some commentaries mention in this regard *4 Ezra* 2:1–13, but this section (*4 Ezra* 1–2) is usually recognized as a Christian edition, so Metzger, "Fourth Book of Ezra," 517.

49. Charlesworth, "Paradise," 154–55.

50. Klauser, "Baum," 24–34.

rather back to Eden in Gen 2–3 (cf. Ezek 31:1–9) and also to the broader setting of the sacred tree in the ancient Near East.[51] These concepts from the ancient Near East and Jewish Scriptures provide a much more reasonable and probable background to the tree of life imagery than any suggested connection with the cult of the Ephesian Artemis.[52]

Figure 71

The phrase "paradise of God" points to the symbolism of the Garden of Eden, since the term "paradise" (*paradeisos*, παράδεισος) means garden and is repeatedly associated in the Greek text of Genesis with the Garden of Eden (LXX Gen 2:8, 9, 10, 15, 16; 3:1, 2, 3, 8, 10, 23, 24; 13:10). The symbolism of the "garden of God" (or the Lord) is also employed in exilic and postexilic settings (Isa 51:3; Ezek 28:13; 31:8–9; cf. water of life in Ezek 47:1–12; Zech 14:8; Joel 4:16–18).[53] The vision of

Figure 72

51. In general see York, "Heiliger Baum," 269–82.

52. While Hemer did not originate this theory about a connection between the tree of the Ephesian Artemis cult and the tree of life, he is surely one of the best known advocates of it in recent years; Hemer, *Letters*, 41–48. Hemer's reasoning and use of evidence, however, are not cogent in my judgment; regarding the deficiencies of Hemer's approach see Friesen, "Revelation," 291–314.

53. Kraft, *Die Offenbarung*, 59 helpfully points out that the wording he "will make her wilderness like Eden" of Isa 51:3 becomes "I will make her desolate places like the garden of the Lord" in the LXX of Isa 51:3.

John is clearly pointing to eschatological rather than historical realities since in Genesis the Garden of Eden could not be located, like it is in Rev 22, in the heavenly city of Jerusalem.

The combination of "tree of Life" and "paradise of God" gives John's audience the opportunity to be assured of the eschatological blessing of total peace and intimacy with God, for eternity. A related assurance is also cherished in the words of *4 Ezra:* "It is for you that Paradise is opened, the tree of life is planted, the age to come is prepared, plenty is provided, a city is built, rest is appointed, goodness is established and wisdom perfected beforehand" (8:52).

5

The Prophecy to Smyrna

Figure 73

Rev 2:8 "And to the angel of the church in Smyrna write: These are the words of the first and the last, who was dead and came to life: 9 "I know your afflic-tion and your poverty, even though you are rich. I know the slander on the part of those who say that they are Jews and are not, but are a synagogue of Satan. 10 Do not fear what you are about to suffer. Beware, the devil is about to throw some of you into prison so that you may be tested, and for ten days you will have affliction. Be faithful until death, and I will give you the crown of life. 11 Let anyone who has an ear listen to what the Spirit is saying to the churches. Whoever conquers will not be harmed by the second death.

THIS SECOND LETTER BEGINS with the familiar "to the angel" and follows the basic literary pattern of the other letters (see notes on introduction to the letters and Rev 2:1). The phrase "the first and the last," adapted from Isa 41:4; 44:6; and 48:12, serves as the christological focus (see notes on 1:17) leading to the joint themes of death and resurrection. The particular phrase "first and last" (*ho prōtos kai ho eschatos*, ὁ πρῶτος καὶ ὁ ἔσχατος) anticipates the later association with the alphabetic designations "Alpha and Omega," "I am the Alpha and the Omega, the first and the last, the beginning and the end" (22:13). This christological focus clearly pertains to the contextual issue of "be faithful until death" (2:10).

Afflictions and poverty are high on this congregation's résumé, facts interpreted by God as the basis of riches. Afflictions (*thlipsis*, θλῖψις always in the singular in the Greek text of Revelation) is the general condition of John's ministry (1:9) as well as his readership's Christian existence (7:14).[1] The association of poverty with affliction and its strong contrast with "you are rich" suggest to many interpreters a literal meaning for the term "poverty," at least in this verse. Their literal poverty, in turn, should perhaps be associated with their disenfranchisement from the labor unions. This might explain why the letter contains no criticism of the congregation's assimilation to the surrounding culture.[2]

This letter to Smyrna depicts a church that more than others experiences sufferings, death, and imprisonment. Since harassment and pogroms vary from city to city and province to province, it is noteworthy that the severity of suffering at Smyrna is associated with a congregation that is already economically marginalized. Undoubtedly this declaration of the wealth of the believers from Smyrna is best viewed from the perspective of Jewish eschatological idiom where terms of wealth and poverty, want and satisfaction, are familiar in the language of affirmation, blessing, and encouragement (Luke 1:53; 6:20; 2 Cor 6:10; James 2:5).

The letter to Smyrna is the first to reflect (see notes also on Rev 3:9) the explicit debate between "church and synagogue" over who is the true Israel of God. As Trebilco noted: "For John, these Jews have forfeited the

---

1. It is lamentable that this term in Rev 7:14 has been sucked into the vortex of "The Great Tribulation" debates with their pre-, post-, and mid-tribulation speculations.

2. Others suggest that the believers' refusal to participate in pagan labor unions provides the better explanation, esp. Harland, *Associations*, 251–64; cf. Aune, *Revelation 1–5*, 161; Witherington, *Revelation*, 98; for a suggested gnostic setting for this imagery cf. Prigent, *Apocalypse*, 166–67.

right to be called Jews by their rejection of Jesus, and through their opposition to the Christians they deserve the title of Satan's agents. Thus we can suggest that in Smyrna and Philadelphia the Jewish communities actively opposed the Christian churches."[3] John's invective here anticipates Tertullian's observation approximately one century later that "synagogues of the Jews [are] fountains of persecution—before which the apostles endured the scourge."[4] Even before his life and ministry were close to an end the Jewish Apostle Paul noted that five times he had already endured the thirty-nine lashes "from the Jews" (2 Cor 11:24).

The reader of texts such as these often reasonably wonders about the possibility and extent of Jewish contribution to pagan hostility toward followers of Christ. The ubiquitous phenomenon of "Godfearers"[5] naturally presupposes a degree of Jewish influence on the surrounding culture. The cultural and legal presence of Judaism in Roman western Asia Minor should never be underestimated.[6] The numerous legal documents preserved by Josephus in his *Antiquities*[7] make clear the rigor of Jewish political clout in this region of Roman Asia. Admittedly it is difficult to gage the exact "spiritual interaction between Jews and pagans"[8] in many areas of life, especially because the evidence is so diverse. A few examples beyond the typical Godfearers evidence are instructive.

Barely a century after the writing of Revelation, the western Anatolian city of Apameia began, first under the pagan Emperor Septimius Severus, a six decade practice of minting coins depicting Noah's Ark, including the figures of both Noah and his wife.[9] This fact should not be seen as an isolated event, but rather as a point on a trajectory of Jewish cultural

---

3. Trebilco, *Jewish Communities*, 27.

4. Tertullian *Scorp.* 10.10, *synagogas Iudaeorum fontes persecutionum*. Earlier than Tertullian are the words of Justin Martyr: "They [i.e., the Jews] kill and punish us whenever they have the power, as you can well believe. For in the Jewish war which lately raged, Barchochebas [=Simon bar Kokhba], the leader of the revolt of the Jews, gave orders that Christians alone should be led to cruel punishments, unless they would deny Jesus Christ and utter blasphemy," 1 *Apol.* 31.6.

5 .The modern literature on this topic is voluminous. By way of introduction one should consult Levinskaya, *Acts in Its Diaspora*, 51–82, 83–103, 105–16, 117–26. One should consult Bonz, "Jewish Donor," 281–99.

6. Trebilco, *Jewish Communities*.

7. In general these sources can be located in *Ant.* 14.185–267; 16.160–78.

8. Strubbe, "Curses," 105.

9. Numismatic evidence is found in Head, *Catalogue*, 101, no. 182, 1906; also note Strabo's (*Geogr.* 12.8.13) comment about Apameia and its moniker "boxes"; Trebilco, *Jewish Communities*, 86–95.

influence with antecedents as far back as the first century AD.

One thinks of a second-century AD pagan curse inscription found on Euboea, the second largest island in the Aegean Sea, which draws many of its curses from Jewish Scripture.[10] This seems to be a pagan inscription because of the multiple references to pagan deities in this document,[11] but the curse itself comes explicitly from the Greek translation (LXX) of Deut 28:22,

Figure 74

28.[12] Specifically the curses state, "May God strike this one with difficulty and fever and cold and irritation and blight and derangement and blindness and insanity."

Also on this trajectory of Jewish religious and cultural influence in its pagan setting is the record of the pagan woman Julia Severa, from the Asia Minor city of Acmonia, who during the reign of Nero built the Jewish synagogue in Acmonia (cf. Luke 7:5 for pagan construction of synagogues).[13] Other extant evidence about this important patroness indicates that she was also highpriestess of the Cult of the Emperor and held important civic positions in the city.[14]

"This building was erected by Julia Severa; P(ublius) Tyrronios Klados, the head for life of the synagogue (*ho dia biou archisunagōgos, ὁ διὰ βίου ἀρχισυνάγωγος*), and Lucius, son of Lucius, head of the synagogue (*archisunagōgos, ἀρχισυνάγωγος*), and Publius Zotikos, archon, restored it with their own funds and with money which had been deposited, and they donated the (painted) murals for the walls and the ceiling, and they reinforced the windows and made all the rest of the ornamentation, and the synagogue (*hē sunagōgē, ἡ συναγωγὴ*) honoured them with a gilded shield on account of their virtuous disposition, goodwill and zeal for the synagogue (*tēn sunagōgēn, τὴν συναγωγὴν*)" (translation taken from Trebilco, *Jewish Communities*, 58-9).

Figure 75

---

10. Philo, *Legat.* 282 mentions Jews in Euboea in the early Empire.

11. Erinyes, Graces, Health, *IG* 9, no. 995, 12, 16.

12. "May the Lord strike you with difficulty and fever and cold and irritation and murder and with blight and paleness. . . . May the Lord strike you with derangement and blindness and distraction of mind" (Deut 28:22a, 28, NETS). For curses "written in Deuteronomy" in Jewish inscriptions consult Trebilco, *Jewish Communities*, 60–68; likewise consult Deissmann, *Light*, 413–24.

13. Trebilco, *Jewish Communities*, 58–60.

14. Numismatic and epigraphical testimony is collected by Ramsay, *Cities*, 637–40.

One final, though more controversial, piece of evidence is the Augustan era Sabbatistes inscription from Elaiussa (Cilician coast).[15] This inscription records the decree of a religious association whose deity and members bear the name "Sabbath."[16] Even though the peculiar content of this text has lead some scholars to interpret the term "Sabbath" in ways unrelated to the Jewish seventh day observance, the original editor's comments bear repeating,[17] "On the other hand the derivation from *sabbatas* (Σάββατα) is the most obvious, and there is really nothing against it." The modern interpreter is then left to decide whether this is a group of Jewish worshipers or an example of non-Jewish worshipers influenced by Jewish religious idiom and practices. If the latter, then this would be one testimony to Josephus's (over)statement that pagans everywhere had been so influenced by the Mosaic Law that they are even given to "resting on the seventh day" (*Ag. Ap.* 2.40 (282)).

This slander (*blasphēmia*, βλασφημία)[18] against the Messiah and his congregation arose from local Jews, Satan's own congregation, who rejected the Christian message that Jesus is the Messiah and that his followers are now the Israel of God. The synoptic gospels and Acts record examples of Jewish "blasphemy" against both Jesus (Luke 22:65) and later the apostles of Christ (Acts 13:45; 18:6). Paul even regarded his "earlier life in Judaism" as one that characterized him as a blasphemer (1 Tim 1:13) since he, like these devout non-Christian Jews in Smyrna, had "violently persecut[ed] the church of God and [tried] to destroy it " (Gal 1:13).

The explicit synagogue-church hostility that occurs in Smyrna has been explained in various ways. One explanation for the epithet "synagogue of Satan" imagines that the Christian community at Smyrna has been the object of imperial mistreatment because of Jewish betrayal and accusations. A longstanding rapprochement between Judaism and Roman emperors (and law) came to an abrupt end with the First Jewish Revolt (AD 66–70) that resulted in the destruction of Jerusalem and the Jerusalem Temple. As a result of the Jewish abandonment of this rapprochement

15. First edition is given by Hicks, "Inscriptions," 233–37; later editions and notes given in *OGIS* 573, Sokolowski, *Lois Sacrées*, no. 80, 181–82.

16. A brief summary of modern opinions is available in Harland, *Associations*, 49–50.

17. Hicks, "Inscriptions," 236; LSJ, 1579 gives the gloss "member of a religious sect of sabbath keepers."

18. Typically in Revelation this term *blasphēmia* (βλασφημία) is associated with Satan's minions (13:1, 5, 6) or unrepentant pagans (16:11). It is noteworthy that in Rev 3:9 the unrepentant Jews of Philadelphia are regarded as pagans in the sight of God.

the Emperor Vespasian: "also laid a tribute upon the Jews wheresoever they were, and enjoined every one of them to bring two drachmae every year into the Capitol, as they used to pay the same to the temple at Jerusalem. And this was the state of the Jewish affairs at this time" (Josephus, *B.J.* 7.6.6 (218)). This taxation law was known as the *Fiscus Judaicus* and required of Jews throughout the empire, adult men, women, slaves, and children. This new and large source of revenue was used to rebuild the pagan temple of Jupiter Capitolinus in Rome. Enforcement of this taxation law was severe during the reign of the Emperor Domitian. The later Latin author Suetonius notes the following about the draconian enforcement of the *Fiscus Judaicus*: "Besides other taxes, that on the Jews was levied with the utmost rigor, and those were prosecuted who without publicly acknowledging that faith yet lived as Jews, as well as those who concealed their origin and did not pay the tribute levied upon their people. I recall

Figure 76

being present in my youth when the person of a man ninety years old was examined before the procurator and a very crowded court, to see whether he was circumcised" (Suetonius, *Dom.* 12.2). The rigor of enforcement was so abusive under Domitian that his successor, the Emperor Nerva, softened the regulation and acknowledged such on his coins with the phrase *FISCI IVDAICI CALVMNIA SVBLATA* (the calumny of the Jewish tax is removed), probably meaning that Rome would no longer prosecute those "who without publicly acknowledging that faith yet lived as Jews, as well as those who concealed their origin and did not pay the tribute levied upon their people."[19]

Yet, while Domitian was still alive, it would have been easy for non-Christian Jews at Smyrna to bring legal harassment against two groups of Christians. First of all, *ethnic Jews* who had converted to Christianity would be *persona non grata* in the local Jewish synagogue (=synagogue of Satan) and accordingly would have been reported to the government by the synagogue; Rome would have still regarded these Jewish converts to Christianity as Jews (cf. Acts 18:2–3) and they would have been punished for tax evasion as "those who concealed their origin and did not pay the tribute levied upon their people" (Suetonius, *Dom.* 12.2).

Another component of the congregation at Smyrna that might have been harmed by Domitian's enforcement of the *Fiscus Judaicus* would have been "God-fearing" *Gentile converts* since they "without publicly

---

19. Cf., Goodman, "Nerva," 40–44.

acknowledging that faith yet lived as Jews" (Suetonius, *Dom.* 12.2). Even though it might seem peculiar to modern Christians, in the mind of certain Romans some Gentile converts might appear [partially] like their Jewish neighbors in terms of religious ceremony. Josephus's comment about first-century AD Judaism in Antioch states, "They also made proselytes of a great many of the Greeks perpetually, and thereby, after sort, brought them to be a portion of their own body" (*B.J.* 7.3.3 (45)).[20]

Less than fifteen years after Revelation was composed, the Apostolic Father Ignatius of Antioch wrote to the church at Philadelphia, a city's whose letter from John also refers to the synagogue there as a "synagogue of Satan" (Rev 3:9). The testimony of Ignatius reveals how porous the boundary between Judaism and the church in these cities could be at times. In an attempt to oppose Judaizing heresy at Philadelphia, Ignatius writes, "But if anyone expounds Judaism to you, do not listen to him. For it is better to hear about Christianity from a man who is circumcised than about Judaism from one who is not" (Ign. *Phld.* 6.1). This quotation from Ignatius implies that there were Gentile believers (one uncircumcised) practicing and advocating selected Jewish ceremonies.

In the mind of Roman officials who were not trained in the nuances of either Jewish or Christian theology (cf. Gallio in Acts 18:12–17) these Gentile Christian believers could look "Jewish." Similarly the Roman historian Dio Cassius writes, "The country [of the Jews] has been named Judaea (*Ioudaia*) and the people themselves Jews (*Ioudaioi*). I do not know how this title came to be given them but it applies also to all the rest of mankind, although of alien race [i.e., Gentiles], who affect their customs" (Dio Cassius, *Rom. Hist.* 37.16.5–17.1). That is, those from Gentile heritage who embrace Jewish customs can be called Jews. Accordingly, some Gentile Christians who shunned idols, sexual immorality, and foods sacrificed to idols might well be perceived as not acknowledging their Jewish heritage ("without publicly acknowledging that faith") "yet living as Jews."

While the *Fiscus Judaicus* may well explain some of the hostile rhetoric of John's prophecy toward the synagogue, there is certainly an explanation that is not so speculative. The assertion that not all who claim to be Jews really are (2:9) can easily be viewed against the backdrop of sectarian Judaism. As the writings from the Dead Sea Scrolls community demonstrates, sectarian Jews would often explain the aberration of other Jews, either in doctrine or practice, on the basis of the activity and influence of Belial (=Satan). While many North American Christians would

---

20. Cf. Cohen, "Respect," 409–30.

find such explanations unacceptable, this association of Belial with one's spiritual enemies even made into the Qumran "Hymn Book." "I give you thanks, Lord," one song states: "because you . . . have protected me from all the traps of the pit, for vicious men have sought my soul when I relied on your covenant. They are a council of futility, an assembly of Belial" (1QH 10.20–22).[21] This phrase "assembly of Belial" certainly resonates with John's phrase "synagogue of Satan." Likewise the Apostle Paul at times regarded his Christian opponents as "servants of Satan" if he disagreed vehemently enough with their doctrine or practice of ministry (2 Cor 11:3–15).

Jesus of Nazareth certainly also manifested elements of sectarian thinking and this would be a natural source for the materials in the seven letters. Sectarian statements found on the lips of Jesus include:

- Matt 10:33: "But whoever denies me before others, I also will deny before my Father in heaven."

- Matt 11:27: "All things have been handed over to me by my Father; and no one knows the Son except the Father, and no one knows the Father except the Son and anyone to whom the Son chooses to reveal him."

- Mark 8:38: "Those who are ashamed of me and of my words in this adulterous and sinful generation, of them the Son of Man will also be ashamed when he comes in the glory of his Father with the holy angels."

- Luke 10:16: "Whoever listens to you listens to me, and whoever rejects you rejects me, and whoever rejects me rejects the one who sent me."

- John 14:6: "Jesus said to him, 'I am the way, and the truth, and the life. No one comes to the Father except through me" (cf. Acts 4:12).

Seeing a connection between the sectarian outlook of Jesus of Nazareth as portrayed in the gospels and the risen Son of Man in Revelation provides a better explanation than one that seeks an explanation in putative claims of widespread Christian anti-Semitism at that time.[22]

21. 4QMMT provides another example; sectarian attitudes are also reflected in the epithets used by the Qumran community of their enemies, for example, Baumgarten, "Seekers," 857–59.

22. It is difficult to deny the presence of pagan based antisemitism in the world of nascent Christianity; especially noteworthy are the perspectives given in Tacitus, *Hist.* 5.1–13; consult Stern for numerous pagan examples, *Greek and Latin*, 3:105.

Specifically, John's sectarian outlook considers all synagogue-attending Jews who did not accept the messiahship of Jesus as no longer the true Jews. Their Jewish identity, according to John's message, is only one of lip service (cf. Rev 3:9). This theological struggle regarding Christian criteria in the determination of Jewish identity is also evident in the writings of Ignatius of Antioch. Ignatius writes, "For I heard some people say, 'If I do not find it in the archives, I do not believe it in the gospel.' And when I said to them, 'It is written,' they answered me, 'That is precisely the question.' But for me, the 'archives' are Jesus Christ, the unalterable archives are his cross and death and his resurrection and the faith that come through him; by these things I want, through your prayers, to be justified" (Ign. *Phld.* 8).

Thus Revelation agrees with other New Testament writings in its support of a modified replacement understanding of Israel and the Christ based congregation (cf. 1 Cor 3:11) of God. The apostle Paul, for example, wrote (Rom 2:28–29): "For a person is not a Jew who is one outwardly, nor is true circumcision something external and physical. Rather, a person is a Jew who is one inwardly, and real circumcision is a matter of the heart—it is spiritual and not literal. Such a person receives praise not from others but from God." According to John, identification as a real Jew is determined on the basis of devotion to the Lamb rather than upon traditional Jewish criteria, e.g., birth and upbringing, adherence to Jewish statutes and ceremony. Ethnic Jews who do not bear the name of the Lamb on their forehead (cf. Rev 14:1–5) cannot be counted within the 144,000 who come from "every tribe of the people of Israel" (Rev 7:4–8); they simply do not qualify.

In harmony with Paul and other New Testament authors this is a plain demonstration of the fact that John's ecclesiology is deeply rooted in the language and thought of the Old Testament.[23] This essential connection to Old Testament ecclesiology is manifest, to mention only a few examples, in the language of marks on the forehead of the elect (Rev 7), the use of the twelve tribes and the number 144,000 (Rev 7) and the Jerusalem imagery (Rev 21–22).

John demonizes these Jews by calling their assembly a "synagogue of Satan." The Greek term translated, or rather transliterated, "synagogue" (*sunagōgē*, συναγωγή) could refer both to a congregation of Jews or to the building in which the congregation assembled, notwithstanding the assertion by some scholars to the contrary.[24] The fact that this Greek term

23. E.g., Rom 2:25–29; Gal 6:14–16; Eph 2:11–3:6; 1 Pet 2:9–10.
24. Aune, *Revelation 1–5*, 165; Kee, "Transformation," 1–24.

sunagōgē (συναγωγή) can refer both to the congregation and to the building where the congregation meets is attested in an early Roman epigraphical document dated prior to the date of the writing of most of the New Testament.[25]

Moreover, this Greek word *sunagōgē* (συναγωγή) is not a term belonging solely to the religious vocabulary of Judaism and Christianity. That is, this term *sunagōgē* (συναγωγή) is not a word that was immediately and naturally associated only with Judaism in the early Roman Empire; thus, in some situations it was helpful to state "synagogue of the Jews." It has often gone unnoticed that a Greek inscription from Ephesus contemporary with the writing of the book of Revelation uses this term *sunagōgē* (συναγωγή) in the context of pagan religion. In this particular Ephesian inscription, this term is used in regard to an assembly of religious officials of the cult of the Ephesian Artemis.[26]

The preceding reference to affliction and the subsequent reference to imprisonment suggest the satanic character of the Jews is their involvement in the social and legal mistreatment of believers. This paradigm of anti-Christian feelings flamed by Jews is well attested in the Acts of the Apostles (Acts 9:23; 13:45, 50; 14:19; 17:5, 13; 20:19) as well as other early Christian literature (1 Thess 2:14; cf. 2 Cor 11:24). Perhaps it is not a coincidence that years later the Christian leader Polycarp was martyred in this very city of Smyrna and the record mentions the involvement of Jews: "The entire crowd, Gentiles as well as Jews living in Smyrna, cried out with uncontrollable anger and with a loud shout: 'This is the teacher of Asia, the father of the Christians, the destroyer of our gods, who teaches many not to sacrifice or worship'" (*Mart. Pol.* 12.2.).

As will become clearer in Rev 12–19, the Devil (= Satan, 12:9; 20:2) stands behind such legal proceedings and the subsequent incarceration and death of those who follow the Lamb. While no other piece of New Testament literature so graphically portrays the deaths of believers, John's reference to the imprisonment of believers resonates with other literature within the New Testament.[27]

---

25. Dating from AD 56 the following Greek inscription reads, in part, ἐφάνη τῇ συναγωγῇ τῶν ἐν Βερνεικίδι Ἰουδαίων τοὺς ἐπιδιδόντες (sic) εἰς ἐπισκευὴν τῆς συναγωγῆς ἀναγράψαι αὐτοὺς εἰστήλην λίθου Παρίου, in Lifshitz, *Donateurs*, no. 100, 81; also *SEG* 17, 1960, no. 823, 215. In general see Oster, "Supposed," 178–208 for an assessment of Kee, "Transformation."

26. *Inschriften von Ephesos*, vol. 2, no. 419a: τῆς συναγωγῆς τῶν νεοποιῶν, not listed in the examples of συναγωγή given in Moulton and Milligan, *Vocabulary*, 600–601.

27. Matt 25:36–44; Luke 21:12; Acts 8:3; 9:2; 12:4–9; 16:23–40; 20:23; 22:4–5; 27:1;

It is not surprising to see similar themes among pre-Christian Jews fighting assimilation in Judaea. In a document from the Dead Sea Scrolls, an interpretation of the canonical Psalm 37, the Qumran writer mentions the poverty of God's people (Rev 2:9), the need for the saints to endure a period of testing (Rev 2:10), the conviction that the trials are a result of the Devil (Rev 2:10), and the assurance that faithfulness to God wins (Rev 2:10-11).[28]

It could be helpful and insightful to know how pagans might have viewed this suffering and imprisonment of believers. Although it comes from a few decades after Revelation we do possess one such direct report. The author is Lucian, a pagan author who is skeptical of all religions, and in one of his many essays against religious leaders and their followers he mentions Christians. The point of this particular essay is to attack a pagan religious leader named Peregrinus Proteus who spent part of his life as a Christian. The important comments from Lucian come from his description of the attention Christians gave to fellow Christians during their imprisonment. "The poor wretches (=Christians) have convinced themselves, first and foremost, that they are going to be immortal and live for all time, in consequence of which they despise death and even willingly give themselves into custody" (Lucian, *Peregr.* 13).

The phrase "ten days" is usually interpreted as a symbol for a short period of time.[29] I really doubt that John's audience made an association between the number ten and "the sum of the fingers of both hands"[30] as some interpreters have suggested. A congregation struggling within the crucible of assimilation and harassment would more likely associate ten days with the theme of being tested for ten days found in the book of Daniel, an Old Testament book that greatly impacted the themes and iconography of Revelation.[31]

In that episode, Daniel and his three Jewish friends were tested for ten days as part of their trial to reject assimilation to Babylonian culture (Dan 1:5-16). The trial aspect of this imprisonment in Smyrna was not primarily characterized by patiently awaiting release from jail, but rather faithfulness awaiting probable death. John knows that this symbolic "ten

---

28:20; Rom 16:7; 2 Cor 11:23; Eph 3:1; 4:1; 6:20; Phil 1:7, 13, 14, 17; Col 4:3, 18; 2 Tim 1:16; 2:9; Phlm passim; Heb 10:34; 13:3.

28. 4Q171 (=4QPsalms Pesher) 2.9-22.

29. Witherington, *Revelation*, 101; Reddish, *Revelation*, 57.

30. Aune, *Revelation 1-5*, 166.

31. Beale, *Revelation*, 242.

days" is a long enough period to give some believers the opportunity to deny their Lord rather than suffer torture and possible execution.

The wording "until death" must refer to martyrdom, given the general tenor of this letter and the preceding references to the terms "devil" and "prison." Those believers who accept martyrdom rather than deny Christ will receive the crown of life[32] and be protected from the second death. In the context of this epistle, the phrase "crown of life" denotes the reward for a martyr, making it therefore a ceremonial object and part of the believer's postmortem (spiritual) jewelry.

The translation "crown" is somewhat misleading to English language audiences since the underlying Greek term *stephanos* (στέφανος, 2:10; 3:11; 4:4, 10; 6:2; 9:7; 12:1; 14:14)[33] connotes more a wreath rather than a modern crown. Wreaths were often made of organic materials such as vines, celery, twigs of oak, pine, or olive trees.

Figure 77

Figure 78

Figure 79

Wreaths were a common reward for victory and achievement in John's world. This included victory in athletic competition, gladiatorial victory, musical accomplishments, and civic achievement.[34] A golden

32. Aune, *Revelation 1–5*, 172–75 for collection of secondary resources and primarily literary sources.

33. The NIV, unlike the NRSV, contributes to this difficulty by translating both στέφανος and διάδημα with the single English term "crown."

34. Stevenson, "Conceptual Background," 257–72.

Figure 80

wreath crown often used gold leaf to imitate the appearance of natural vegetation. The other term used in Revelation is *diadēma* (διάδημα, 12:3; 13:1; 19:12) and it connotes more of a royal headband or crown.[35]

In some pagan eschatological traditions the dead received a wreath at burial to affirm that they were victors in life as well as in death. Those of high wealth or status would also receive golden wreaths.[36] There is a noteworthy inscription from the Aegean area that has often gone unnoticed in the study of this issue.[37] In the mid-first century AD the Lycian League (*Lukiōn to koinon kai hoi archontes*, Λυκίων τὸ κοινὸν καὶ οἱ ἄρχοντες), a region directly south of the location of the seven churches awarded a golden wreath (*stephanon chrusoun*, στέφανον χρυσοῦν) to Junia Theodora in anticipation of her death. According to the inscription, they believed she would arrive in

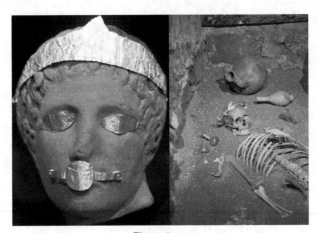

Figure 81

35. BDAG, 227.

36. Pliny, *Nat.* 21.2.1–9.1; Aune, *Revelation 1–5*, 174–75.

37. For additional studies of this inscription consult Winter, *Roman Wives*, communities; Walters, "'Phoebe,'" 167–90.

the presence of the gods (*hotan eis theous aphikētai,* ὅταν εἰς θεοὺς ἀφίκηται) after her death.[38]

Unlike Junia Theodora, the martyrs of Christ did not receive a literal crown and they did not need to bring with them into eternity a crown of gold awarded by a local provincial federation. Rather, the crown of life that John mentions is for those who were faithful at martyrdom, regardless of their social status and civic recognition, and is appropriately granted by the one who "came to life again."

This divine assurance to the churches completes the reward for mar-

Figure 82

tyrdom mentioned in 2:10. Just as 2:10 states the reward for the martyrs, 2:11 assures the martyrs who overcome that they no longer need to fear. The phrase "second death" is also known in pagan eschatology, but there it refers to the further purification after death and not punishment in the afterlife.[39] The Jewish Targums, on the other hand, seem to provide the closest conceptual and verbal affinities to this notion.[40]

In John's work this phrase "second death" refers to the "fiery lake of burning sulfur" (21:8). There are few Old Testament references to post mortem punishment. One of these is Dan 12:1–2, "At that time Michael, the great prince, the protector of your people, shall arise. There shall be a time of anguish, such as has never occurred since nations first came into existence. But at that time your people shall be delivered, everyone who is found written in the book. Many of those who sleep in the dust of the earth shall awake, some to everlasting life, and some to shame and everlasting contempt."[41]

38. Pallas et al., "Inscriptions Lyciennes," 496–508 [=*SEG* XVIII (1962) no. 143, 51–4].

39. Plutarch, *Fac.* 942f and notes by William A. Beardslee, "De facie," 295–96.

40. Beale and McDonough, "Revelation," 1093–94.

41. Some interpreters include Isa 66:23b–24, "'All flesh shall come to worship before me,' says the Lord. 'And they shall go out and look at the dead bodies of the people who have rebelled against me; for their worm shall not die, their fire shall not be quenched, and they shall be an abhorrence to all flesh.'" This text from Isaiah is clearly taken by Jesus to refer to hell, Mark 9:47b–48: βληθῆναι εἰς τὴν γέενναν, ὅπου ὁ σκώληξ αὐτῶν οὐ τελευτᾷ καὶ τὸ πῦρ οὐ σβέννυται (= Isa 66:24b ὁ γὰρ σκώληξ αὐτῶν οὐ τελευτήσει καὶ τὸ πῦρ αὐτῶν οὐ σβεσθήσεται); also consult Koole, *Isaiah III*, 530;

Although not known from the Jewish Scriptures, images of a "fiery lake of burning sulfur" were well known to John and his audience because this imagery was popular in both Jewish writings outside Scripture and non-Jewish eschatology.[42] The "fiery lake" represented the place where the damned would receive eternal punishment.[43] In Second Temple Judaism this imagery is clearly known (1 En. 10:13–15; cf. 21:7–10): "In those days they will lead them into the bottom of the fire—and in torment—in the prison (where) they will be locked up forever. And at the time when they will burn and die, those who collaborated with them will be bound together with them from henceforth unto the end of (all) generations. And destroy all the souls of pleasure and the children of the Watchers, for they have done injustice to man."[44] Likewise, the authors behind the Dead Sea Scrolls knew of postmortem punishments associated with fire and sulfur. For example, "those who derided and insulted God's chosen will go to the punishment of fire" (1QpHab 10.13). In another document entitled "Rule of the Community" found in Cave 1 one reads that those who have given themselves to Belial (=Satan) will be treated by God "according to the darkness of your deeds, and sentenced to the gloom of everlasting fire" (1QS 2.7–8). Finally, in the Essenes' essay that has been entitled "Wiles of the Wicked Woman" one reads: "Her lodgings are couches of darkness and in the heart of the night are her tents. In the foundations of gloom she sets up her dwelling, and camps in the tents of silence, in the midst of eternal fire" (4Q184 frag. 1.6–7).

Even earlier than it appeared in Judaism, this idea was well known in Greek literature and religion. To be sure there were many significant differences between the eschatology of John on the one hand and the eschatology of paganism on the other. They both agreed, however, that they had: "a firm hope (euelpis, εὔελπις) that there is something in store for those who have died, and, as we have been told for many years, something much better for the good (agathois, ἀγαθοῖς) than for the wicked (kakois, κακοῖς)" (*Phaed.* 63c).[45] Closer than Plato to the time of John is the Roman

---

Hemp, "'esh," 428.

42. Glasson, *Greek Influence.* For sepulchral epigraphy consult Peres, *Griechische Grabinschriften.*

43. If New Testament authors were annihilationists, it seems that they would have felt the need to declare it and explain it, since the eschatological terminology they employed was in use in their milieu and was not understood from the perspective of annihilationism.

44. Commentary on these texts available in Nickelsburg, *1 Enoch 1.*

45. Naturally Greek grave inscriptions also illumine points of similarity and

author Cicero who acknowledged the important contributions made to society by mystery religions. When discussing in particular the Eleusinian Mysteries he noted that "we have learned from them the beginnings of life, and have gained the power not only to live happily, but also to die with a better hope" (Cicero, *Leg.* 2.36).

Notwithstanding the profound differences between pagan and Judeo-Christian eschatology, they often spoke with similar terminology and cosmology. In both Greek literature and the New Testament (2 Pet 2:4) Tartarus was a well known[46] term for the place of punishment for wicked and unholy behavior.[47] In Graeco-Roman thinking the fiery river/lake associated with Tartarus was sometimes known as Phlegethon (=Pyriphlegethon).[48] In Plato's writings, for example, one reads that: "The man who had led a godly and righteous life (*ton men dikaiōs ton bion dielthonta kai hoiōs*, τὸν μὲν δικαίως τὸν βίον διελθόντα καὶ ὁσίως) departs after death to the Isles of the Blessed (*eis makarōn nēsous*, εἰς μακάρων νήσους) and there lives in all happiness (*oikein en pasē eudaimonia*, οἰκεῖν ἐν πάσῃ εὐδαιμονίᾳ) exempt from ill, but the godless and unrighteous man (*ton de adikōs atheōs*, τὸν δὲ ἀδίκως καὶ ἀθέως) departs to the prison of vengeance and punishment (*to tēs tiseōs te kai dikēs desmōtarion*, τὸ τῆς τίσεώς τε καὶ δίκης δεσμωτάριον) which they call Tartarus" (*Gorg.* 523a–b).[49] Tartarus is naturally under ground and there are in that location "subterranean rivers . . . of fire too, great rivers of fire" (*kai aenaōn potamōn amēchana megethē hupo tēn gēn . . . polu de pur kai puros megalous potamous*, καὶ ἀενάων ποταμῶν ἀμήχανα μεγέθη ὑπὸ τὴν γῆν . . . πολὺ δὲ πῦρ καὶ πυρὸς μεγάλους ποταμούς) (*Phaed.* 111d) or "a great place burning with sheets of fire" (*eis topon megan puri pollō kaomenon*, εἰς τόπον μέγαν πυρὶ πολλῷ καόμενον) (*Phaed.* 113a) and a "river called Pyriphlegethon, whose fiery stream belches forth jets of lava" (*eponomazousin Puriphlegethonta, hou kai hoi rhuakes apospasmata anaphusōsin*

---

difference, Peres, *Griechische Grabinschriften.*

46. BDAG, 991.

47. For generally excruciating punishment, terrifying tortures, and "suffering throughout eternity" in the afterlife see Plato *Gorg.* 525c; 523a–527e; *Phaed.* 107c; 111d; 113b.

48. Schlapbach, "Phlegethon," 132.

49. See also *Gorg.* 522e. For additional contrasts between the Isles of the Blessed and Tartarus see *Gorg.* 524a, or between general rewards and punishments see *Leg.* 10.904d–e; *Phaedr.* 249a–c; *Phaed.* 108a–c; *Resp.* 1.330d–331a; 2.363c–e; 10.614b–616a.

hopē an tuchōsi tēs gēs ἐπονομάζουσιν Πυριφλεγέθοντα, οὗ καὶ οἱ ῥύακες ἀποσπάσματα ἀναφυσῶσιν ὅπῃ ἂν τύχωσι τῆς γῆς) (*Phaed.* 113b).

While the Jewish writer Philo of Alexandria does not mention the characteristic of fire, he does reveal a belief in Tartarus. Philo, like his younger contemporary John, teaches that burning fire awaits unfaithful believers. In particular, he consigns to Tartarus apostate Jews of first-century Alexandria who have been assimilated to surrounding paganism. "But the man of noble descent (i.e., from Abraham), who has adulterated the coinage of his noble birth, will be dragged down to the lowest depths, being hurled down to Tartarus and profound darkness, in order that all men who behold this example may be corrected by it" (Philo, *Praem.* 152).

Perhaps the text of 2 Pet 2:4, "God . . . sent them to hell" reveals one of the best examples of the transcultural ubiquity of eschatological terms from the period of the early church. The text of 2 Peter uses the Greek term *tartaroō* (ταρταρόω).[50] Rather than acknowledging the origin of the term "Tartarus" from Greek religion and then rendering the Greek *tartaroō* (ταρταρόω) with the words "cast into Tartarus,"[51] most English translations provide a dynamic equivalent by using the word "hell." The price paid for this practice of not translating the Greek term *tartaroō* (ταρταρόω) in a way that reveals its origin is the shielding of the modern reader from the knowledge of the shared vocabulary on certain aspects of postmortem eschatology.

Following the literary pattern of the previous letters Christ warns the hearers not to surrender to spiritual self deception by hearing but not listening to the voice of God. As in Rev 20:6, John emphatically offers martyrs the assurance that they will never (οὐ μή) have to face the possibility of the second death (cf. Rev 20:14).[52]

---

50. See Bauckham, *2 Peter, Jude,* 249.

51. See BDAG, 991; Thayer, *Lexicon.*

52. The use of the phrase *ou mē* (οὐ μή) with the subjunctive mood communicates "the strongest way to negative something in Greek," Wallace, *Greek Grammar,* 468.

6

The Prophecy to Pergamum

Figure 83

Rev 2:12 "And to the angel of the church in Pergamum write: These are the words of him who has the sharp two-edged sword: 13 "I know where you are living, where Satan's throne is. Yet you are holding fast to my name, and you did not deny your faith in me even in the days of Antipas my witness, my faithful one, who was killed among you, where Satan lives. 14 But I have a few things against you: you have some there who hold to the teaching of Balaam, who taught Balak to put a stumbling block before the people of

Israel, so that they would eat food sacrificed to idols and practice fornica-
tion. 15 So you also have some who hold to the teaching of the Nicolaitans.
16 Repent then. If not, I will come to you soon and make war against them
with the sword of my mouth. 17 Let anyone who has an ear listen to what the
Spirit is saying to the churches. To everyone who conquers I will give some
of the hidden manna, and I will give a white stone, and on the white stone is
written a new name that no one knows except the one who receives it.

THIS LETTER TO PERGAMUM contains the stylistic features present in the
other letters sent by John (see notes on introduction to the seven letters).
This use of the "sharp, double-edged sword" christology is particularly
germane in a congregation chastised for its egregious syncretism, since
execution by the sword (and sometimes a spear) was a frequent penalty
in the Jewish Scriptures for those guilty of syncretism (see notes on 2:16).
The risen Christ comes armed and prepared to deal appropriately with
those guilty of assimilation in the congregation at Pergamum. A poignant
presentation of this correlation of sword and syncretism is evident in this
text from Exodus 32:23–29:

> They said to me, "Make us gods, who shall go before us; as for
> this Moses, the man who brought us up out of the land of Egypt,
> we do not know what has become of him." So I said to them,
> "Whoever has gold, take it off"; so they gave it to me, and I
> threw it into the fire, and out came this calf! . . . then [Moses]
> said to them, "Thus says the Lord, the God of Israel, 'Put your
> sword on your side, each of you! Go back and forth from gate
> to gate throughout the camp, and each of you kill your brother,
> your friend, and your neighbour.'" The sons of Levi did as Moses
> commanded, and about three thousand of the people fell on that
> day. Moses said, "Today you have ordained yourselves for the
> service of the Lord, each one at the cost of a son or a brother, and
> so have brought a blessing on yourselves this day."

In addition, the mention of assimilation associated with Balaam (2:14)
justified such a pointed response in John's prophecy since Num 25:7–8
and Num 31:8 highlight the use of sword and spear to punish the syncretism introduced by Balaam among the elect of God.

The mention of the location of the throne of Satan is intended to acknowledge the severity and hostility of the congregation's context in Pergamum. Many solutions have been given to solve the enigma of the phrase
"Satan's throne." Some have judged that it was an allusion to Judaism and
its satanic synagogue, while others have suggested the extensive cult of the

Greek healing god Asclepius[1] and its shrines. Others favor seeing it as a reference to the seat of Roman loyalty with its *Neokoros* temple,[2] begun under Augustus, and the attendant Emperor Cult. Others see this as a reference to the large altar of Zeus found at Pergamum.[3] In light of the two ideas associated with the two occurrences of the phrase "where Satan" in 2:13, the throne of Satan is possibly a reference to the totality of the vibrant pagan environment in which the Pergamene believers lived.[4]

Several ideas expressed in 2:13 point to the legal setting of the death of Antipas. The issues of the "name of Christ" (*onoma sou*, ὄνομά μου),[5] "renouncing faith" (*apnoumenos tēn pistin*, ἀρνοῦμενος τὴν πίστιν),[6] "faithful witness" (*ho marus ho pistos*, ὁ μάρτυς ὁ πιστός),[7] and "put to death" (*hos apektanthē*, ὃς ἀπεκτάνθη) cumulatively lead to this conclusion.[8] It is clearly no accident that the only other use of the phrase "faithful witness" in Revelation is when it is applied to Christ and his death before au-

Figure 84

thorities (1:5; 3:14), serving thereby as a paradigmatic death for all Christian martyrs. Nothing is known of Antipas other than what is mentioned

---

1. "From the reign of Domitian (AD 83–96) onwards, Asclepius and the deities associated with him frequently occurred on the city's coinage, thus emphasizing the god's importance for Pergamum," Weisser, "Pergamum," 136. The magnificent Asklepieion that can be seen today in Pergamum was not yet constructed when Revelation was written; in general consult Hoffmann, "Roman Remodeling," 41–61.

2. For *Neokoros* temples see Burrell, *Neokoroi*, 273–330.

3. Beale, *Revelation*, 246–47; Collins, "Pergamon," 172–73 suggests it is the Altar of Zeus and the temples of Athena and Zeus. See Reddish, *Revelation*, 59 for a list of suggested interpretations.

4. Osborne's comment, *Revelation*, 144, "Most Romans did it [imperial cult] out of civic duty rather than actual worship" reflects an unfamiliarity with both primary sources and with very important discussions in the last three decades regarding the imperial cult in Roman Asia.

5. Acts 4–5; 1 Pet 4:14.

6. Cf. Matt 10:17–33; Acts 3:13–14; Rev 3:8.

7. Acts 7:58; 23:11; 26:16–22; Rev 3:14.

8. Cf. Osborne, *Revelation*, 142.

Figure 85

here by John. The phrase "in the days of" reveals nothing about how much time had elapsed since the martyrdom of Antipas.

In contrast to the faithfulness of Antipas in resisting assimilation and syncretism, there are a number in the congregation at Pergamum who adhere to "the teaching of Balaam." The faithfulness of Antipas cannot, however, vicariously atone for the sins of other Pergamene believers who have surrendered to assimilation so that they could more fully enjoy the amenities of urban life in Ro-

Figure 86

man Pergamum. Specifically, the assimilation is manifested in the sins of "eat[ing] food sacrificed to idols and practic[ing] fornication."

Osborne's analysis that these two "relate to practice rather than doctrine"[9] is an odd bifurcation based upon what we know from other New Testament authors. It is noteworthy in this regard that according to John the similar assimilation advocated by Jezebel was associated with doctrine (2:24, *tēn didachēn tautēn*, τὴν διδαχὴν ταύτην). It is evident from Paul that this issue of eating food sacrificed to idols can be addressed, in part,

9. Ibid., 144.

Figure 87

on the basis of the doctrine of monotheism (1 Cor 8:4-6) as well as the doctrine of creation (1 Cor 10:26=Ps 24:1).

The pejorative depiction of Balaam here is based upon only a few verses in Scripture and later extrabiblical versions of the Balaam stories.[10] Most of the Balaam materials in the Old Testament are located in Num 22-24 and reflect Balaam's blessings upon Israel. Nevertheless, Num 25:1-2 blames Israel's syncretism on the cult of Baal of Peor, eventuating in sexual immorality and idolatry (ἐβεβηλώθη ὁ λαὸς ἐκπορνεῦσαι εἰς τὰς θυγατέρας Μωαβ καὶ ἐκάλεσαν αὐτοὺς ἐπὶ ταῖς θυσίαις τῶν εἰδώλων αὐτῶν καὶ ἔφαγεν ὁ λαὸς τῶν θυσιῶν αὐτῶν καὶ προσεκύνησαν τοῖς εἰδώλοις αὐτῶν, Num 25:1-2). Then Numbers places the blame at the feet of "Balaam's advice" (Num 31:16).

Beale correctly points out the verbal influence of Num 31:8 and Josh 13:22 upon the language of condemnation and punishment recorded in Rev 2:16: "And *Balaam son of Beor they killed with a sword* (apekteinan en rhomphaia, ἀπέκτειναν ἐν ῥομφαίᾳ) together with their slain" (Num 31:8b).

Figure 88

10. Beale, *Revelation*, 248-51; Hackett, "Balaam," 569-72; Chavalas, "Balaam," 75-78; The ideas on Balaam and the book of Revelation by Greene are too brief and simplistic to be of any help, "Balaam Figure," 228.

"And Balaam the son of Beor, the diviner, they slew (*apekteivav en tē rhopē*, ἀπέκτειναν ἐν τῇ ῥοπῇ) at the decisive moment" (Josh. 13:22).

Even though a specific event at which Balaam "taught Balak to entice the Israelites" (2:14) is missing from Scripture, this tradition and understanding is known to the Jewish author Philo (ca. 20 BC–AD 50), an older contemporary of John. According to Philo, "the advice which Balaam gave to Balak," arose from his awareness: "that the only way by which the Hebrews could be subdued was by leading them to violate the law, . . . seducing them by means of debauchery and intemperance . . . [by] putting pleasure before them as bait" (*Mos.* 1. 295–300). Moreover, a Midianite adulteress would require a Hebrew man to join "in the same sacrifices and libations which I use . . . [so that the Hebrew man] then offer[s] together at the same images and statues, and other erections in honour of my gods."

This combination of idolatry and immorality is part of the stock Jewish characterization of pagan existence, known, for example, from texts such as Rom 1:18–32 and Wis (14:22–27): "Then it was not enough for them to err about the knowledge of God, but though living in great strife due to ignorance, they call such great evils peace. . . . they no longer keep either their lives or their marriages pure, but they either treacherously kill one another, or grieve one another by adultery, and all is a raging riot . . . sexual perversion, disorder in marriages, adultery, and debauchery. For the worship of idols not to be named is the beginning and cause and end of every evil."[11]

We cannot discern the numerical size or strength of this lapsed group within the congregation, but it seems to have been influential enough to convince other believers to assimilate to the pagan mores of sexual fornication and idolatry, pagan practices akin to those opposed by Paul at Corinth (1 Cor 10:1–22). Unless one opted to flee the cities, there was no way to completely avoid contact with all idolatry (cf. 1 Cor 5:10), which may explain why John focuses more on the avoidable activity of eating food sacrificed to idols and sexual immorality. John's hostility toward idols certainly resonated with other earlier Christian preaching that always characterized pagan religion as idolatrous, intellectually inferior, and illusory (1 Thess 1:9; Acts 19:26; cf. Isa 44:9–20). This two pronged concern of immorality and idolatry also forms two of the four concerns in the edict associated with the Jerusalem Conference (Acts 15:19–20).

11. Wis 14:22–27 (NRSV); Num 25:1–2 LXX contains the phrases ἐκπορνεῦσαι εἰς τὰς θυγατέρας . . . . ἐπὶ ταῖς θυσίαις τῶν εἰδώλων αὐτῶν; in general see Wis 12–14, tersely summarized with ἀρχὴ γὰρ πορνείας ἐπίνοια εἰδώλων, "For the idea of making idols was the beginning of fornication" Wis 14:12 (NRSV).

Regarding the sin of eating "things sacrificed to idols," it is noteworthy that the meteoric burst of Christian monotheism in nearby Bithynia a decade or so later noticeably diminished the practice of pagan temple sacrifice. Consequently there was a marked decline in the attendant sales of food offered to idols in the towns and cities. This is the best historical explanation for the concluding remark of the governor Pliny to the Emperor Trajan in his letter concerning "What to do with Christians?" Pliny writes, after having oppressively thinned the ranks of the Bithynian congregations through multiple executions and brutal intimidation: "It is certainly quite clear that the temples, which had been almost deserted, have begun to be frequented, that the established rites, long neglected, are being resumed, and that from everywhere sacrificial animals are coming, for which until now very few purchasers could be found" (Pliny, *Ep. Tra.* 10.96).

Figure 89

One generation later the Christian philosopher Justin dialogues with the non-Christian Jew, Trypho, who criticizes Christianity by observing, "I believe, however, that many of those who say that they confess Jesus, and are called Christians, eat meats offered to idols, and declare that they are by no means injured in consequence." Justin's response is to label those believers who eat idol food as heretics who:

139

blaspheme the Creator of the universe, and Christ, whose Advent was foretold by Him, and the God of Abraham, and of Isaac, and of Jacob. They are all outside of our communion, for we know them for what they are, impious atheists and wicked sinners, men who profess Jesus with their lips, but do not worship Him in their hearts. These men call themselves Christians in much the same way as some Gentiles engrave the name of God upon their statues, and then indulge in every kind of wicked and atheistic rite. Some of these heretics are called Marcionites, some Valentinians, some Basilidians, and some Saturnilians, and others by still other names.[12]

John's accusation that the teaching of Balaam promotes, or at least tolerates, sexual immorality (*porneusai*, πορνεῦσαι) has raised questions whether this immorality is literal or metaphorical. To be sure, the Old Testament is replete with examples characterizing Israel's assimilation and syncretism as "spiritual" adultery.[13] The issue is whether John is being redundant to mention idolatry and then metaphorical adultery. It seems best, especially in light of the Balaam paradigm, to view the sexual sins here as literal sexual aberration and immorality and not solely a metaphor for covenant unfaithfulness.[14]

In the context of the following passage from Lucian's *The Passing of Peregrinus*, Peregrinus is expelled from the Christian community for consuming unlawful foods. Perhaps this was meat offered to idols:

"For a time [Peregrinus] battened himself thus; but then, after he had transgressed in some way even against [the Christians]—he was seen, I think, eating (ἐσθίων) some of the food that is forbidden them—they no longer accepted him, and so, bring at a loss, he thought he must sing a palinode and demand his possessions back from his city" (Lucian, *The Passing of Peregrinus* 16).

Figure 90

A second form of heretical teaching in the congregation is associated with "the teaching of the Nicolaitans" (on Nicolaitans see notes on 2:6), a teaching probably cut from the same cloth as the teaching of Balaam. In

---

12. Justin Martyr, *Dial.* 35. It should not be forgotten that the pagan author Lucian describes the expulsion ("they no longer accepted him") of Peregrinus from Christianity because of the fact that Peregrinus "was seen . . . eating some of the food that is forbidden them"; in all probability this was food that had been sacrificed to idols.

13. E.g., Ps 136:39; Nah 3:4–5; Hos; Ezek 16; Jer 3:6–10, 20.

14. An alternative view is given by Beale and McDonough, "Revelation," 1094.

all probability this group likewise encouraged pluralism, syncretism, and building bridges in the direction of societal norms and values.

The only acceptable response from the congregation is repentance. The "repent or else" paradigm is well known in the narrative of Scripture and indeed on the lips of Jesus in the Gospel of Luke (Luke 13:3–5), "But unless you repent, you too will all perish." Typically repentance is required in the hope that God will relent of his promise of punishment and that God's prophecies of destruction will not come to pass. That is, if the prophetic call to (re)turn is effective, then the attendant divine threats will be revoked (see Appendix B).

If repentance is lacking, the horrific Son of Man from the christophany of chapter one will "make war" against the congregation at Pergamum. This bellicose terminology (*polemos*, πόλεμος; *polemeō*, πολεμέω) associated with the Son of Man is often directed in Revelation against Satan (Rev 12:7; 19:11), or it can depict Satan's assault on believers (11:7; 12:17; 13:7; 20:8). Here, however, it is directed against two groups within the congregation. This threatened divine war will be directed against Balaamite believers who have become so comfortable with pagan mores and activities that they participate in them. Secondly, this wrath of Jesus will also be revealed against believers (associated with the angel of Pergamum, "against you") who refuse to practice the biblical virtue of intolerance. Specifically, they will be punished for their patience toward the sinful behaviors of these lapsed believers. Osborne aptly summarized Christ's warning in these words: "the wrath will be especially addressed to the heretics and their followers. Nevertheless, the judgment will be upon the whole church, for undoubtedly if the church had taken a strong stand, there would have been far fewer defections to the Nicolaitan camp."[15] Beale correctly concurs by noting that "the church had a responsibility to cease tolerating

---

"He shall not judge by what his eyes see, or decide by what his ears hear; but with righteousness he shall judge the poor, and decide with equity for the meek of the earth; he shall strike the earth with the rod of his mouth, and with the breath of his lips he shall kill the wicked. Righteousness shall be the belt around his waist, and faithfulness the belt around his loins" (Isa 11:3b-5).

"He made my mouth like a sharp sword, in the shadow of his hand he hid me; he made me a polished arrow, in his quiver he hid me away" (Isa 49:2).

Figure 91

---

15. Osborne, *Revelation*, 146.

this movement" and to "immediately discipline the idolaters" in order to "escape the same fate" of the sharp sword of Christ's wrath.[16]

In addition to the influence of the Balaam story on the sword imagery, there is also influence from the messianism of Isaiah. The phrase "sword of my mouth" represents a combination of Royal-Davidic messianism (Isa 11:4) and servant messianism (Isa 49:2). This imagery of Isa 11 was certainly in use among the community of the Dead Sea Scrolls when it alluded to texts such as Isa 11:4, "With your sceptre may you lay waste the earth. With the breath of your lips may you kill the wicked."[17] The same imagery is also used of Jesus's combat against the beast and false prophet in Rev 19:15, 21. Although it is quite shocking to followers of Christ, both ancient and modern, the militarism of Jesus will apparently vanquish erring Christian believers who have abandoned first commandment loyalty (Exod 20:3=Deut 5:7) and those who tolerate them just like it will vanquish the beast and the false prophet.

Christ's threat to spiritually kill even his own followers "with the sword of my mouth" resonates with and affirms the biblical doctrine of the impartiality of God's discipline and justice. This fundamental doctrine of impartiality is seen earlier in Moses (Deut 1:17; 10:17), Amos (Amos 1:3–2:8; 3:2), Jewish history (2 Chr 19:7), Paul (Rom 2:11, 12–16, 25–29; Gal 2:6; Eph 6:9; Col 3:25) and Peter (Acts 10:34; 1 Pet 1:17). Based upon the words and teaching of Jesus no amount of pious lobbying can alter the impartiality of God (cf. Matt 7:21). Lest pluralistic believers in the modern church in the Christian West think that this imagery is just so much divine saber rattling by Christ, a look at Rev 19:11–21 shows that phrases like "make war against them" and "sword of my mouth" refer to combat situations resulting in casualties. When Christ "makes war" against the church there are no POWs, only those who suffer "the same precise fate" of Balaam "on an escalated spiritual scale . . . if they do not repent."[18]

Since those of Balaam and the Nicolaitans are current realities in the Pergamene congregation against whom Christ threatens to fight, it seems probable that the threat "I will soon come to you" anticipates a visitation and judgment by God in the near future, a divine threat that will be revoked only if repentance occurs. This threat, then, points to an immediate rather than an eschatological visitation by Christ (see notes on 2:5).

16. Beale, *Revelation*, 251.

17. 1Q28b (=1QRule of Benediction) 5.24–25 and 4Q161 (=4QIsaiah Pesher) frags. 8–10.11–19.

18. Beale, *Revelation*, 251.

Prior to the blessings given to the faithful at Pergamum, the reader is reminded of the necessity for true spiritual hearing of Christ's message. The listening and obedient believers at Pergamum are promised a new reward. The reward for the faithful will be hidden manna. Those believers who forego pagan feasts and polluted food offered to idols will be rewarded with God's sustaining manna.[19] The concept of the hidden manna may reflect a post-biblical Jewish tradition recorded

Figure 92

in 2 Macc 2:4–8.[20] This story reports that at the time of the imminent destruction of the Temple by the Babylonians, the prophet Jeremiah was instructed by God to take with him the ark of the covenant, the symbol of God's spiritual presence with the people. Jeremiah was to go to Mt. Nebo, the story records, and to hide the ark in a cave. Jeremiah, the text continues, "came and found a cave-dwelling, and he brought there the tent and the ark and the altar of incense; then he sealed up the entrance" until "God gathers his people together again and shows his mercy" (2 Macc 2:5–7). Since the ark of the covenant contained a golden vessel that held manna (Heb 9:4; Exod 16:32–4), this Johannine reference to hidden manna may connote the idea of the ark of God hidden during the conditions of exile and duress. Thus the Pergameme believers will not be left desolate, but will be given sustenance of manna, which was, after all, viewed as a divine meal (in contrast to pagan feasts), the "bread of angels" (Ps 78:24–25).[21]

The whiteness of the stone given to victors has several possible meanings.[22] Probably John intends to emphasize the assured victory of the faithful believers, since in the Graeco-Roman world being "black stoned" (similar to black balled) meant failure and rejection. Whiteness, like whiteness of garments, also connotes purity and acceptance in the presence of the divine (on the use of the color white in Revelation and in the contemporary cultures see notes on Rev 3:4–5). It is noteworthy that there are numerous inscriptions from the Hellenistic and Roman periods that prescribe that particular inscriptions be engraved on white stones.

---

19. Beale and McDonough, "Revelation," 1094 associate this manna with an "end-time feast."

20. See Goldstein, *II Maccabees*, 184.

21. LXX Ps 77:24–25 (καὶ ἄρτον οὐρανοῦ ἔδωκεν αὐτοῖς ἄρτον ἀγγέλων ἔφαγεν ἄνθρωπος).

22. Beale, *Revelation*, 252–53.

Some of the spiritual assurances given to harassed believers in Roman Asia are described by the term "new": new names (Rev 2:17), a new Jerusalem (Rev 3:12; 21:2), new songs (Rev 5:9; 14:3), new heaven and new earth (Rev 21:1), and indeed all things become new (Rev 21:5). In biblical idiom, the theme of newness focuses upon consolation and hope for a people alienated from its surrounding culture and struggling under the oppressive regime of the Babylonians. It is rooted in the prophecies and idiom of the latter part of Isaiah. There messages are first given in light of the Babylonian exile, words that speak to them of a newness soon to be brought about by God.[23] In John's day this idiom reaffirms hope to a people of God struggling under the Roman Babylon.

Isa 42:9: "See, they have come; also new things, which I myself will declare (*kai kaina ha egō anaggelō*, καὶ καινὰ ἃ ἐγὼ ἀναγγελῶ) and before they sprang forth, they were made plain to you (NETS)."

Isa 65:17: "For heaven will be new, and the earth will be new, (*estai gar ho ouranos kainos kai hē gē kainē*, ἔσται γὰρ ὁ οὐρανὸς καινὸς καὶ ἡ γῆ καινή). and they shall not remember the former things, nor shall they come upon their heart (NETS)."

Isa 66:22: "For as the new heaven and the new earth, which I am making (*ho ouranos kainos kai hē gē kainē ha egō poiō*, ὁ οὐρανὸς καινὸς καὶ ἡ γῆ καινή ἃ ἐγὼ ποιῶ) remain before me, says the Lord, so shall your offspring and your name stand (NETS)."

Interpreters have debated the nature of the new name (*onoma kainon*, ὄνομα καινόν).[24] Whose name is this? Is it the new name of the Messiah, perhaps King of Kings and Lord of Lords (Rev 19:12–16; cf. Phil 2:9–10) or is it a name given by God to the elect who have overcome? The weight of the evidence seems to point to the latter. This promise of a new name seems to be a clear allusion to Isa 62:2, though in the case of Isaiah the symbolic name Hephzibah (Isa 62:4) is given to Zion and the city of Jerusalem. In Revelation the new name is awarded to the individual believer who has eschewed the errors of the Nicolaitans and resisted the teaching of Balaam.

---

23. Isa 43:19: "Look, I am doing new things (ἰδοὺ ποιῶ καινὰ) that will now spring forth, and you will know them, and I will make a way in the wilderness and rivers in the dry land." Isa 48:6: "You have heard all things, and you yourselves have not known. But I have also made to be heard by you, from now on, the new things that shall come to pass; (καὶ ἀκουστά σοι ἐποίησα τὰ καινὰ) yet you did not speak." Isa 62:2: "And nations shall see your righteousness, and kings your glory, and he shall call you by your new name, which the Lord will name" (καὶ καλέσει σε τὸ ὄνομά σου τὸ καινόν ὃ ὁ κύριος ὀνομάσει αὐτό, NETS).

24. Beale, *Revelation*, 257–58.

In a world where "Satan's throne" and its attendant activity and influence still abound (2:13), recognition by God and the reward of the new name is something known only to the elect of God, for the reality of the believer's true identity "is now hidden with Christ in God" (Col 3:3). After all, prior to the end of time, history, and the casting of death and Hades into the lake of fire (20:14), even the Messiah must go into battle bearing only "a name written on him that no one knows but he himself" (19:12).

7

The Prophecy to Thyatira

*Rev 2:18 "And to the angel of the church in Thy-
atira write: These are the words of the Son of
God, who has eyes like a flame of fire, and whose
feet are like burnished bronze: 19 "I know your
works—your love, faith, service, and patient endurance. I know that your last works are greater
than the first. 20 But I have this against you:
you tolerate that woman Jezebel, who calls herself a prophet and is teaching and beguiling my
servants to practice fornication and to eat food
sacrificed to idols. 21 I gave her time to repent,*

Figure 93

*but she refuses to repent of her fornication. 22 Beware, I am throwing her
on a bed, and those who commit adultery with her I am throwing into great
distress, unless they repent of her doings; 23 and I will strike her children
dead. And all the churches will know that I am the one who searches minds
and hearts, and I will give to each of you as your works deserve. 24 But to the
rest of you in Thyatira, who do not hold this teaching, who have not learned
what some call 'the deep things of Satan,' to you I say, I do not lay on you any
other burden; 25 only hold fast to what you have until I come. 26 To everyone
who conquers and continues to do my works to the end, I will give authority
over the nations; 27 to rule them with an iron rod, as when clay pots are
shattered—28 even as I also received authority from my Father. To the one
who conquers I will also give the morning star. 29 Let anyone who has an ear*

listen to what the Spirit is saying to the churches.

JOHN BEGINS THIS LETTER by drawing upon two attributes of the Son of Man christophany, namely the eyes and feet of the Son of God. It is noteworthy that this is the only instance of the title "Son of God" in the seven letters, indeed in the entire book of Revelation. The idea of "son of god" was frequently used in emperor veneration[1] and in numerous inscriptions. This imperial setting, however, hardly provides the explanation for this occurrence here. Some have suggested an association of the "Son of God" with burnished bronze feet with the "Son of Man" in Rev 1:13–15 (based upon Dan 10).[2]

It seems the best explanation of this unique usage, however, is that it contextually anticipates the Davidic "Son of God" christology found later in this letter to the congregation at Thyatira (2:26–27). Since the Son of God christology is not one dimensional in the New Testament, it is crucial to understand that this letter to Thyatira rests upon a Davidic Son of God theology. The imagery in 2:26–7 is clearly based upon the Davidic Covenant wording that began in 2 Sam 7:13–14, "He shall build a house for my name, and I will establish the throne of his kingdom for ever. I will be a father to him, and he shall be a son to me." This wording and theology is then later interpreted in Ps 2:7 regarding David, "I will tell of the decree of the Lord: He said to me, 'You are my son; today I have begotten you." This theology continues in this letter with its attendant Davidic "Son of God" messianism.[3]

As noted earlier (1:14), fiery eyes were often a part of theophanies in antiquity, though here the specific origin of the imagery is Dan 10:6. The fiery eyes may also anticipate the later reference to Christ's "searching hearts and minds" (2:23). Notwithstanding a long commentary tradition to the contrary, it is not at all clear that the bronze feet of the Son of God are meant to interface with the "local patron God Apollo" or local labor unions.[4]

John begins his analysis of the church at Thyatira with kudos for their spiritual achievements in crucial areas such as faith and love (*tēn agapēn*

1. In some regions and contexts, the preferred term was "son of the 'divinized' one," when the term "divinized" was preferred over "god."

2. Beale, *Revelation*, 259–60.

3. Ps 2:8–9: "Ask of me, and I will make the nations your heritage, and the ends of the earth your possession. You shall break them with a rod of iron, and dash them in pieces like a potter's vessel."

4. As suggested by Osborne, *Revelation*, 153; Beale, *Revelation*, 259–60 critiques this mis(use) of the concept of "local allusion."

kai tēn pistin, τὴν ἀγάπην καὶ τὴν πίστιν), their service oriented lifestyle (*tēn diakonian,* τὴν διακονίαν), and the tenacity of their faith in light of duress (*tēn hupomonēn sou, kai ta erga sou,* τὴν ὑπομονήν σου, καὶ τὰ ἔργα σου). In fact, in many ways their works and programs were improving and expanding all the time. "Contrary to the Ephesians," as Osborne notes, "the quality of life in this church was not diminishing"[5] and it certainly had not reached a plateau in growth.

For John's "Son of God," however, all of this congregational achievement can be inadequate in itself. For Christ there are even more foundational issues than all these applauded ecclesiastical virtues, virtues that many modern churches and their pastors would greatly covet. What modern congregation, after all, would not greatly desire a résumé that reflected love, faith, service, and perseverance and would not feel largely satisfied when those were attained? There is a fundamental sin, however, which cannot be brooked under any circumstances. John knows that Christ has little tolerance for violations of first commandment loyalty—"you shall have no other gods" (Exod 20:3). This means that all the applause for the congregation's achievements is muted both because of the adoption of a Jezebel perspective, by some of its members, and equally by the congregation's tolerance of those fellow members who have followed Jezebel.

In light of the direction of some of the ecclesiastical culture in Thyatira, the Son of God (2:18) must make every effort through John's prophetic ministry to subvert the values of spiritual toleration and nonjudgmentalism that are guiding some of the interpersonal relationships among the members. In this instance of the violation of first commandment loyalty, when religious syncretism has gained the upper hand, Jesus regards intolerance rather than tolerance as the virtue. Even though spiritual intolerance is currently the "unforgiveable sin" in most areas of comtemporary culture, both sacred and secular, this prevailing Western perspective does not represent the outlook revealed to John by Christ.

The believers in Thyatira were tolerating an idolater in their midst, a false prophetess. It is evident from the text that John's concern is not that this woman is a prophetess (cf. Luke 2:36; Acts 2:17; 21:9; 1 Cor 11:5), but that she is a false prophetess. Obviously this situation would not have arisen at all if women had had no voice in the early church. In the early Roman era the religion of the Jews, of the Christians, and of the pagans all had women prophets.[6] The essential problem with Jezebel's teaching is its

5. Osborne, *Revelation,* 155.
6. Flower, *Seer,* 211–39.

content; it is false and therefore she misleads[7] the saints. This sentiment of John's judgment is reminiscent of the analysis of the prophetic errors that led to the downfall of the congregation of Judah (Lam 2:14): "Your prophets have seen for you false and deceptive visions; they have not exposed your iniquity to restore your fortunes, but have seen oracles for you that are false and misleading."

Generations before Revelation traditional Jews had fought a losing battle against the assimilation forces of Hellenism and Romanism in Judea. This to, in their judgment, was facilitated by the work of false prophecy. One of the hymns that came from this anti-assimilationist movement was preserved among the Dead Sea Scrolls and reads: "But you, O God, abhor every plan of Belial and your counsel remains, and the plan of your heart persists endlessly. But they, hypocrites, plot intrigues of Belial . . . they search for you among the idols, place in front of themselves the stumbling block of their iniquities, they go to search for you in the mouth of prophets of fraud attracted by delusion" (1QH (=1QHodayot) 12.12–16). By setting up Jezebel as an Old Testament "type" of the false prophetess at Thyatira, John is underscoring a threefold spiritual reality: the gravity of *1.* her sins, the sinfulness of her excessively tolerant fellow believers, and the *3.* inevitable doom and failure that await her and her followers (2:23, "her children," *ta tekna*).

Much like those at Pergamum who promoted the teaching of Balaam, this Jezebel is guilty of inculcating syncretism in the forms of sexual immorality and the practice of eating food sacrificed to idols (2:20). Debate exists regarding John's charge of "sexual immorality" and whether it should be interpreted literally or metaphorically (see note on 2:14 for my own views). Reddish represents many other commentators when he writes: "Because the biblical tradition often used sexual imagery to describe idolatry, Jezebel was accused of being guilty of 'many whoredoms' (2 Kgs. 9:22). This metaphorical use of sexual imagery explains the charge of fornication leveled against the Thyatiran 'Jezebel.'"[8] She accomplishes this by means of her "prophetic-teaching" ministry. The words of the Son of God to this congregation assume that the elect of God can be deceived and led into apostasy and embracing "Satan's so-called deep secrets."[9]

7. The Greek term used here is *planaō* (πλανάω), a term employed seven other times in Revelation, 12:9 (the deceiver), 13:14 (deceives), 18:23 (were deceived), 19:20 (he deceived), 20:3 (deceive), 20:8 (deceive), 20:10 (deceived).

8. Reddish, *Revelation*, 64.

9. Prior theological commitments occasionally make it difficult for interpreters to acknowledge the possibility of apostasy. The NIV's unusual rendering of Mark

The phrase "time to repent" (*chronon hina metanoēsē*, χρόνον ἵνα μετανοήσῃ) reflects the specific character of God attested throughout Scripture, but revealed especially in Yahweh's self revelation in Exodus 34:5–6: "The Lord descended in the cloud and stood with him there, and proclaimed the name, 'The Lord.' The Lord passed before him, and proclaimed, 'The Lord, the Lord, a God merciful and gracious, slow to anger, and abounding in steadfast love and faithfulness.'"[10] Since God is "slow to anger" by nature, he had given Jezebel sufficient time to abandon both her destructive teachings and practices. Although John has been accused at times of advocating a rigor of discipline similar to the later heresy known as Montanism, this is patently not the case. The concept of *agapē* (ἀγάπη) is in John's opening doxology (1:5b–6), and so it is not a surprise that in John's message we read of a God who gives opportunity and time for repentance (9:20; 16:9, 11). At some point, however, like the proverbial Amorites, Jezebel's sin would have "reached its full measure" and God's wrath would be revealed.

In the case of Jezebel John's words are very clear; she did not repent and come back to God because "she is unwilling," not because her choice was preordained by God himself from eternity. This text does not say why she was unwilling, but one of John's point it that it was her choice to remain rebellious and immoral and therefore unacceptable to God. A possible answer to the question regarding her unwillingness to repent might be found in the words of sixth-century BC Jews who themselves were similarly unrepentant in the face of Jeremiah's preaching against their assimilation (Jer 44:16–18): "As for the word that you have spoken to us in the name of the Lord, we are not going to listen to you. Instead, we will do everything that we have vowed, make offerings to the queen of heaven and pour out libations to her, just as we and our ancestors, our kings and our officials, used to do in the towns of Judah and in the streets of Jerusalem. We used to have plenty of food, and prospered, and saw no misfortune. But from the time we stopped making offerings to the queen of heaven and pouring out libations to her, we have lacked everything and have perished by the sword and by famine." Like these Judean opponents of Jeremiah in Egypt, *mutatis mutandis*, the Christian Jezebel knew that she and her followers

---

13:22, "to deceive the elect—if that were possible" reveals this tendency since it takes a general Greek conditional clause and without justification turns it into a condition contrary to fact clause. Whereas Jesus leaves open the possibility of deceiving the elect, the NIV makes it into an impossibility.

10. This divine characteristic is also revealed in Num 14:18; Neh 9:17; Pss 86:15, 103:8, 145:8; Joel 2:13; Jonah 4:2; Nah 1:3.

could have material satisfaction, be better off, not perish by the sword, and suffer no harm if they followed the gods of their culture and the religion of the surrounding empire. She and her followers probably asserted that "Christian pluralism" entitled them to have both Christ and the religious benefits of the surrounding culture and that John's theology was far too culturally subversive and religiously restrictive for them.

The NRSV's phrase "great distress" is its translation of the Greek phrase *thlipsis megalē* (θλῖψις μεγάλη). A more literal translation might be "great tribulation," which would at least make the modern reader aware that this Greek phrase must not necessarily be understood as a technical term for the "great tribulation" (cf. Rev 7:14) associated with certain forms of Christian millenarianism.

In biblical anthropology "hearts and minds" are the sphere in which decisions and loyalties are shaped.[11] On the basis of searching these, God critiques one's deeds and then either rewards or punishes. Rev 2:23b certainly should be seen as an paraphrase of Jer 17:10, "I the Lord test the *mind* and search the *heart*, to *give* to all according to their ways, according to the *fruit* of their doings." This connection between works and reward is based upon a biblical theme attested in the Old Testament, Jesus, and Paul. The particular wording can be traced back to Ps 62:12, "And steadfast love belongs to you, O Lord. For you repay to all according to their work." (cf. Jesus's affirmation of eschatological judgment based upon works, Matt 16:27). These covenant breaking behaviors of immorality and eating foods offered to idols are not depicted as mere peccadilloes but rather as pernicious deeds according to which Jezebel and her followers will be judged and punished.

John threatens quick and visible discipline of this woman and her colleagues who stand in opposition to John's theology. There is no clear indication in the text whether the threat of death (*apoktenō en thanatō*, ἀποκτενῶ ἐν θανάτῳ) was to be taken literally or spiritually, although the latter clearly seems more probable. John's older Jewish contemporary, Philo of Alexandria, had similar struggles with his fellow Jews who assimilated to the diverse and pervasive polytheism of the pagan culture of Graeco-Roman Alexandria. Philo also knew of pseudo-prophetic figures within Egyptian Judaism who, like the Christian Jezebel, claimed inspiration and guidance by the Holy Spirit as a prophetic means to lead Jews "to the worship of those who are accounted gods in the different cities" (Philo,

---

11. Schuele, "Heart," 764–66; Wan, "Mind," 90–91.

Spec. 1.315).[12] Philo's draconian recommendation is that such a person should be killed by the local community of the Jews (cf. Zech 13:3), "judging it a virtuous action to be zealous for his execution" (Philo, *Spec.* 1.316). Even though in many ways Philo is regarded as more urbane and sophisticated than John of Patmos, Philo's attitude on this issue of the treatment of apostates certainly points in another direction since he calls for execution by the hands of fellow Jewish believers. This suggests that early Christian references to Jewish brutality against them need not necessarily be viewed as merely anti-Semitic rhetoric.

The reference to "all the congregations" (*pasai hai ekklēsiai*, πᾶσαι αἱ ἐκκλησίαι) underscores the importance of the statement given at the end of each letter, "What the Spirit says to the churches." Both the praise and censure revealed to each congregation should be a matter of deep concern to each of the other congregations. Irrespective of whatever form the death manifested itself in, the text states that this punishment will be recognized (*gnōsontai*, γνώσονται) by believers in other congregations (2:23).

The references to repentance in this letter provide another example of the conditional nature of some of the predictions in the book of Revelation (see Appendix B). That is, God's promised wrath is provisional in nature and consequently will be aborted on the basis of repentance manifested in the lives of those threatened by God's punishment (2:22b, *ean mē metanoēsōsin*, ἐὰν μὴ μετανοήσωσιν).

In contrast to the previously mentioned believers who are aligned with "what some call 'the deep things of Satan'" and must repent or perish, the rest of the believers at Thyatira are commended for their orthodoxy and orthopraxy. They have not participated in "this teaching" of Jezebel that advocates and leads to immorality and idolatry.

John's terminology "what some call 'the deep things of Satan'" is replete with difficulties. Does this idea "what some call" emerge from those aligned with Jezebel, or by those at Thyatira "who do not hold to" her teachings? It is not possible to give a certain answer, though I doubt that these assimilated believers in the congregation at Thyatira associated their own doctrine with Satan, any more than they themselves would have used the term "Jezebel" as a moniker for their leader. To state the obvious, church history is not filled with heretics who thought they were. If, however, this designation comes from nonassimilated, faithful, believers at Thyatira, then they are stating an outlook very similar to one given earlier by Jesus and later the Apostle Paul. A popular and false Jewish

12. Sandelin, "Danger," 109–50.

messianism embraced by the Apostle Peter was attributed by Jesus to Satan (Mark 8:31–33=Matt 16:21–23). When assimilation to paganism took place among members of the congregation of God, Paul himself directly attributed this assimilation to the work of Satan (2 Cor 6:14–7:1).[13]

"And this is the time of salvation for the nation of God and a period of rule for all the men of lot, and of everlasting destruction for all the lot of Belial" (1QM 1.5).

"I [shall obtain] for you [rest] from all your enemies: (it refers to this,) that he will obtain for them rest from a[ll] the sons of Belial, those who make them fall, to destroy th[em on account of] their [sins]" (4Q174 (=4QFlorilegium) 7-8).

Figure 94

Jesus places no other burden on them except that they are to remain faithful until his eschatological return. Since the faithful recipients of John's prophecy at Thyatira are told to "hold fast to what you have until I come" (ὃ ἔχετε κρατήσατε ἄχρι[ς] οὗ ἂν ἥξω, 2:25) and to persevere "to the end" (ἄχρι τέλους) it appears that these followers of the Lamb would have anticipated the Parousia of Jesus in their own lifetime. Jesus's imperative (2:25) to those believers to "hold on to what you have" seems a bit hollow if believers ultimately had no choice in the matter, but *had* to manifest perseverance in all circumstances. Overcoming in 2:26 is closely associated with keeping the very works of Jesus (ὁ τηρῶν ἄχρι τέλους τὰ ἔργα μου), including one's devotion to first commandment loyalty. This language of doing works, and especially the works of Jesus, resonates with the language of the Fourth Gospel, "Very truly, I tell you, the one who believes in me will also do the works (i.e., the works, *ta erga*, τὰ ἔργα) that I do" (14:12).[14]

Though there is much debate concerning the interpretation of Rev 2:26b–27, there is a general consensus regarding the intertextual background to the wording of these verses. In fact, if there is an exception to the adage that Revelation never directly quotes the Old Testament but only alludes to it, these verses would be the exception.[15] The promise of 2:26b–27 is based upon a prior christological interpretation of the earlier verse in Psalm 2 (LXX), specifically Ps 2:7: "I will tell of the decree of the Lord: He said to me, 'You are my son; today I have begotten you.'" The

13. Garland, *2 Corinthians*, 334–35.

14. The NIV has a noticeable hesitancy in translating the Greek terms *ergon/erga* (ἔργον/ ἔργα) with the word "work/works."

15. *Novum Testamentum*, 27th ed. regards 2:27 as a quotation from the LXX of Ps 2:9 and the UBS 4th rev. ed. of *The Greek New Testament* regards 2:26b–27 as a "poetic" statement of Ps 2:8–9.

reliance here on Davidic Covenant theology from the Old Testament reflects again its pervasiveness in Revelation. Built upon that foundation of Jesus's kingly sonship, the further description includes (Ps 2:8b–9): "I will make the nations your heritage, and the ends of the earth your possession. You shall break them with a rod of iron, and dash them in pieces like a potter's vessel."

When looking at this section of Revelation, at least two significant and profound problems require attention. The first question regards who Psalm 2, which Richard Bauckham notes is John's "favourite psalm,"[16] is addressing. Specifically, is the promise of Ps 2:8–9 as used by John spoken to Christ, to Christ's faithful followers in John's congregations, or both?[17] The second problem focuses upon the brutality of the language found in this Davidic text from Psalm 2 and how this imagery of brutal domination is to be interpreted within the context of Christian faith and values.[18]

The first issue is extraordinarily complex since it involves decisions about uncertainties in the areas of grammar, intertextuality, and both John's messianism and eschatology. Numerous interpreters believe that followers of Christ are included in this promise. This outlook is found both in the writings of futurist[19] and nonfuturist scholars.[20] The details, however, of this believer centered interpretation are not uniform.

Many interpreters who regard Christian overcomers as the recipients of the promises of Ps 2 make Rev 2:26–27 part of a large dispensational patchwork, gathering verses from numerous centuries and diverse contexts to sew together a millenarian cloth. Osborne, for example, invokes Psalm 149:6–7, "Let the high praises of God be in their throats and two-edged swords in their hands, to execute vengeance on the nations and punishment on the peoples" and makes these verses from the Psalter part of a Christian eschatological jihad that Rev 2:26–27 supposedly depicts.[21]

16. Bauckham, *Climax*, 314.

17. See for example, Quek, "I Will," 175–87.

18. Although this fact does not obviate the difficulties of the brutal imagery used here, it should be pointed out that the wording of the LXX, Revelation, and the Latin Vulgate all disagree with the Hebrew wording in Ps 2:8. The Hebrew text is typically rendered "You shall break them with a rod of iron." Revelation 2:27 and the LXX use the Greek term *poimainō* (ποιμαίνω) which often means "to shepherd." As Beale points out, however, the sense of *poimainō* (ποιμαίνω) in Revelation and certainly in LXX texts such as Mic 5:5(6) and Jer 6:3; 22:22 means to destroy or to devastate (Beale, *Revelation*, 267).

19. Osborne, *Revelation*, 166–67.

20. Aune, *Revelation*, 166–67.

21. Osborne, *Apocalypse*, 166–67.

There are other scholars who take the same language and understand it very differently. In a seminal essay entitled "The Apocalypse as a Christian War Scroll"[22] Richard Bauckham fully examines the imagery of militancy and vocabulary of war found in the book of Revelation, but concludes: "Revelation makes lavish use of holy war language while transferring its meaning to nonmilitary means of triumph over evil. . . . In the eschatological destruction of evil in Revelation there is no place for real armed violence, but there is ample space of the imagery of armed violence."[23] Accordingly, "The messianic army is an army of martyrs who triumph through their martyrdom, because they are followers of the Lamb . . . by following his path to death."[24]

Notwithstanding the popularity of the interpretation that regards Rev 2:26b–27 as a promise of reward only to believers, it seems that perspective needs to be questioned. One possible issue is that it makes believers rather than the Messiah the recipient and fulfillment of this obviously Davidic Psalm. Premillenialists often see this promise as "the first definitive reference in Revelation to the coming millennial kingdom, which Jesus is to establish when He returns to earth . . . [and when] The overcomer will join Christ in destroying the nations who oppose Him."[25]

Typically these interpreters understand the word "him" in the phrase "to him I will give authority" as the faithful believer who overcomes. The NASB translation (2:26b) seems more accurate, however, when it views this "him" as part of the quotation that comes from Ps 2:8 rather than the overcomer mentioned in 2:26a. This believer-centered fulfillment seems problematic because it diminishes the Christ-centered nature of this text in Ps 2:8–9 and neglects the significant evidence that throughout the New Testament this particular Psalm is focused on the Messiah and not the Messiah's followers.[26]

John would not have been the first author of the period to believe that his second Psalm pertained to the Messiah. A well known example is the seventeenth chapter of the *Psalms of Solomon*. This particular Psalm mentions early on (*Pss. Sol.* 17:4) 2 Sam 7, an essential text for the Davidic

22. Bauckham, "Climax," 210–37.

23. Bauckham, "Climax," 233.

24. Bauckham, "Climax," 229.

25. Thomas, *Revelation 1–7*, 233.

26. Prigent, *Apocalypse*, 189 concludes otherwise with these words, "On the other hand, what is less traditional and widespread is the making of this text into a promise addressed to Christians. . . . the fulfillment of a prophecy so surprising that until then it had been reserved for the Messiah."

Covenant in the Jewish Scriptures, and later expresses its Davidic hopes in these words using Ps 2:9 (*Pss. Sol.* 17:21, 24): "See, Lord, and raise up for them their king, the son of David, to rule over your servant Israel in the time known to you, O God. Undergird him with the strength to destroy the unrighteous rulers . . . to smash the arrogance of sinners like a potter's jar; to shatter all their substance with an iron rod; to destroy the unlawful nations with the word of his mouth." Furthermore, both concepts from Ps 2, "rule the nations" and "with an iron scepter" are used only of the Christ elsewhere in Revelation.[27]

The christological focus of these verses (2:26b–27a) might be taken as the direct object (which is otherwise lacking) of the words of Christ in Rev 2:27b (=2:28 in Greek text). A more literal translation of the Greek text is "just as I have received _____ from my Father." Most English translations insert a word that they deem appropriate and then make it the direct object of the verbal phrase. Their word choice is often the word "authority," derived from Rev 2:26b. Their choice of the term "authority" is not inappropriate, but then they seem to forget that this choice assumes that Christ is the referent of the words of Ps 2. From this perspective it makes more theological sense to understand Christ as the primary heir and fulfillment of this promise "from my Father." In hoping to solve this conundrum other interpreters seek to interpret these verses as teaching that believers are currently participating in Christ's rule as the Davidic King (Rev 1:5–6).

Beyond the issue of whether Christ or his followers or both are the intended fulfillment of the quotation from Psalm 2, one needs to interact with the issue of the brutality of the imagery of Ps 2:8–9 and its use in Rev 2:26–27. The brutal image remains, whether one understands Christ or his followers to be its fulfillment. Even when one takes this language as metaphorical for the advancement of the Christian mission, it is still important to observe the scriptural origin of the language and its imagery.

Can this iron scepter, nation smashing imagery be made compatible with Christian values and ethics? Many times there have been attempts, often subtle, to bowdlerize particular christological texts and themes, especially those like Psalm 2. How, it is asked, could Jesus (or his followers) be portrayed as being involved in dashing nations "to pieces like pottery?" The problem does not necessarily leave whether one takes the domination

27. Rev 12:5: "And she gave birth to a son, a male child, who is to rule all the nations with a rod of iron"; 19:15: "From his mouth comes a sharp sword with which to strike down the nations, and he will rule them with a rod of iron"; cf. Rom 15:12 taken from the Royal Davidic chapter Isa 11:10.

literally or spiritually. That is, the Messiah is either presented as physically destroying Rome or destroying its culture, values, and religions by means of the Christian gospel. Domination is there in both ideas. Notwithstanding the awkwardness, and at times painfulness, of these claims, God's interaction with pagan nations is rarely depicted as a gentle experience or tranquil scene in biblical piety. Indeed, the Lord considers all nations, *qua* nations, "as less than nothing and emptiness" (Isa 40:17) before him. This depiction of harsh treatment against the nations, painted with the phrases "ruling with an iron scepter" and "dash them to pieces," reflects Jewish idiom, especially in terms of the messianic Davidic King (cf. *Pss. Sol.* 17:21–45).[28]

Interpreters have given theodicies for this graphic and violent language of Davidic Sonship in Revelation. There are modern interpreters who understand these verses and their images from a believer centered perspective that sees the fulfillment manifest in the gospel's destruction of unbelieving nations through evangelism.[29] G. B. Caird finds the fulfillment of this promise in Christians since "John sees this ancient hope [of Ps 2:9] transfigured in the light of the Cross . . . and God will use no other iron bar than the death of his Son and the martyrdom of his saints."[30] From a similar perspective Beale suggests that: "If it also has a present application to the 'overcomers,' who are said to participate already in the messianic kingdom (Rev 1:5–6, 9; 5:10), then the 'authority' they exercise in beginning to fulfill the Psalm is the witness that they bear through suffering to Christ's death and resurrection."[31]

Although disturbing to many, it should be pointed out that this "iron scepter" Jesus is not an anomaly appearing only in this chapter; rather, it fits into the overall picture of Jesus in Revelation, even when this extended graphic imagery is not found. For John's theology, God's recapturing of his creation does not occur apart from the militant work of Christ since "Jesus Christ . . . [has become] the ruler of the kings of the earth" (1:5). Furthermore, Christ's kingdom is always subversive and has appeared explicitly to destroy alternative nations, empires, and their values, until "the kingdom

28. Collins, *Scepter*, 49–73.

29. These interpreters tend to see this "domination" manifested in the surrender of non-Christian civilizations to the gospel, Prigent, *Apocalypse*, 189; Harrington, *Revelation*, 66; Swete, *Apocalypse*, 47; Murphy, *Messages*, 321, on the other hand, affirms "and the righteous would be crowned with absolute dominion over all the realms of earth, and all the thrones of mankind."

30. Caird, *Revelation*, 46.

31. Beale, *Revelation*, 268.

of the world has become the kingdom of our Lord and of his Messiah, and he will reign for ever and ever" (11:15).

It should not be forgotten that Revelation was written in a world where life was cheap and violence was ubiquitous. The *Pax Romana* was neither achieved nor maintained by beating swords into plowshares, but rather by harsh and inexorable force. When the drama of Revelation shows scene after scene of battered Christians and believers being cruelly assaulted and unjustly killed (2:13; 6:9–11; 7:13–14; 11:7–8; 13:6–7; 13:15; 14:12; 16:6; 17:6; 18:24; 19:2; 20:4), biblical justice demands that this pogrom against the followers of the Lamb be addressed.[32] With the virtual rape of the Bride of the Lamb (19:7; 21:9) in Revelation, it is little wonder that the pagan rapists beg to be covered with an avalanche of boulders rather than face the dominion and justice of her enraged husband, the Lamb (6:16; cf. 14:10).

The radical violence against believers taking place in a culture and empire of gratuitous violence[33] provides the best justification for John's association of the Lamb with such brutal language of domination, whether viewed literally or metaphorically. A biblical theology of the justice of God and God's defense of the oppressed were rightly employed by John in this particular prophetic ministry to the congregations of western Asia Minor. In fact, there may never have been a more appropriate setting in which to present this Davidic imagery of Psalm 2 than in John's own pastoral setting. If the Old Testament teaches anything, it teaches that YHWH is a defender of the oppressed and the victimized and especially when the victims are the elect of Israel.[34]

Taking the Christ-centered approach means, moreover, that just as Christ received his Royal Davidic sonship from his Father 2:26b–27, so the overcomer who faithfully keeps "the works" of Christ (*ho tērōn achri telous ta erga mou*, ὁ τηρῶν ἄχρι τέλους τὰ ἔργα μου) will also receive the morning star (2:28b). It is strange that Thomas comments that Thyatira is

---

32. Christian interpreters understandably wrestle with the violent language of Revelation, sometimes excusing John on the basis of his use of "apocalyptic language" or his use of "traditional materials," implying thereby that he did not really believe it.

33. Every interpreter of Revelation should read Kyle, *Spectacles*.

34. "'Then I will draw near to you for judgement; I will be swift to bear witness against the sorcerers, against the adulterers, against those who swear falsely, against those who oppress the hired workers in their wages, the widow, and the orphan, against those who thrust aside the alien, and do not fear me,' says the Lord of hosts," Mal 3:5; cf., Zech 2:8; Gen 12:3; cf. Isa 10:1–3 for the association of destruction with the oppression of the defenseless.

"the only overcomer to receive a double promise"[35] since a double promise is found in the preceding letter to Pergamum (2:17, namely hidden manna and a white stone).

One suggested background for this "morning star" christology is Num 24:17, "a star shall come out of Jacob, and a sceptre shall rise out of Israel," especially since the scepter of Num 24:17 would be associated with the "rod of iron" of Ps 2:9.[36] We do know now that certain forms of ancient Judaism saw significant themes of messianism in Num 24. The War Scroll from the Dead Sea Scrolls quotes Num 24:17–19 in a highly enthusiastic militarism sprinkled with numerous slogans (e.g., For the battle is God's!) that refers to God's past defeat of Pharaoh and his imminent destruction of the Kittim, all of whom were guided by the Devil.[37]

Rev 22:16 shows clearly that John associated this astral symbolism of the morning star with Royal Davidic christology, "I am the root and the descendant of David, the bright morning star." It is quite probable that this is a messianic adaptation of the "star of Jacob" imagery since similar interpretations are seen in the earlier Jewish documents from the Qumran community.[38]

The particular wording about the reward of the morning star to the overcomer is noteworthy since it is the exact opening words of the quotation about the Messiah from Ps 2:8 (LXX).

- Ps 2:8 (LXX): δώσω σοι (*dōsō soi*); "I will give to you"

- Rev 2:26b: δώσω αὐτῷ (*dōsō autō*); "I will give to him"

- Rev 2:28b: δώσω αὐτῷ (*dōsō autō*); "I will give to him"

Jesus the Messiah receives the Davidic kingdom and the Christians receive the Davidic Messiah Jesus. Many interpreters suggest that this imagery of receiving the morning star (i.e., Christ) may be another idiom for emphasizing the faithful believer's participation in the rule of the Messiah. Aune writes, "The gift of the morning star must refer to the fact that the exalted Christ shares his messianic status with the believer who conquers."[39]

There is still, however, an unanswered question about this "morning star" christology. There is nothing in the text from Num 24:17 that requires, or even points to, the star being the morning star. The phrase

---

35. Thomas, *Revelation 1–7*, 232.

36. The LXX of Num 24:17 does not contain the word "scepter."

37. 1QM (=1QWarScroll) 11.6; similarly 4Q175 (=4Q Testamonia) 12–13.

38. See Collins, *Scepter*, 71–78, 84–87; see the notes also on Rev 3:20–21.

39. Aune, *Revelation 1–5*, 212.

"morning star" refers to the planet Venus. Why would John's prophecy use such astral nomenclature, with overtones of pagan astrology, to refer to Christ? A very plausible answer is found when one recalls the background and occasion for the writing of the seven letters. These prophetic letters were written against the backdrop of "competition" with the Imperial Cult and the mythological ideology that undergirded it.

Specifically, some have suggested John's use of the planet Venus is best explained against the backdrop of the use of the goddess Venus in association with the mythology of the divinity of Julius Caesar, the first "Caesar," who worshiped Venus with the epithets *Venus Victrix* (Venus the Victorius) and *Venus Genetrix* (Mother Venus).[40] Devotion to *Venus Genetrix* continues, in fact, to appear on Ro-man coins of the imperial family at least as late as Antonius Pius in the second century AD.[41] In Roman mythology it was the star of Venus that led Aeneas on his journey from Troy to the historic founding of Rome. This association between Venus and the Julian family is well attested in the world of the Ro-man Republic and early Roman Empire. An early Roman era Ephesian inscription makes the connection between Julius Caesar and

Figure 95

Venus/Aphrodite clear when Caesar is described as "god manifest, born of Ares and Aphrodite and the common Savior of human life" (*ho apo Areōs kai Aphrodeitēs theos epiphanēs kai koinos tou anthrōpinou biou sōtēr,* ὁ ἀπὸ Ἄρεως καὶ Ἀφροδείτης θεὸς ἐπιφανὴς καὶ κοινὸς τοῦ ἀνθρωπίνου βίου σωτήρ).[42] The iconography of Roman coinage likewise attests the dissemination of this concept of the divine association of Venus and Ro-man Emperors.[43] Accordingly John's use of the "morning star" christology would place Christ in competition with Caesar, in a way similar to the use of the seven stars in the christophany of chapter 1.

This epistle to Thyatira concludes with the typical admonition to take heed to the Spirit's instruction to all the churches.

40. Weinstock, *Divus Julius*, 80–90.

41. See American Numismatic in Primary Source Bibliography.

42. *Inschriften von Ephesos*, vol. 2, no. 251.

43. See Staatliche Museen in Primary Source Bibliography.

8

The Prophecy to Sardis

Figure 96

Rev 3:1 "And to the angel of the church in Sardis write: These are the words of him who has the seven spirits of God and the seven stars: "I know your works; you have a name of being alive, but you are dead. 2 Wake up, and strengthen what remains and is on the point of death, for I have not found your works perfect in the sight of my God. 3 Remember then what you received and heard; obey it, and repent. If you do not wake up, I will come like a thief, and you will not know at what hour I will come to you. 4 Yet you have still a few persons in Sardis who have not soiled their clothes; they will walk with me, dressed in white, for they are worthy. 5 If you conquer, you will be clothed like them in white robes, and I will not blot your name out of the book of life; I will confess your name before my Father and before his angels. 6 Let anyone who has an ear listen to what the Spirit is saying to the churches.

FOLLOWING THE INITIAL REFERENCE to the angel of the congregation, Christ's identity is associated with the "seven stars" of the initial christophany (see notes on 1:16, 20) and the "seven spirits" of the initial salutation (1:4). Other texts likewise mention the "seven spirits" and associate them with seven lamps of fire before the throne, "a paraphrased allusion to Zech 4:2–7 ... which identified the 'seven lamps' as God's one Spirit."[1] It is also probable that the seven spirits are to be associated with the number of the congregations being addressed by Christ since the scene contains the imagery of Christ having the seven spirits.

This congregation receives little commendation from Jesus; in fact, Jesus's message to this congregation "is the most strongly negative"[2] of all his exhortations to the seven churches. Sardis takes its place among the other rebuked churches and is put on notice that it will be judged by God on the basis of its works (cf. Rev 2:2, 5, 19, 22, 26; 3:1, 8, 15). This stern tone is also seen in the fact that Jesus addresses this congregation with more Greek imperatives (3:1, 3:2{2x}, 3:3{3x}, 3:6) than any other of the seven churches.

The works of the church in Sardis exist in name only; although it possesses a reputation[3] for spiritual life, it, in fact, is quite dead. This connection between the concepts of "your deeds" and "being alive" reflects the well attested biblical understanding of covenantal nomism (Rev 3:2). Faithful deeds indicate the path to life (Deut 30:19), or in Paul's words, "obedience leads to righteousness" (*ē hupakoēs eis dikaiosunēn*, ἢ ὑπακοῆς εἰς δικαιοσύνην; Rom 6:16c). As Moses emphasized to the Israelites, the keeping of the deeds of the covenant constituted the very possibility for life (Deut 32:46–47a): "Take to heart all the words that I am giving in witness against you today; give them as a command to your children, so

---

1. Beale and McDonough, "Revelation," 1089.

2. Witherington, *Revelation*, 105.

3. For this use of ὄνομα see BDAG, 711–14.

that they may diligently observe all the words of this law. This is no trifling matter for you, but rather your very life."

Notwithstanding the esteemed reputation of the congregation at Sardis among other congregations, from God's perspective the congregation is quite dead. This demonstrates once again an obvious truth from Judeo-Christian history, namely that communities of the elect cannot always be trusted as the guarantor of God's truth. Just because one congregation has the reputation among other congregations and believers of being dynamic and alive does not mean that it is so in the eyes of God. Hypocrisy is kept alive and thrives exactly because God's people often cannot see past the "you have a reputation" that is characteristic of certain congregations.

Scripture is replete with examples of God's people revealing a significant gap between the reality of their lives as seen by God and their mere reputations. A well known example comes from the apostle Paul (Rom 2:21b–23): "Will you not teach yourself? While you preach against stealing, do you steal? You that forbid adultery, do you commit adultery? You that abhor idols, do you rob temples? You that boast in the law, do you dishonour God by breaking the law?"

While the spiritual term "dead" (*nekros*, νεκρός) is typically associated with the condition of nonbelievers and the unsaved,[4] that is clearly not the case here (cf. Eph 5:14). The language then shifts (3:2) and John sees embers that might still be fanned back to life. Building perhaps upon the important link between the ideas of death and sleep,[5] John moves from spiritual death to the imagery of spiritual slumber. A similar coalescence of imagery is preserved in Pauline theology, "Sleeper, awake! Rise from the dead, and Christ will shine on you." (Eph 5:14). The danger of spiritual slumber is alluded to elsewhere in the New Testament (e.g., Rom 13:11; Eph 5:14; 1 Thess 5:7; Rev 16:15; cf. Isa 56:10; Joel 1:5). In addition, "γρηγορῶν [*grēgorōn*] is often used eschatologically to depict the spiritual watchfulness that is necessary to be ready for Christ's return (Mark 13:35, 37; Matt 24:42; 25:13; Luke 12:36–38; 1 Thess 5:6)."[6]

At this point John's prophecy focuses upon the questionable future of this congregation and the uncertain salvation of some of the members in the congregation. The ultimate salvation of this congregation cannot

---

4. Eph 2:1; Col. 2:13; Rom 6:13.

5. E.g., 1 Cor 7:39; 11:30; 15:6, 18, 20, 51; 1 Thess 4:13; 2 Pet 3:4; Likewise the Greek term *egeirō*, ἐγείρω, BDAG, 271–2, can mean either "wake up" or "rise from the dead."

6. Osborne, *Revelation*, 174.

rely solely upon beginning well; it must be strengthened in order to survive.[7] As Craig Keener observed: "Those who do not persevere are lost. But many (especially in my own Baptist tradition) have wrongly reinterpreted the Calvinist teaching so as to allow into heaven anyone who once professed salvation, an idea refuted both here and regularly throughout the New Testament. . . . [These verses offer] a serious warning to many nominal Christians in our culture who depend purely on a past profession of faith to ensure their salvation."[8] The phrase "what remains" includes, "both persons and the elements of Christian character."[9] They are at the very brink of spiritual destruction and the language suggests that they barely have time and opportunity to recover from a fatal situation. Direct and immediate action is required to recover from the inadequate and defective works that characterize their current lives as believers. In contrast to the reputation their works have among other churches,[10] in "the sight of my God" they are insufficient, incomplete. The danger in which these church members find themselves is a direct result of their own impenitent and disobedient hearts; otherwise, repentance would not be commanded.

John's directive is for the congregation to retrace its steps back to its early core of beliefs and lifestyle, to repent of its departure from these earlier commitments, and to embrace afresh its original faith. This shares some similarity with Paul's demand that the Galatians return to the true gospel they had received and heard at his first preaching in Galatians (cf. 2 Cor 11:1–4). Often Scripture employs the theme of "remember."[11] As here, it "was a device frequently used in early Christian texts to encourage those addressed to live up to or to recapture earlier moral and spiritual standards," including typically their initial teachings and experiences with God.[12]

Osborne seems to be over interpreting the two verbs "received" and "heard" when he suggests that these "tell the two ways these truths came

7. This resonates well with this Pauline emphasis seen in his letters (Rom 1:11, 16:25; 1 Thess 3:2, 13; 2 Thess 2:17, 3:3) and Acts (14:22; 15:41; 18:23).

8. Keener, *Revelation*, 147.

9. Beckwith, *Apocalypse*, 473.

10. Contrary to this study, Reddish *Revelation*, 71 believes that the deception was not among other churches but rather "to those outside the church, it still seemed alive . . . because it readily accepted and involved itself in the cultural, social, and political activities of the larger society."

11. E.g., Deut 7:18, 8:2, 9:7, 15:15, 24:22; Josh 23:4; 1 Chr 16:12; Ps 105:5; Isa 46:9; Jer 51:50; Mal 4:4; Luke 22:19; 1 Cor 11:24–5; Eph 2:11; 2 Thess 2:1–5, 3:10; 2 Tim 2:8.

12. Aune, *Revelation 1–5*, 147.

to them, through apostolic tradition ("received") and the teaching of the church ("heard").[13] Based upon the content of several epistles of the New Testament, upon several of the seven letters of Revelation, and upon what is known of early Christian heresy, "the teaching of the church" is probably the last place John would point to for spiritual certainty. As this very letter to Sardis demonstrates (3:1), some of the churches of Roman Asia were not very successful in discerning the difference between a pseudo-truth based upon ecclesiastical perception and the real truth as God himself saw it. The analysis of H. B. Swete is more appropriate when he associates the aorist verb "heard" with original reception of faith (cf. Rom 10:17) and not with later ecclesiastical teaching.[14]

John's prediction of catastrophic and sudden punishment from Christ[15] may well have reminded the Sardian Christians of memorable events in the city's history. Most scholars think of two times in Sardian history when the city was captured because those in the city slept.[16] A more recent story that those at Sardis might have also remembered, as the later Roman historian Tacitus did, was the memory of the historic earthquake of AD 17. Like a nocturnal thief, this earthquake's nighttime arrival "increased the surprise and destruction" it unleashed upon twelve important cities of Roman Asia. Tacitus's report portrays the catastrophic and almost apocalyptic nature of this occurrence: "In the same year, twelve important cities of Asia collapsed in an earthquake, the time being night, so that the havoc was the less foreseen and the more devastating. Even the usual resource in these catastrophes, a rush to open ground, was unavailing, as the fugitives were swallowed up in yawning chasms. Accounts are given of huge mountains sinking, of former plains seen heaved aloft, of fires flashing out amid the ruin. As the disaster fell heaviest on the Sardians, it them brought the largest measure of sympathy" (*Ann.* 2.47.1-2).

This imminent punishment threatened by Christ, like many divine threats in the prophecies of John, can be stopped by the repentant actions of believers (see Appendix B). The "if" (*ean, ἐὰν*) clause in 3:3 shows that

---

13. Osborne, *Revelation*, 176.

14. Swete, *Apocalypse*, 50.

15. Thief imagery can be found in the synoptic gospels (e.g., Matt 24:43) and Paul (1 Thess 5:2)--though the imagery was well known in the events of everyday life (Job 24:14; Philo, *Spec.* 4, 10).

16. Examples would include Ramsay, *Letters* 376-85; Swete, *Apocalypse*, 49; Osborne, *Revelation*, 177; Witherington, *Revelation*, 106; Talbert, *Apocalypse*, 21; this urban historical background seems less likely to me since these defeats took place in 549 BC (Cyrus) and 218 BC (Antiochus III).

a positive response by the local Sardian believers to these threats can halt the fulfillment of these threats, which is the normal way biblical prophecy works (cf. Jer 18:5–10). Nothing less than obedience and repentance can spare this congregation from the undesirable and harsh visitation from Christ. Most commentators rightly regard this punitive visit as one that would not occur in conjunction with the Second Coming, but rather would be "the invisible coming of Christ to judge this particular church in the present."[17]

Even though the majority of the congregation at Sardis lives on the precipice of destruction, there are a "few people" (*oliga onomata*, ὀλίγα ὀνόματα) who are victors. As a self-acknowledged prophet John knows well the significance of "the few" and their place in a long history of believers regarded as the faithful remnant of God (Judg 7:1–8). Prophets are rarely permitted to applaud the majority, since the majority typically does not follow the path of God, and this analysis of Sardis corresponds closely to Jesus's own observation (Matt 7:13) that "the many" (πολλοί) move steadily down a wide path to destruction, while the narrow way that leads to life is walked by only a few.

It should be noted that this dichotomy of the "few" and the "many" was also well known among certain philosophical moral teachers of the Hellenistic and Roman periods. One example comes from the first century AD work associated with the name Cebes and entitled *Tabula*, 15.1–3.[18] In this story the traveler asks his guide: "Now what kind of path is this that leads to true Education (*paideia*, παιδεία)? [I said].

"Do you see this place up here," he said, "where no one dwells, but seems instead to be deserted?"

"I see."

"Then do you also see a small gate and in front of the gate a path which is not much frequented; very few pass this way (*all' oligoi panu poreuontai*, ἀλλ᾽ ὀλίγοι πάνυ πορεύονται), as it were through a trackless waste which seems both rough and rocky?"

"Certainly," I said.

"And there seems to be a high hill, and a very narrow ascent with a deep precipice on either side."

"I see."

17. Witherington, *Revelation*, 106; Osborne, *Revelation*, 177–78 chooses both, with Jesus arriving both in the present and in eschatological judgment.

18. *Tabula*, 15.1–3. This same dichotomy is assumed in Plato's famous "Allegory of the Cave."

"Now this," he said, "is the path that leads to true Education (παιδεία)."

These victorious believers at Sardis are wearing unsoiled garments. Clothes (*stolē*, στολή; *himation*, ἱμάτιον) play an important role in the symbolism of Revelation, as does their cleanness (3:5, 18; 4:4; 6:11; 7:9, 13, 14; 22:14). In this context "soiled clothes" refers to inadequate and incomplete deeds. The Greek verb for "soiled" (*molunō*, μολύνω) often carries the idea of polluted or defiled. One of the best examples of this use of "dirty clothes" to represent a spiritual condition is recorded in Zech 3:3–5: "Now Joshua was dressed in filthy clothes as he stood before the angel. The angel said to those who were standing before him, 'Take off his filthy clothes.' And to him he said, 'See, I have taken your guilt away from you, and I will clothe you in festal apparel.' And I said, 'Let them put a clean turban on his head.' So they put a clean turban on his head and clothed him in the apparel; and the angel of the Lord was standing by."

Since these "few" believers do not have soiled garments, Jesus promises them white garments for their clothing as they walk with him. Two reasons demand that special attention be given to the significance of the color white. First, this term "white" receives extraordinary attention in Revelation. This word occurs more times in Revelation (17x) than in the rest of the New Testament documents combined. Indeed, in all of Scripture the only competitor with Revelation for frequency of the word "white" is Leviticus chapter 13 (16x), but there white is used in regard to the color of sores, skin, and hair. Since the Jewish Scriptures are generally devoid of any cultic use of the idea of white garments (cf. Eccl 9:7–8),[19] John's use relies upon ubiquitous and deeply engrained visual symbolism of white garments that was well known primarily from the surrounding Graeco-Roman culture[20] and secondarily from Graeco-Roman culture's impact on contemporary Judaism.[21]

---

19. Some have thought that the Jewish Scriptures do contain references to the cultic use of the term "white" since it mentions the use of "linen" cloth in the tabernacle (Exod 26:1) and as a garment for the priests (Exod 28:42; Lev 16:4). Linen, however, was naturally a dull white, tan or ecru in color, and only became "white" when it was bleached to become white. If the Old Testament had intended to convey the cultic idea of the color "white," they would have mentioned "white linen." Since these cultic texts in fact do not mention the term "white," even though there were many opportunities to do so, it does not seem prudent to assume or conclude that the term "white" was a cultic term at that time in Jewish history.

20. In general one can consult Herrmann, "Farbe," 391–93; in Plato's *Resp.* 10.617c the three celestial Fates were "clad in white vestments."

21. Synoptic texts include Matt 17:2; 28:3; Mark 9:3; John 20:12; other New Testament texts include Acts 1:10; Rev 4:4; 6:11; 7:9, 13; 20:11.

There are numerous examples from the Graeco-Roman setting that highlight the pervasive presence of white garments. One well known instance of this from Roman culture was: "When a boy assumed the toga virilis, [and] any Roman onlooker knew that regardless of his young age, he was a freeborn citizen male. This was apparent first and foremost because his toga was completely white. Persius (Sat. 5.33) calls it candidus umbo, 'shining white toga,' while an inscription from Sardis that commemorates Augustus' grandson and adopted son Gaius' ceremony, speaks of his 'brilliant white toga in all its splendour.'"[22] Perhaps even more significant is the fact that the normal term for this toga was *toga pura*, highlighting ethical connotations. "The boys were emerging from childhood" and therefore this white garment reflected a "period of protective benefits that left them ritually and sexually unspoiled."[23]

Practices in pagan mysteries and temples also shed light on this issue since at times they required devotees to be dressed in white clothes in order to be acceptable for the sacred ceremonies and in order to come before the deity associated with the temple.[24] One such Hellenistic era testimony comes from the famous Asclepius sanctuary at Epidaurus. It refers to the participation of "those who have in their hearts virtue and reverence" and who will lead the religious procession "dressed in white raiment" (*heimasin en leukoisi*, εἵμασιν ἐν λευκοίσι).[25] The color white obviously symbolizes their hearts of virtue and reverence, a correlation that clearly resonates with Rev 3:4–5.[26] Another Hellenistic era inscription from the Asia Minor city of Priene contains the command for the devotees to enter the temple with white raiment (*esthēti leukē*, ἐσθῆτι λευκῇ).[27]

The Greek author Pausanias (4.33.5) mentions with great praise the mysteries at Andania. The fortuitous discovery of a Greek inscription from that very site sheds significant light on the nature and practice of this

---

22. Dolansky, "Togam," 54. The inscription from Sardis referred to in the above article is found in *IGRR* vol. 4, no. 1756, lines 6–7.

23. Dolansky, "Togam," 54.

24. An inscription dated 61–60 BC reveals the deity himself forbidding anyone entering the sacred cave of Pan when wearing either colored or dyed garments, *SEG* XXXVI, no. 267 [=Lupu, ed., *Religion*, doc. 4].

25. *IG* 4.1, no. 128, an inscription dedicated by Isyllus, son of Socrates, the Epidaurian, dedicated to Apollo Maleatas and to Asclepius (=Edelstein and Edelstein, *Asclepius*, 1:145).

26. On the importance of "inner purity" in the heart of the worshiper see Veyne, *Die griechisch-römische*, 41–45.

27. Sokolowski, *Lois Sacrées*, no. 35, 100–1.

Greek cult in the early first century BC. One of the numerous stipulations in the divine arrangement of this cult's ceremonies is that the males who have been initiated into these mysteries are to wear white clothing to the ceremonies (*ton heimatismon leukon,* τὸν εἱματισμὸν λευκόν).[28] From the second century AD comes the testimony of Aelius Aristides, a devoted worshiper of the healing god Asclepius, who remarks about standing: "within the entrance of the temple and that many others had assembled, just as when a purification takes place, and that they were clad in white and otherwise too in suitable fashion."[29]

One final and important piece of evidence to illumine John's concern for the spiritual significance of the color white is found in the Latin novel *Metamorphoses,* written by Apuleius (c. AD 125–80).[30] In Book 11 of this novel the reader is introduced to elaborate religious ceremonies associated with the goddess Isis, one of the most worshiped goddesses of the Roman world. Prior to this religious ceremony for the goddess, a ceremony repeated many times throughout Graeco-Roman cities, the women who were preparing the procession in honor of the savior goddess Isis were "radiant in white garments" (11.9). In addition Apuleius mentions that the sacred youth choirs for the celebrations of Isis were dressed "radiant in snow-white festal tunics" (11.9). Next the reader is introduced to the large crowd of people who had been initiated in the divine rites of the goddess and who were "shining in the immaculate whiteness of linen raiment" (11.10; cf. 11:15). It comes as no surprise that in the *Metamorphoses* the priests of the Isis religion were "clad in white linen" (11.10).

The purpose of assembling this Graeco-Roman testimony is to challenge uncritical thinking on two issues. Hopefully it will challenge the idea that Old Testament materials provide all the important concepts necessary to interpret the imagery in the book of Revelation. Equally unacceptable and in need of being challenged is the suggestion that the symbolism of "white garments" should automatically be understood through the lens of later ecclesiastical theology. Stephen Smalley, for example, mistakenly suggests: "It is reasonable to conclude, therefore, that the white garments mentioned in this verse (as in verse 4) represent attire belonging to those who are with Christ in heavenly dimension. They are the clothing of the

28. Sokolowski, *Lois Sacrées des Cités,* no. 65.16, 120–34.

29. Aelius Aristides, *Oration* 48.31 (cf. *IG* IV2 no. 128 l.19); a generally contemporary inscription from Pergamum mentions the wearing of a white chiton during incubation in the temple of Asclepius there, *Inschriften von Pergamon* II, no. 264 (=Sokolowski, *Lois Sacrées,* no. 14, 42).

30. The following translations are taken from Griffiths, *Isis-Book,* 81–83.

faithful in the resurrection life. . . . As they are made white by the blood of the Lamb (Rev 7:13-14), the image is an appropriate expression for justification by faith."[31] A better perspective, it seems to me, would avoid suggesting "justification by faith," since this is a doctrine with minimal significance in Revelation. In their various urban settings John's readers were constantly aware of the close association between white garments and piety, spirituality, and divine acceptance. Christians from Roman Asia had frequently observed this close association in the festive occasions and celebrations of the surrounding pagan milieu. Accordingly, this correlation between divine realities and white garments should be viewed from the perspective of the visual experiences and urban life of those early Roman Asian believers.

Faithful believers in Sardis are told that the reward of walking with Christ is guaranteed "for they are worthy." This term "worthy" (axios, ἄξιος) occurs often enough in Revelation (3:4; 4:11; 5:2, 4, 9, 12; 16:6) to see that the status of worthiness is based upon the actions of the person described by the term worthy (cf. Matt 10:37; Luke 15:21; 23:41; Col 1:10). In particular in this letter this worthiness belongs to "the few people in Sardis" who have no need to be told to "wake up" or to "strengthen what remains" or to "remember" to "obey" or to "repent" (3:2-3). Those believers at Sardis who are "alive" are such because their works and lives are acceptable to God (3:1-2).

Beyond the guarantee to the overcomers that they will be dressed in white, Christ also pledges to them two additional promises. Christ promises that he will never, ever[32] remove their names from the book of life. When referring to the book of life, one naturally thinks of the Mosaic petition addressed to God, "blot me out of the book you have written" (Exod 32:32-33). Moses's plea probably refers to a divine book that registers the people of God, though with no necessary association with judgment in the afterlife.[33] Similarly Ps 139:15-16 points to a divine book without any

31. Smalley, *Revelation*, 85.

32. The use of the phrase οὐ μή with the subjunctive mood communicates "the strongest way to negative something in Greek," Wallace, *Greek Grammar*, 468, though his later assessment that it negates "the possibility of the loss of salvation" certainly contradicts the conditional nature (ἐάν) of security expressed in Rev 3:3.

33. Εἰ δὲ μή ἐξάλειψόν με ἐκ τῆς βίβλου σου ἧς ἔγραψας. Ps 69:23-5, 28 first uses the phrase "book of life," though still without direct reference to the afterlife, "Let their eyes be darkened so that they cannot see, and make their loins tremble continually. Pour out your indignation upon them, and let your burning anger overtake them. May their camp be a desolation; let no one live in their tents. . . .Let them be blotted out of the book of the living; let them not be enrolled among the righteous."

particular eschatological significance: "My frame was not hidden from you, when I was being made in secret, intricately woven in the depths of the earth. Your eyes beheld my unformed substance. In your book were written all the days that were formed for me, when none of them as yet existed." Perhaps on John's mind when thinking of names blotted from the Book of Life would also be the well known Jewish Eighteen Benedictions (*Shemoneh Esreh*). The twelfth statement (*birkat-ha-minim*) states: "And let them [i.e., Christians and heretics] be blotted out of the Book of Life and not be inscribed together with the righteous. Blessed art thou, O Lord, who humblest the arrogant."[34] This prophetic message to the congregation at Sardis, unlike verses in the Hebrew Scriptures, points to the broadened eschatological concept of the "book of life" where the book contains the names of those that will receive eternal life and postmortem reward.

"Erasure" or "blotting out" of one's name depicts removal of an individual from a particular community and the attendant loss of its benefits and blessings (cf. Rev 20:15). The Greek author Dio Chrysostom (ca. 40–ca. 120), for example, mentions the erasure of a citizen's name prior to his criminal execution: "In Athens, for instance, whenever any citizen has to suffer death at the hands of the state for a crime, his name is erased (*autou to onoma exaleiphetai*, αὐτοῦ τό ὄνομα ἐξαλείφεται) first. Why is this done? One reason is that he may no longer be considered a citizen when he undergoes such a punishment but, so far as that is possible, as having become an alien. Then, too, I presume that it is looked upon as not the least part of the punishment itself, that even the appellation should no longer be seen of the man who had gone so far in wickedness, but should be utterly blotted out" (*Oration* 31.84–85). Jesus's promise to those at Sardis offers permanent security to believers who maintain their spiritual wakefulness, repentance, and obedience (3:3). Witherington captures the clear teaching of this section when he writes, "The image suggests it is possible to be in such a book and then to be blotted out of it because of unacceptable beliefs and practices."[35] A similar observation is made by Mitchell Reddish: "those who are not faithful will have their names expunged from the Book of Life and will lose their place in God's fellowship. This is a sobering wakeup call to those who take their relationship to

---

34. Skolnik, "Birkat, Ha-minim," 711–12; see Marcus, "Birkat Ha-Minim Revisited," 523–51 and Horbury, "Benediction," 19–61.

35. Witherington, *Revelation*, 106.

God for granted."[36] In his treatment of this teaching, Craig Keener[37] rightly gives the heading "On those who do not persevere!"

The third promise that the heavenly Son of Man makes to the conquerors resonates with teachings of the earthly Jesus. In particular, Jesus admonished his audience that, "I tell you, whoever acknowledges me before men, the Son of Man will also acknowledge him before the angels of God" (Luke 12:8; cf. Mark 8:38; Luke 9:26). Those at Roman Sardis who are loyal to Christ will have their names acknowledged "before my Father and his angels" by the Son of Man himself. This wording assumes the presence of "his angels" at the time of eschatological judgment. This imagery finds its early roots in the postexilic prophet Zechariah (Zech 14:5). Jesus repeatedly referred to the presence of angels at the final judgment: "For the Son of Man is to come with his angels in the glory of his Father, and then he will repay everyone for what has been done" (cf. Matt 13:39, 41, 49; 24:31; 25:31; Mark 8:38; Luke 9:26; 12:8–9). The Apostle Paul likewise mentions angels at the final judgment (2 Thess 1:7; cf. 1 Cor 6:3) as well as the presence of their leader, the "archangel" (1 Thess 4:16, *archangelou*, ἀρχαγγέλου), known elsewhere in the New Testament as Michael (Jude 9; cf. Rev 12:7).[38]

This epistle ends with the well known admonition for the hearers to pay attention to the Spirit's instruction to the other six congregations (see notes on 2:7).

36. Reddish, *Revelation*, 72.

37. Keener, *Revelation*, 147.

38. Mach, "Angels," 24–27.

9

The Prophecy to Philadelphia

The value of this Greek inscription is to demonstrate that in some instances non-Christian religions were also very concerned about morality and ethics. This Greek inscription dates from the late second or first century BC. It was discovered in the city of Philadelphia (*SIG* 3.985; translation from Barton and Horsley, "Hellenistic," 9-10).

"To this man Zeus has given ordinances for the performance of the purifications, the cleansings and the mysteries, in accordance with ancestral custom and as has now been written. When coming into this *oikos* let men and women, free people and slaves, swear by all the gods neither to know nor make use wittingly of any deceit against a man or a woman, neither poison harmful to men nor harmful spells. They are not themselves to make use of a love potion, abortifacient, contraceptive, or any other thing fatal to children . . . Apart from his own wife, a man is not to have sexual relations with another married woman, whether free or slave, nor with a boy nor a virgin girl; nor shall he recommend it to another. Should he connive at it with someone, they shall expose such a person, both the man and the woman, and not conceal it or keep silent about it. . . . These ordinances were placed with Agdistis, the very holy (ἁγιωτάτην) guardian (φύλακα) and mistress of this *oikos*. May she create good (ἀγαθὰς) thoughts (διανοίας) in men and women, free people and slaves, in order that they may obey the things written here. At the monthly and annual sacrifices may those men and women who have confidence (πιστεύουσιν) in themselves touch this inscription (γραφῆς) on which the ordinances of the god have been written, in order that those who obey these ordinances and those who do not may be manifest."

Figure 97

Rev 3:7 "And to the angel of the church in Philadelphia write: These are the words of the holy one, the true one, who has the key of David, who opens and no one will shut, who shuts and no one opens: 8 "I know your works. Look, I have set before you an open door, which no one is able to shut. I know that you have but little power, and yet you have kept my word and have not denied my name. 9 I will make those of the synagogue of Satan who say that

*they are Jews and are not, but are lying—I will make them come and bow
down before your feet, and they will learn that I have loved you. 10 Because
you have kept my word of patient endurance, I will keep you from the hour
of trial that is coming on the whole world to test the inhabitants of the earth.
11 I am coming soon; hold fast to what you have, so that no one may seize
your crown. 12 If you conquer, I will make you a pillar in the temple of my
God; you will never go out of it. I will write on you the name of my God, and
the name of the city of my God, the new Jerusalem that comes down from my
God out of heaven, and my own new name. 13 Let anyone who has an ear
listen to what the Spirit is saying to the churches.*

This letter begins with the customary address to the angel of the
congregation. "Like the message to Smyrna, the message to Philadelphia
contains no words of criticism or judgment on the church. Both churches
receive only praise and encouragement."[1] The phrase "holy and true" is
used only one other time in Revelation (6:10) and there it is used of God,
though the individual terms "holy" and "true"[2] are found frequently in
Scripture as divine epithets.

The reference to holding the "key of David" is but one facet of the
rich Davidic christology presented in Revelation. This particular imagery
stems from one brief episode in the Old Testament (Isa 22:22). In this
little known story one reads of the forceful removal of an "official" steward
of God, namely Shebna, who had previously been in charge of the royal
household of God. He is replaced by another steward, a loyal steward "my
servant Eliakim son of Hilkiah" (Isa 22:19–22): "I will thrust you from
your office, and you will be pulled down from your post. On that day I
will call my servant Eliakim son of Hilkiah, and will clothe him with your
robe and bind your sash on him. I will commit your authority to his hand,
and he shall be a father to the inhabitants of Jerusalem and to the house
of Judah. I will place on his shoulder the key of the house of David; he
shall open, and no one shall shut; he shall shut, and no one shall open."
As "father to the inhabitants of Jerusalem" this Eliakim will bear the key
of David.

At different periods both Shebna and Eliakim had been God's designated servants. However, Shebna was "ousted" by God and replaced
by Eliakim. The use of this somewhat obscure narrative in the letter to
Philadelphia is quite intentional since the imagery facilitates a modified

1. Reddish, *Revelation*, 74.

2. The Johannine letters has a greater concentration of the term "true" (and cognates) than any other portion of New Testament texts. The Gospel of John has more
occurrences than the entire Pauline corpus.

replacement theology of Judaism in redemptive history. There is now a new servant who wears the robe, the sash, and receives the authority of the previous servant of God (Isa 22:22). But this modified replacement theology is not told in terms of the well known "Law versus Gospel" theology where the Jews are replaced by the Gentiles, but rather a replacement of unbelieving Jews who do not follow the Messiah "who holds the key of David" by those Jews and Gentiles who do follow the Davidic Christ. This particular replacement theology anticipates the replacement reflected in the strong wording of Rev 3:9. In this ecclesiastical adaptation of the Shebna-Eliakim episode, Jesus is now the agent for replacement since he is the only legitimate holder of the prerogatives of the Davidic covenant. Christ alone holds the key of David, a point made earlier in 3:7.[3]

This particular Davidic reference to the term "key" anticipates upcoming phrases and concepts in the next section of the letter to Philadelphia, including the "open-shut" language of 3:8. The "open door" imagery of the Philadelphian letter points to access to the benefits of the Royal Davidic covenant. These benefits now come solely through the Davidic Jesus, who opens the door to salvation for believers and shuts out those who do not listen to his voice (cf. John 10:1–9).

The works of the Philadelphian congregation that Christ knows are its obedience to the words of Christ and its refusal to deny his name (3:8). God's provision of an "open door" is a rich theme in the New Testament, whether doors of faith (Acts 14:27), jail doors (Acts 16:26), doors for service (1 Cor 16:9), or door for the gospel (2 Cor 2:12, cf. Col 4:3). In the Philadelphian setting, this open door probably relates to the openness derived from the Davidic key. This congregation may have had "little strength," e.g., in numbers, wealth, influence, or stature,[4] but they have a divine tenacity and loyalty to Christ's word and name.

The temptation for followers to deny the name of Jesus is well treated in the gospels themselves. The disciples of Jesus are warned by Jesus himself that they will be hated "because of my name" (Matt 10:22) and be delivered to tribulation and killed and "hated by all nations because of my name" (Matt 24:9). Within less than twenty years of the writing of Revelation believers were being executed in an adjacent province for refusing to curse the name of Christ, a practice that no true Christian could do, so the pagan governor Pliny had been told. Pliny reports: "Those who denied

---

3. The basis of Witherington's suggestion that the key is "to the New Jerusalem" remains unclear and would benefit from further development, Witherington, *Revelation*, 106.

4. Beckwith, *Apocalypse*, 481.

they were . . . Christians, who repeated . . . an invocation to the gods, and offered adoration to your image . . . with those of the gods, and . . . cursed Christ . . . I thought it proper to discharge. Others who . . . at first confessed themselves Christians and then denied it . . . all worshiped your statue and the images of the gods and cursed Christ" (*Ep. Tra.* 10.96).

As seen earlier (see notes 2:9) John embraces a modified replacement doctrine, where "Israel according to the flesh" (to use Paul's terminology, Rom 9–11) is displaced by an Israel defined by loyalty to the words of Jesus Christ (cf. Acts 3:22–26). No one can open the door of salvation that has been closed to these Jews "who say that they are Jews and are not, but are lying," since they attend not the synagogue of Christ in Philadelphia, but the "synagogue of Satan."

The phrase "fall down at your feet" adds particular poignancy, indeed truculence, to John's particular replacement theology. It is an example of divine reversal, which is always painful. This phrase was a well established Jewish idiom used to show pagan supplication and subservience to Israel as God's elect (Isa 45:14; 49:7, 23; 60:14). Other Jewish groups of the Second Temple period also continued this Isaianic picture. The Essenes War Scroll reads: "Rejoice Zion, passionately! Shine with jubilation, Jerusalem! Exult, all the cities of Judah! Open your gates continuously so that the wealth of the nations can be brought to you! Their kings shall wait on you, all your oppressors lie prone before you, the dust of your feet they shall lick" (1QM 12.13–15; 19.5–7). By utilizing this Jewish idiom from Isaiah, the letter to Philadelphia shows that because Jesus "has the key of David" the Philadelphian congregation is now God's Israel. Accordingly, disbelieving Jews at Philadelphia are now in some sense regarded as unbelievers.[5] The rhetorical concept that Jews could be regarded as pagans is certainly already stated in the Jewish Scriptures. Isaiah's (1:10) identification of Jerusalem and its leaders with Sodom and Gomorrah clearly demonstrate this, as does Hosea's comment "for you are not my people, and I am not your God" (Hos 1:9; cf. Jer 3:8; Isa 50:1). Stated graphically, pseudo-Jews in the Philadelphian synagogue of Satan will grovel as sycophants at the feet of Christians, just as Israel had earlier imagined pagans would bow before it.

This sycophancy even requires that the unbelieving Jews must recognize that now the object of God's redemptive love is the congregation of Christ. Osborne suggests that the statement "I have loved you" stems

---

5. Beale and McDonough, "Revelation," 1097.

from Isa 43:4 (*kago se ēgapēsa*, κἀγώ σε ἠγάπησα).[6] If so, the comforting sentiments of the following words of Isa 43 anticipate the contrasting "hour of trial" in Rev 3:10. Isaiah states: "Do not fear, for I have redeemed you; I have called you by name, you are mine. When you pass through the waters, I will be with you; and through the rivers, they shall not overwhelm you; when you walk through fire you shall not be burned, and the flame shall not consume you. For I am the Lord your God, the Holy One of Israel, your Savior" (Isa 43:1b–3a).

Christ's promise of preservation to the Philadelphian congregation is not offered unconditionally (cf. John 14:21; 15:10), but is offered because (*hoti*, ὅτι) his followers have kept his "command to endure patiently." Jesus's promise to "keep you" resonates with Johannine language preserved in the Fourth Gospel (17:11, 15).

The phrase "hour of trial" is, according to Osborne, a reference: "to the final end-time trials that precede the eschaton. This is differentiated from the local 'ten-day tribulation' of Smyrna (2:10), by its involvement of the 'whole world' . . . and so connotes a worldwide conflagration, the messianic judgments of the rest of the book (cf. Dan 12:1–2; Matt 24:21–22; 2 Thess. 2:1–12)."[7] Although the view expressed by Osborne is found in many commentaries, it is not the working assumption of this commentary.[8] The frequent expression of fictive globalism, both in and out of Scripture, diminishes the need to take the phrase "whole world" literally.[9] Of the remaining two examples of the term *oikoumenē* (οἰκουμένη) in Revelation (12:9; 16:14), neither demands a geographical referent larger than the Roman region about which John prophecies in his messages to the seven churches.

The globalism in John's wording "the whole world" need not be taken any more literally than the globalism of these two non-Christian documents also from the same century, one in Latin and the other in Greek. A Latin inscription dated AD 4, while mourning the death of the son of Augustus, describes the Emperor Augustus as "guardian of the Roman Empire and defender of the whole world."[10] In AD 67 an honorific de-

---

6. Osborne, *Revelation*, 191, following Swete, *Apocalypse*, 55.

7. Osborne, *Revelation*, 193; also Beckwith, *Apocalypse*, 483.

8. Beale, *Revelation*, 433–35 advocates a "great Tribulation" that culminates at the end of history but began in antiquity; Harrington, *Revelation*, 71 concludes that this "is the only explicit reference in the messages to a worldwide ordeal, which is the theme of the rest of the book."

9. See materials regarding this issue in the introduction.

10. *ILS* vol. 1, no. 140, 9–10 *Augusti . . . custodis imperi Romani totiusque orbis*

cree issued by the high priest of the imperial cult at Akraiphia (Boeotia) proclaims Nero "the Lord of the whole world" (*ho tou pantos kosmou kurios*, ὁ τοῦ παντὸς κόσμου κύριος).[11]

In Rev 3:10 the phrase "the whole world" should be interpreted in light of the associated circumstances, promises, and threats, given to the original readers. For example, in the clauses "Because *you* have kept my word" and "I will keep *you*," the singular pronoun "you" (*se*, σε) pertains to those specific readers in Philadelphia who have manifested the particular virtue of endurance. From the perspective of this commentary, there is no justification for transforming the referent of this singular pronoun "you" (*se*, σε), found in this occasional document of the late first century, into some eschatological, worldwide "you." Aune prudently observed: "the promise made here pertains to Philadelphian Christians *only* and cannot be generalized to include Christians in the other churches of Asia, much less all Christians in all places and times."[12]

The impending time "of trial" (*peirasmos*, πειρασμός) is to be characterized by "testing" (*peirazō*, πειράζω), two terms found only in the seven letters within the book of Revelation (2:2, 10; 3:10 2x). Here it refers primarily to impending punishment and wrath from God poured out on pagans, from which the followers of the Lamb will be spared.[13]

Special attention needs to be given to the phrase "the inhabitants of the earth" (*hoi katoikountes epi tēs gēs*, οἱ κατοικοῦντες ἐπὶ τῆς γῆς) since it often serves as an important pillar in the hermeneutic of a person who is a futurist and embraces global literalism. From the perspective of global literalism it is considered to be a clear reference to the worldwide inhabitants of the earth at the end of time. Even Bauckham embraces the global, worldwide interpretation of this phrase and shockingly asserts that the "general use of *hoi katoikountes epi tēs gēs* (οἱ κατοικοῦντες ἐπὶ τῆς γῆς) has no particular Old Testament source, but follows general apocalyptic

---

terrarum praesidis.

11. *SIG* no. 814; In an epistle from Tiberius to the Greek city of Gytheion, in which he declines divine honors for himself, he refers to Augustus and the greatness of Augustus's benefactions "to the entire world" (εἰς ἅπαντα τὸν κόσμον), *SEG* vol. 11, no. 922,19–20.

12. Aune, *Revelation 1–5*, 240.

13. This term is also used in the LXX of God's punishment of pagans, Deut 4:34; 7:19; 29:2; Beale and McDonough, "Revelation," 1097 notes that this is a time of "purifying and strengthening believers while being at the same time a divine punishment on unbelievers."

usage."[14] In reality the Old Testament does indeed provide a very important usage of this phrase. In its basic form this Greek phrase occurs eleven times in Revelation (3:10; 6:10; 8:13; 11:10 [2x]; 13:8, 12, 14 [2x]; 17:2, 8). A search of the TLG[15] makes a strong case for the fact that the Septuagint provides an important linguistic and idiomatic background to the use of this phrase in the letter to the congregation at Philadelphia.

What emerges when this phrase is examined in the LXX is that it does not point as futurists assert to all the inhabitants of the entire planet, but "in the Pentateuch it usually means 'native Palestinians.'"[16] The phrase often points to those who occupy the Land of Promise and serve as a spiritual snare for assimilation and a nemesis of God's elect.

The following representative list of LXX occurrences of this phrase makes transparent a conceptual background that the LXX provides for the use of this idiom in the book of Revelation. From this perspective the phrase refers to those individuals and cultures that serve as a catalyst for assimilation and syncretism among God's people. That is, those who "dwell in the land" are the foil against which devotion to God is urged. They are depicted as a snare since they attempt to entice the elect into idolatry, worship of the Emperor, and immorality.

An appreciation of this phrase in the Old Testament setting and its typological use in Revelation certainly removes the presumption that these words in Revelation must point primarily or necessarily to a literal globalism.

- Num 14:14: "But also, all those who dwell upon this land (*pantes hoi katoikountes epi tēs gēs*, πάντες οἱ κατοικοῦντες ἐπὶ τῆς γῆς) have heard that you are Lord among this people" (NETS).

- Num 32:17: "And, having taken up arms, let us be a vanguard ahead of the sons of Israel until we bring them to their place. And our chattel will settle in walled cities, because of those that inhabit the land (*dia tous katoikountas tēs gēs*, διὰ τοὺς κατοικοῦντας τὴν γῆν)" (NETS).

- Num 33:55: "But if you do not destroy those living on the land from before you (*tous katoikountas epi tēs gēs*, τοὺς κατοικοῦντας ἐπὶ τῆς γῆς), then it shall be that whomever of them you leave shall be thorns

14. Bauckham, *Climax*, 240n3.

15. The Thesaurus Linguae Graecae (TLG) is a computerized database that contains "virtually all Greek texts surviving from the period between Homer (eighth century BC) and AD 600 and the majority of surviving works up the fall of Byzantium in AD 1453," adapted from www.tlg.uci.edu.

16. Aune, *Revelation 1–5*, 240.

in your eyes and missiles in your sides, and they shall act with hostility upon the land on which you will settle" (NETS).

- Josh. 9:24: "And they answered Iesous, saying, "It was reported to us what the Lord your God instructed his servant Moyses, to give you this land and to destroy us and all its inhabitants from before you (*pantas tous katoikountas ep' autēs*, πάντας τοὺς κατοικοῦντας ἐπ' αὐτῆς), and we greatly feared for our lives before you and did this thing" (NETS).

- Judg. 1:32: "And Aser lived in the midst of the Chananite who inhabited the land (*tou katoikountes tēn gēn*, τοῦ κατοικοῦντος τὴν γῆν), for he could not remove him" (NETS).

- 2 Sam 5:6: "And Dauid departed, and his men, to Ierousalem against the Iebousite who inhabited the land (*ton katoikounta tēn gēn*, τὸν κατοικοῦντα τὴν γῆν)" (NETS).

- 2 Chr. 20:7: "Are you not the Lord who utterly destroyed the inhabitants of this land (*tous katoikountas tēn gēn tautēn*, τοὺς κατοικοῦντας τὴν γῆν ταύτην) from before your people Israel and gave it forever to the seed of Abraham, your beloved?" (NETS).

Basically, then, the faithful at Philadelphia are assured that they will be spared from the divine visitation that is coming against their antagonists. This theme of protection of the elect of God from his coming wrath is fundamental to New Testament soteriology, including Paul (e.g., Rom 5:9; 1 Thess 1:10; Eph 5:6), and is also found later in Revelation (e.g., 6:16–7:3)

Christ's promise to come soon is given often in Revelation (see notes on 2:5). When Christ threatened to return to Ephesus (2:5) or to return soon to Pergamum (2:16) it was to bring punishment. Since the congregation at Philadelphia has nothing to be punished for, it is not explicitly stated whether Christ's return is to bless the congregation during the lifetime of the original readers or to return in an eschatological sense. Ben Witherington notes, however, that this section "sounds congenial to dispensationalism at first. . . . Notice, however, that the author says nothing about taking the Christians out of the world; rather he speaks of Christ coming and protecting Christians."[17]

The "what you have" phrase clearly includes all the spiritual rewards and prerogatives already mentioned in this letter and that would represent the totality of the believer's salvation and blessings from God. The

17. Witherington, *Revelation*, 106–7; Reddish, *Revelation*, 76 makes similar observations.

imperative mood of the Greek verb *krateō* (κρατέω, "hold," "hold on to") is spoken twice by Jesus in the seven letters (2:25; 3:11), and both times the imperatival mood means that believers themselves contribute decisively to whether they retain or forfeit their reward of eternal salvation; otherwise the use of the imperative mood is insignificant. In this instance the Christian's reward is the crown of life (for crown imagery see notes on 2:10). Some interpreters consider this forfeiture of salvation impossible. Accordingly, James Rosscup writes: "To be finally deprived of the crown does not infer, then, that a person at one time was genuinely saved and qualifying for it but later is not. The idea is not the forfeiture of salvation one has. It is the tragedy of losing out on what potentially might be given. None of the truly elect will turn away from Christ. . . . all will gain 'the crown which consists of [eternal] life'" (Rev 2:10)."[18]

For the one who overcomes, the reward is expressed in terms of temple architecture and building materials. Interpretations of the phrase "pillar in the temple of my God" are understandably very diverse.[19] The interpretation of this architectural idiom that builds best upon the known evidence from the Graeco-Roman world is that of Gregory Stevenson, who sees the background in the widespread ancient practice of "the sculpting of human columns or pillars," especially in sacred architecture.[20]

Figure 98

18. Rosscup, "Overcomer," 272–73.

19. Stevenson, *Power and Place*, 244–47 for an overview of different interpretations and perspectives. Reddish, *Revelation*, 77–78 mentions the metaphorical use of pillar language in Gal 2:9 to emphasize pillars as "symbols of strength." The suggestion by Beale and McDonough seems strained when they point to Isa 56:3–5 as a background to this concept, "Revelation," 1097.

20. Stevenson, *Power and Place*, 247; the following information comes primarily from Stevenson, *Power and Place*, 247–51.

The best, but not only,[21] known example of this would be the caryatids of the Acropolis's Erechtheum in Athens. John is emphasizing not only the stability associated with pillars, but the pregnant symbolism of human pillars who "symbolically served the deity whose building it was. [And] as cultic servants . . . they stood in perpetual service to the deity."[22] The permanency of Christ's promise, "you will never again (*ou mē*, οὐ μὴ) go out of it" (3:12) follows very naturally upon the fact that Christ is addressing those who overcome (*ho nikōn poiēsō auton*, Ὁ νικῶν ποιήσω αὐτὸν).

The inscription of the divine name certainly connotes divine ownership. This theme is related to texts in the Old Testament such as: "Make a plate of pure gold and engrave on it as on a seal: Holy To The Lord," (Exod 28:36; cf. Exod 39:30) or "On that day there shall be inscribed on the bells of the horses, 'Holy to the Lord'" (Zech 14:20). More pertinent, though, to John's contextual imagery of temple columns is the fact that columns in many Graeco-Roman temples contained the name of the deity in whose temple it stood. Inscriptional remains from the temple of the Ephesian Artemis, to mention one instance, provide examples of names of individuals and deities on columns.[23]

Christ's fourfold repetition of the phrase "my God" clearly undergirds the theocentric views recorded elsewhere in Revelation. It is unclear whether John's vision has in mind the Jewish Tetragrammaton YHWH or merely *kurios* when he mentions "I will write on him the name of my God" (3:12; cf. esp. Num 6:27). It is well known that the Tetragrammaton was still in use among Jewish authors in the period of the Second Temple and in the patristic era.[24]

The reference to the "the new Jerusalem, coming down out of heaven from God" anticipates the embellished description given in Rev 21, yet another example of Johannine intertextuality between the seven letters and the final chapters of the new heavens and new earth (21–22).[25] The idea of a new Jerusalem was very vibrant is the period of the Second

---

21. Pliny *Nat.* 36.38: "The Pantheon of Agrippa was embellished by Diogenes of Athens; and among the supporting members of this temple there are Caryatids."

22. Stevenson, *Power and Place*, 248.

23. *Inschriften von Ephesos*, vol. 5, nos. 1518 and 1519, pp. 49–50.

24. Philo, *Mos.* 2.38 (206) and Josephus, *Ant.* 2.12, 4. For Qumran see Rösel, "Names," 600–602. For Greek evidence one should still consult Deissmann, *Bible Studies*, 319–36. POxy 7.1007, lines 4 and 14 record a third-century example of the Tetragrammaton transcribed as ZZ.

25. The concept of the "new Jerusalem" will be treated more fully at the discussion of Rev 21:2.

Temple following the return from Babylonian captivity. Ezekiel chapters 40–48 provided the basis of much of the postexilic utopian thought about Jerusalem (supplemented by texts such as Isa 54; Zech 2 and Tob 13). Seven fragments coming from five different caves at Qumran reveal an extensive pre-Christian document, written in Aramaic, and called "The New Jerusalem" text.[26] In contrast to John's new Jerusalem that is the people of God (21:9–10),[27] the various depictions of the new Jerusalem in Jewish thought point to the utopian city of God.

The concept of "new name" was already introduced in Rev 2:17. The suggestion of some patristic authors that the "new name" of Isa 62:2 and 65:15 was the name "Christian"[28] is exceedingly improbable, as is Ramsay's idea that the new name concept would especially resonate with Philadelphia believers because their city's name had been changed.[29] The epistle ends with standard wording that encourages believers at all seven congregations to give heed to the prophecy to the Philadelphians (see notes on 2:7).

---

26. Nickelsburg. *Jewish Literature,* 177–79; also DiTommaso, "New Jerusalem," 996–97 and Martínez, "New Jerusalem," 606–10.

27. Gundry, "New Jerusalem," 254–64.

28. Sources given in Aune, *Revelation 1–5,* 244.

29. Ramsay's material given in Aune, *Revelation 1–5,* 244, though without an opinion given by Aune.

10

The Prophecy to Laodicea

Rev 3:14 "And to the angel of the church in Laodi-
cea write: The words of the Amen, the faithful and
true witness, the origin of God's creation: 15 "I know
your works; you are neither cold nor hot. I wish that
you were either cold or hot. 16 So, because you are
lukewarm, and neither cold nor hot, I am about to
spit you out of my mouth. 17 For you say, 'I am rich,
I have prospered, and I need nothing.' You do not
realize that you are wretched, pitiable, poor, blind,
and naked. 18 Therefore I counsel you to buy from

Figure 99

me gold refined by fire so that you may be rich; and white robes to clothe
you and to keep the shame of your nakedness from being seen; and salve to
anoint your eyes so that you may see. 19 I reprove and discipline those whom
I love. Be earnest, therefore, and repent. 20 Listen! I am standing at the door,
knocking; if you hear my voice and open the door, I will come in to you and
eat with you, and you with me. 21 To the one who conquers I will give a place
with me on my throne, just as I myself conquered and sat down with my
Father on his throne. 22 Let anyone who has an ear listen to what the Spirit
is saying to the churches."

EVEN THOUGH THIS FINAL letter to the congregations of Asia begins with a
traditional address to its angel, there is remarkably no significant influence
of the opening christophany (1:12–16) seen in the letter itself. This absence
of any impact from the revealed Christ of chapter one may anticipate the

harshness of the letter and Christ's stern warnings and patent disapproval of this congregation. Christ, in fact, is pictured at the end of the letter as still trying to gain entrance into the life of even a single member of the Laodicean congregation. At the time of the writing of the letter all doors to Christ are yet closed.

Christ's opening words to the congregation at Laodicea contain three christological titles. The use of the titular term "the Amen" is unique in John's christology. Some have suggested that this is a direct reference to Isa 65:16 where, it is suggested, it occurs as a title for God.[1] The ambiguity of the Hebrew vocalization and of the ancient translations is quite mixed, which means that Aune's conclusion that "this title is significant since it attributes to Christ a title associated only with God"[2] ought to be taken with some reservation. The evidence is not as straightforward as his conclusion suggests. Interestingly, the majority of the occurrences of "amen" in the Hebrew Old Testament are not transliterated in the LXX by the Greek term *amēn* (ἀμήν) that is used in Revelation, but rather by *genoito* (γενοίτο, "may it be").[3]

The designation of Christ as "the origin of God's creation" requires some special comments. The term translated "origin" is the Greek term *archē* (ἀρχή),[4] a term also used of Christ in Paul's letter to the congregation in Colossae (Col 1:18). This designation for Christ was perhaps already known by these Laodicean believers since their grandparents had been instructed to read Paul's letter to the Colossians (Col 4:16).[5] This same term *archē* is found in pagan religious and philosophical texts in reference to the chief pagan deity Zeus.[6] Declaring Christ as the *archē* of God's creation captures the sense of related themes seen in other New Testament texts, where Christ's role as sole agent in God's creation is described. It bears repeating that important New Testament "christology" texts highlight Christ's role in creation, but not that he is Creator.

- All things came into being through him, and without him not one thing came into being. What has come into being . . . He was in the

---

1. Aune, *Revelation 1–5*, 255.

2. Ibid.; see also comments by Osborne, *Revelation*, 203.

3. BDAG, 53–54.

4. Other translations render this term *"archē"* as "beginning" (KJV, NASB, ASV, NLT), "origin" (NRSV), "first" (Message), or "originator" (NET, HCSB).

5. Reddish, *Revelation*, 80–81; see also Osborne, *Revelation*, 204 and Swete, *Apocalypse*, 59.

6. BDAG, 138.

world, and the world came into being through him; yet the world did not know him. (John 1:3, 10).

- Yet for us there is one God, the Father, from whom are all things and for whom we exist, and one Lord, Jesus Christ, through whom are all things and through whom we exist. (1 Cor 8:6).

- He is . . . the firstborn of all creation; for in him all things in heaven and on earth were created, things visible and invisible, whether thrones or dominions or rulers or powers—all things have been created through him and for him. (Col 1:15–16).

- God . . . in these last days he has spoken to us by a Son, whom he appointed heir of all things, through whom he also created the worlds. (Heb 1:1–2).

In John's view, then, God's work in Christ includes both creation and cross, a perspective sometimes lost on the modern Western church that acts at times as though God's self revelation and work began at the Exodus and not in the Creation. In Rev 1:5 Jesus himself has already been called "faithful witness" as he is here.

Jesus's critique of the Laodicean congregation has produced more than one interpretation of the metaphorical terms "cold," "hot," and "lukewarm." A longstanding view interprets the term "hot" as a positive spiritual trait and the term "cold" as a pejorative spiritual trait. The term "lukewarm" is then taken to mean something like spiritual apathy. The words of G. B. Caird are representative of this outlook: "This is the church in an affluent society, without either hot enthusiasm or cold antagonism towards religious matters. Even open hostility would be preferable to this lukewarm and repulsive indifference, for it would at least suggest that religion was something to be in earnest about."[7]

A second perspective, often advocated to refute the preceding one, regards the different water temperatures as a "local allusion" (from the Lycus Valley) to the nearby hot springs at Hierapolis and the cold waters at the springs in nearby Colossae.[8] From this second perspective: "The tepid water of Laodicea does not produce any obvious benefit, unlike the healing properties of the hot baths at Hierapolis Spa or the refreshingly cool drinking water available to the Colossians (both of which are equally beneficial). The Laodicean angel has lost his effectiveness."[9]

7. Caird, *Revelation*, 56–57.
8. Boxall, *Revelation*, 76; a view also taken by Osborne, *Revelation*, 205–6.
9. Boxall, *Revelation*, 76.

Another view, certainly less convincing than the two previous, is that the "cold" person is not a believer at all, but rather is either one who has never heard the Christian message[10] or one who has heard it but, in Thomas's view, is "an unbeliever who has rejected the gospel openly and aggressively."[11]

A fourth and more recent view avoids any connection with the "local allusion" approach. This fourth perspective comes from the conviction that this letter: "Does not rely on special inside knowledge of the locale for its effectiveness. The author uses the imagery to define and speak to the situation in a way that could be understood not only by the Laodicean Christian but by a wider group of readers."[12] Koester asserts that the hot-cold-lukewarm imagery arose from widespread dining practices in the Graeco-Roman world.[13] In support of this interpretive model Plato is mentioned (*Resp.* 437d) when he notes that if someone's surroundings are hot he prefers a cold drink and if someone's surroundings are cold he prefers a hot drink. Related to the Laodicean setting, Koester continues, John: "expected readers to know that cold and hot beverages stand in contrast to their environment, and that diners find them refreshing. In contrast, the temperature of a cup of lukewarm water or wine is more like that of its surroundings; it does not distinguish itself to the touch."[14] Applied to the congregation at Laodicea, the Son of Man is warning them "that their works in no way distinguish them from others in their society."[15] This accusation from Christ then would be intended to undermine claims that they are truly his followers.

If the traditional view is correct then Christ is telling the Laodiceans that he would prefer no deeds over apathetic deeds. The second perspective gives the message that God is desirous of useful deeds rather than worthless ("neither hot nor cold") deeds. From the third perspective, advocated by Thomas, "Lukewarm is a description of church people who have professed Christ hypocritically but do not have in their hearts the reality of what they pretend to be in their actions."[16] Koester's outlook

10. Trench, *Epistles*, 259–60. Trench regards cold "as one hitherto untouched by the powers of grace. . . . He is not one on whom the grand experiment of the Gospel has been tried and has failed" (260).

11. Thomas, *Revelation 1–7*, 306.

12. Koester, "Message," 424.

13. Ibid., 412–6.

14. Ibid., 415.

15. Ibid., 415.

16. Thomas, *Revelation 1–7*, 308.

concludes that Christ is calling the lukewarm believers in Laodicea to distinguish themselves from the values of complacency and materialism that characterize the surrounding Graeco-Roman culture. These ambient values would also include sexual immorality, worship of manmade gods and goddesses, and the idolatry of using brute force against Christian dissension.

Certainly the Laodiceans' lukewarmness stems from a misperception of their spiritual situation. Although they are on the verge of becoming expectoration (cf. Lev 18:27–29), they have a falsely elevated view of their spiritual richness, vitality, and security. Rev 3:17–18 is replete with spiritual metaphors, metaphors that highlight both the self delusion of the Laodiceans and the remedy that Christ offers. Grant Osborne correctly observes (*Revelation*, 208) about Christ's response to this Laodicean delusion that: "Their actual state is described by five successive adjectives that separate naturally into two groups: their general situation (wretched and pitiful [=pitiable in NRSV]) and their specific description (poor, blind, and naked)." The specific terms of redemption that the Son of Man offers correspond to the description of their lost circumstances. The congregation is poor and Christ offers "gold refined by fire;" the congregation is blind and Christ offers "salve to anoint your eyes;" the congregation is naked and Christ offers "white robes to clothe you." These metaphors are in the literature of antiquity, in both pagan and Jewish sources.

The arrogance of their self evaluation summarized by the statement that they "do not need a thing" because they can rely upon their own resources is cut from the same cloth of spiritual delusion seen among the people of God in Jeremiah's time (Jer 2:13). Jeremiah observed: "for my people have committed two evils: they have forsaken me, the fountain of living water, and dug out cisterns for themselves, cracked cisterns that can hold no water." The paradoxical theology and imagery of "buying" from God what is already "free" is clearly present in the prophet Isaiah (55:1–2): "Ho, everyone who thirsts, come to the waters; and you that have no money, come, *buy* and eat! Come, *buy* wine and milk without money and without price. Why do you spend your money for that which is not bread, and your labour for that which does not satisfy? Listen carefully to me, and eat what is good, and delight yourselves in rich food." Commenting upon Isaiah 55 John Calvin observed: "He shews that we are poor and utterly destitute, and that we have nothing by which we can become entitled to God's favour; but that he kindly invites us, in order that he may freely bestow everything without any recompense."[17]

Even though this congregation has convinced itself that it is at the zenith of spiritual maturity, it is in fact at the nadir of spirituality; its members are "wretched, pitiful, poor, blind and naked." The scenery of Judeo-Christian history is strewn with myriad examples of self deception and its brutal consequences. One does not have to wait to the end of the first century AD to see this phenomenon among congregations of the followers of Christ. Deception and self-deception were frequent characteristics of congregations.

- 1 Cor 3:18: "Do not deceive yourselves. If you think that you are wise in this age, you should become fools so that you may become wise."

- 1 Cor 6:9–10: "Do you not know that wrongdoers will not inherit the kingdom of God? Do not be deceived! Fornicators, idolaters, adulterers, male prostitutes, sodomites, thieves, the greedy, drunkards, revilers, robbers—none of these will inherit the kingdom of God."

- 1 Cor 15:33: "Do not be deceived: 'Bad company ruins good morals.'"

- 2 Cor 13:5: "Examine yourselves to see whether you are living in the faith. Test yourselves. Do you not realize that Jesus Christ is in you?—unless, indeed, you fail to pass the test!"

- Gal 6:3–4: "For if those who are nothing think they are something, they deceive themselves. All must test their own work; then that work, rather than their neighbour's work, will become a cause for pride."

- Gal 6:7: "Do not be deceived; God is not mocked, for you reap whatever you sow."

- Jas 1:16: "Do not be deceived, my beloved."

- Jas 1:22: "But be doers of the word, and not merely hearers who deceive themselves."

- Jas 1:26: "If any think they are religious, and do not bridle their tongues but deceive their hearts, their religion is worthless."

- 1 John 1:8: "If we say that we have no sin, we deceive ourselves, and the truth is not in us."

The only hope for these self deluded believers is to repent, to see themselves as the Son of Man sees them, and to go to him for garments

17. Calvin, *Book of Isaiah*, 4.157.

to cover their nakedness (cf. Gen 3:7–10).[18] They need salve for their eyes in order to heal their spiritual blindness, blind eyes that surely see but do not perceive.

The picture of Jesus at the door has often been too sentimentalized in Christian piety. The well-known painting by Warner Sallman,[19] "Christ at Heart's Door" (based upon the letter to the church at Laodicea, Rev 3:20) may well excite the soul of Christian piety, but it is an unfortunate and anemic representation of the christophany of Revelation 1. There can be little doubt that John intended the horrific Jesus of Revelation 1 to be visualized by the church at Laodicea when hearing Christ's voice at the door. For more than one reason, believers at Laodicea would have been dumbfounded had they opened the door to Christ and seen someone looking like Sallman's Jesus standing there. Since the pastoral ethos of the christology of Revelation 1 stems directly from the counter culture spirit of biblical prophecy, one is hardly surprised to realize that this is not the "Good Shepherd" Jesus or the friendly, smiley, and affirming Jesus of much of American Christianity.

Moreover, since this is a letter to Christians, this scene presented to the Laodicean congregation is patently not a prototype of the evangelical "sinner's prayer" where Jesus is invited into the heart of the unregenerate sinner. The one who stands, knocks, and wishes to enter is the same one that chastises, rebukes, and disciplines (3:19). It is certainly no coincidence that terms of rebuke and discipline immediately precede the "knocking on the door" scene.

Only in conjunction with earnest repentance can one "hear the voice" and open the door. The two imperatives of 3:19b, "be earnest" and "repent," are joined by a "therefore" (*oun*, οὖν) to the previous words of loving rebuke and discipline (3:19a). This means that the loving discipline of God is intended to produce repentance and a change

Figure 100

18. "Nakedness, as an exposure of the most shameful kind, is a sign of or a call for divine judgment," Gorman, "Nakedness," 217.

19. Morgan, "Warner Sallman," fig. 1.14, p. 42.

in behavior. This is certainly the view expressed in texts such as Rom 2:4, "Or do you despise the riches of his kindness and forbearance and patience? Do you not realize that God's kindness is meant to lead you to repentance?" or Heb 12:5–6: "And you have forgotten the exhortation that addresses you as children—'My child, do not regard lightly the discipline of the Lord, or lose heart when you are punished by him; for the Lord disciplines those whom he loves, and chastises every child whom he accepts.'"

It is probably no accident that this admonition to "be earnest" in regard to repentance is addressed to a congregation that has a demonstrable history of self-deception. Once again, Judeo-Christian history reveals that God's elect people have often set up a two tiered system of repentance, a system that reflects a substandard understanding of earnestness and integrity. One kind of repentance is characterized by superficiality and ceremonial manifestations of repentance. The other kind of repentance, and the only one acceptable to God, reflects a profound change in direction, manifested in both internal cleanings of the heart *and* external changes of behavior.

Jeremiah refers to this hypocritical kind of repentance practiced in his day with these words (Jer 3:6–10): "The Lord said to me in the days of King Josiah . . . that faithless one, Israel, I had sent her away with a decree of divorce; yet her false sister Judah did not fear, but she too went and played the whore. Because she took her whoredom so lightly, she polluted the land, committing adultery with stone and tree. Yet for all this her false sister Judah *did not return to me with her whole heart, but only in pretence*, says the Lord." The prophet Joel's oracle (Joel 2:12–13) to his fellow Judeans reveals this same concern: "Yet even now, says the Lord, return to me *with all your heart*, with fasting, with weeping, and with mourning; *rend your hearts* and not your clothing. Return to the Lord." In the midst of the need for profound repentance David (Ps 51:16–17) realizes that: "For you have no delight in sacrifice; if I were to give a burnt-offering, you would not be pleased. The sacrifice acceptable to God is a broken spirit; a broken and contrite heart, O God, you will not despise." John the Baptist (Luke 3:8) demanded those coming to him for salvation needed to: "Bear fruit worthy of repentance. Do not presume to say to yourselves, 'We have Abraham as our ancestor'; for I tell you, God is able from these stones to raise up children to Abraham." And finally, the apostle Paul had to remind the Corinthians (2 Cor 7:9–10) that: "your grief led to repentance; for you felt a godly grief, so that you were not harmed in any way by us. For godly grief produces a repentance that leads to salvation and brings no regret, but worldly grief produces death."

These previous words of Scripture make clear God's displeasure with notions of repentance that mean little more than "to change one's mind." Notwithstanding current practices in Western churches to the contrary, the meaning of repentance in Scripture is to change the direction of one's life, not merely changing elements of intellectual assent. As Calvin correctly wrote: "Hence we infer that the doctrine of repentance ought always to accompany the promise of salvation. . . . And indeed no man will sincerely desire to be reconciled to God and to obtain pardon of sins till he is moved by a true and earnest repentance. . . . Thus repentance embraces a change of the whole man. . . . And if any man boast that he has been changed, and yet live as he was wont to do, it will be vain-boasting; for both are requisite, conversion of the heart and change of life."[20] In Scripture hearing is tantamount to obedience, which explains Moses's words, "*Hear*, O Israel, and be careful to *obey*."

Christ's wording to the Laodiceans, however, "*if* anyone hears," suggests at least the possibility that no one in the congregation is listening to him and that he will always remain on the outside of that particular congregation. Indeed, in the case of the Laodiceans it might be that the entire congregation was listening to other more attractive voices, softer and gentler voices that did not bring the harsh rebuke, discipline, and discipleship that Christ demanded.

If any Laodiceans do "obey the voice" (cf. Exod 19:5; Josh 24:24; 1 Sam 15:22; 2 Kgs 18:12; Jer 7:23) of Christ, then they will grant him entrance. The wording of Christ "if *he opens* the door" certainly seems to indicate that there is an important role for human decision to either accept or to reject Christ's invitation.

Even though a scene as prosaic as 3:20 hardly requires a biblical background, scholars have noted two sets of verses with similar wording. Although an unexpected location, Song of Songs (5:2) reads, "Listen! my beloved is knocking. 'Open to me, my sister, my love, my dove, my perfect one.'" Even though "some Jewish commentators understood 'open to me' in Cant. 5:2 as a call for Israel's repentance,"[21] this hardly seems adequate to establish this as the source of the imagery. After all, in the text of Song of Songs the husband has already left before his wife opens the door to her room (5:6): "I opened to my beloved, but my beloved had turned and was

---

20. Calvin, *Book of Isaiah*, 4.166–67.
21. Beale, *Revelation*, 308.

gone. My soul failed me when he spoke. I sought him, but did not find him; I called him, but he gave no answer."

The other suggested text of Scripture is Luke 12:35–38 which is an eschatological parable that contains the themes of a returning master who knocks on the door, who awaits entrance for a banquet, and who serves his servants who admit him. Revelation 3:20, however, does not seem to point to an eschatological meal.

The significance of fellowship at meals in antiquity can hardly be over emphasized, both fellowship between humans and fellowship between the divine and humans.[22] This widespread cultural sacrament of antiquity had not yet been profaned by fast food and impersonal meals. From the communal Passover meal (Exod 12; cf. 24:9–11) through the Lord's Meal (1 Cor 11:17–33) to the eschatological messianic banquet (Luke 13:29; 22:15), biblical faith always held fellowship meals in high regard.[23] In this regard Isaiah 25:6 makes this significant promise of a divine meal in conjunction with God's eschatological defeat of death, "On this mountain the Lord of hosts will make for all peoples a feast of rich food, a feast of well-matured wines, of rich food filled with marrow, of well-matured wines strained clear."[24] Christ's offer then is to believers at Laodicea who desire an active fellowship and intimacy with him, an experience where the reality of divine fellowship is best captured by the imagery of a meal.

Beyond the above mentioned biblical examples of meals, Graeco-Roman culture and religion likewise gave expression to similar institutions. There are numerous examples of tombstones which depict the deceased participating at a banquet. Some of these are reflecting the widespread idea that in the afterlife one's reward consisted of banqueting.[25] Even though Plato is obviously displeased with the emphasis upon eschatological inebriation, his report does attest the association between the afterlife and banqueting made by some of his contemporaries. "They take them to the other world and provide them with a banquet of the Blest, where they sit for all time carousing with garlands on their heads, as if virtue could not be more nobly recompensed than by an eternity of intoxication" (Plato, *Resp.* 2.363c–d). Meals where deities were present as guests

22. Binder, "Banquet," 488–97; Gutsfeld, "Meals," 525–27.

23. In general see Aune, *Revelation 1–5*, 250–55, although in my judgment his argument about the meal that Christ offers and "Hellenistic magical divination" seems unpersuasive.

24. Interestingly the LXX omits any reference to a meal and mentions only the drinking of wine (LXX πίονται οἶνον).

25. Dunbabin, *Roman Banquet*, 104–10.

(*theoxenia*)[26] and meals where deities were the host(ess) are well attested. An inscription from Panamara (64 miles SE of Ephesus), for example,[27] reads, "god calls all men to the feast and provides a common dinner where they are all treated equally, no matter from where they come." Similarly a papyrus reveals the god Sarapis as host offering an invitation that reads, "The god calls you to a banquet."[28]

A final window into late first century pagan thoughts on the issue of dining with deities comes from the Stoic philosopher Epictetus. Epictetus was exiled from Rome by Domitian in the early 90s and much of his important teaching came from the years following his banishment from Rome. In the work entitled *Enchiridion*, a summary of Epictetus's work written by his student Arrian, he mentions those who will be able to "share the banquet of the gods (*sumpotēs tōn theōn esē*, συμπότης τῶν θεῶν ἔσῃ)" (Epictetus, *Enchiridion*, 15). Two features are notable about this passage in Epictetus. First, those regarded as worthy dining partners with the gods received this recognition based upon their decision to embrace divine perspectives. That is, this status is a reward based upon satisfying godly standards. Second, Epictetus combines the reward of divine dining with the reward of co-enthronement with the gods, "you will not only share the banquet of the gods, but share also their rule (*tote ou monon sumpotēs tōn theōn esē, alla kai sunarchōn*, τότε οὐ μόνον συμπότης τῶν θεῶν ἔσῃ, ἀλλὰ καὶ συνάρχων)." Accordingly, Epictetus joins together the two rewards also mentioned in Rev 3:20–21.

Throne sharing is the particular concept that is found in Christ's promised reward to the overcomers at Laodicea. This motif has roots in the Christian movement prior to Revelation. Paul adapts this theme in his words, "and raised us up with him and seated us with him in the heavenly places in Christ Jesus" (Eph 2:6; cf. Col 3:1–4), and "if we endure, we will also reign with him" (2 Tim 2:12).

The cultures of the ancient Mediterranean Basin were well acquainted with temples and thrones, both terrestrial and celestial. Images and expressions related to temples and thrones provided a rich vocabulary for pagan, Jewish, and Christian authors to communicate their religious beliefs in the Hellenistic and Roman era.

---

26. Kearns, "Theoxenia," 1506–7.

27. Hatzfeld, "Inscriptions," 57–122, πάντας ἀνθρώπους ὁ θεὸς ἐπὶ τὴν ἑστίασιν καλεῖ καὶ κοινὴν καὶ ἰσότιμον παρέχι τράπεζαν τοῖς ὁποθενοῦ[ν] ἀφικνουμένοις, no. 11, lines 2–4, 73; this inscription is also treated in Smith, *From Symposium*, 81–84.

28. *NewDocs*, 1:1, 1c, lines 1–2 καλεῖ σε ὁ θεὸς εἰς κλείνην.

In this context we encounter the concept that an individual could share in the enthroned status of a deity, as already seen in the above quotation from Epictetus. The is also seen in the Dead Sea Scrolls 4Q521, "For he will honor the pious upon the throne of an eternal kingdom." Sometimes in paganism an individual could share a temple with a deity (*sunnaos, σύνναος*)[29] or share an altar with a deity (*sumbōmos, σύμβωμος*).[30] It was possible in paganism, or Judaism, or Christianity to share a throne with a god (*sunthronos, σύνθρονος*). All of these images were designed to confer a degree of elevated status upon the devotee of a god or goddess.

In some instances co-enthronement was imagined to confer divine status to a human ruler or to one of his family members. The following story relates the death of Philip of Macedon, the father of Alexander the Great.

> "While it was still dark, the multitude of spectators hastened into the theatre, and at sunrise the parade formed. Along with lavish displays of every sort, Philip included in the procession statues of the twelve gods wrought with great artistry and adorned with a dazzling show of wealth to strike awe in the beholder, and along with these there was conducted a thirteenth statue, suitable for a god, that of Philip himself, so that the king exhibited himself enthroned among the twelve gods . . . . Such was the end of Philip, who had made himself the greatest of the kings of Europe in his time, and because of the extent of his kingdom had made himself a throned companion (*sunthronos, σύνθρονος*) of the twelve gods" (Diodorus, *Hist.* 16.92.5; 16.95.1).

Perhaps more relevant to the era and to the thoughts of those in John's congregations, there is a very insightful Greek inscription from Anatolian Commagene that "is the most striking and most informative monument of the Hellenistic Ruler Cult."[31] It comes from the mid-first century BC. To be sure Commagene was not adjacent to Roman Asia, but its king was involved enough in Roman Asia for the people of Ephesus to dedicate an inscription to King Antiochus because this king of Commagene had made a benefaction to the temple of Artemis of the Ephesians.[32] As one of the most pietistic documents from the Graeco-Roman period that pertains to the ruler cult, it reveals the religious convictions of King Antiochus I,

---

29. Nock, "Σύνναος Θεός," 202–51.

30. Ibid., 202–51.

31. Goell, "Foreword," xxx.

32. Fraser, "Kings," 359–60 (=*OGIS* 405).

king of Commagene: "And as I have taken forethought to lay the foundation of this sacred tomb, which is to be indestructible by the ravages of time, in closest proximity to the heavenly throne, wherein the fortunately preserved outer form of my person, preserved to ripe old age, shall, after the soul beloved by God has been sent to the heavenly thrones of Zeus Oromasdes (=Ahura Mazda), rest through immeasurable time."[33]

Sitting co-enthroned with the Messiah and participating in his kingdom need not necessarily point only to an eschatological time, since the followers have already become a kingdom and priests (1:6; cf. Eph 2:6), but in this instance it probably does.[34]

This is the first time in Revelation that Christ himself is designated as an overcomer ("just as I myself conquered," 3:21b; cf. 5:5). It is not, however, the first time Christ's identification with followers is noted. The same affirmation is made when John uses the same phrase "faithful witness" for Christ (1:5, *ho martus ho pistos*, ὁ μάρτυς, ὁ πιστός) and for Antipas, "my faithful witness" (2:13, *ho martus mou ho pistos mou*, ὁ μάρτυς μου ὁ πιστός μου).

The phrase "sat down with my Father" refers of course to the central New Testament teaching of the enthronement of Christ as the Royal Davidic King.[35] Even though Royal Davidic christology is well known by the synoptic authors, pervasive in the theology of Acts, used often by Paul, and crucial for the theology of Hebrews, it is barely known in the churches of North America, revealing their preference for a Savior or a Healer rather than the antidemocratic and subversive notion of a King.[36]

Explicit Davidic christology was already found in the letter to the congregation at Philadelphia (Rev 3:7, "Who has the key of David") and will later be closely associated with the central qualification for Christ's opening the seven seals (5:5, "the Lion of the tribe of Judah, the Root of David"). Since the opening of the seven seals on the scroll controls the plot

33. Dörner and Young, "Nomos Inscriptions," 214. Also "[en]throned likewise among the deities who hear our prayers" is stated in the same epigraphical document (214).

34. Some scholars attempt to interpret these verses in Revelation through the lens of Luke 22:28–30 ("You are those who have stood by me in my trials; and I confer on you, just as my Father has conferred on me, a kingdom, so that you may eat and drink at my table in my kingdom, and you will sit on thrones judging the twelve tribes of Israel"), overlooking the facts that these Lukan verses are directed only to the twelve apostles.

35. For human co-enthronement with a divine king and its benefits see 1 Macc 10:59–66.

36. For an advocate of this position see McKnight, *King Jesus*.

of Revelation chapters 4–11 one should not underestimate the significance of Davidic kingship and enthronement theology in John's theology.

The roots of this enthronement christology for Jesus can be located in the Royal Davidic Ps 110:1, "The Lord says to my lord, 'Sit at my right hand until I make your enemies your footstool.'" Sometimes in the New Testament this exact verse is quoted (Matt 22:44; Mark 12:36; Luke 20:42; Acts 2:34; Heb 1:13), while at other times only a part such as "right hand" (Matt 26:64; Mark 14:62; Luke 22:69; Acts 5:31, 7:55; Rom 8:34; Eph 1:20; Col 3:1; Heb 1:3; 8:1; 10:12; 12:2; 1 Pet 3:22) is employed. But in all instances, regardless of whether the Davidic reference is fully quoted, the undergirding theology for the spiritual journey of Christ and for his co-enthroned followers is Royal Davidic christology from Ps 110:1.

This final letter of the seven ends with the admonition to all the congregations to hear what God's Spirit spoke to this congregation.

Appendix A

John's Crisis, Real or Imagined?

IT HAS BEEN ARGUED by some that the entire ethos of Revelation, with its scenes of horrific suffering and believers martyred by the minions of Domitian, should be put aside as historically implausible since the traditional portrait of Domitian has been overturned, in the judgment of some scholars, by more perceptive investigations of the Roman sources of the early second century AD.[1] If traditional interpreters only understood more accurately the urbane and pluralistic demeanor of Domitian and his favorable relations with many Roman Senators, it is argued, then the traditionalists would naturally set aside John's poisoned perspective as nothing more than sectarian, apocalyptic, a "weakly Christianized Judaism,"[2] or perhaps "a curious record of the visions of a drug addict which was absurdly admitted to the canon under the title of Revelation."[3] For better or worse, many traditional interpreters of Revelation are not yet convinced about this "new Domitian."[4]

One possible way to cut this Gordian Knot of uncertainty about Domitian's administrative style and claimed harassment of believers would be to reframe the discussion. Let us imagine for a moment that Domitian was the best of all Roman emperors. The issue then becomes, "Would the best Roman Emperors condone the treatment of believers portrayed by the book of Revelation?" Part of the reframing of the Domitian issue is to

---

1. Thompson, *Revelation* (1990), gives an entire chapter to challenging the traditional perspective, 95–115.

2. Bultmann, *Theology*, 2:175.

3. Thompson, *Revelation* (1990), 4, quoting the famous critique of the book of Revelation by George Bernard Shaw.

4. Slater, "Social Setting."

ask the ancillary question, Is it appropriate to evaluate the social and legal behavior of the best Roman emperor by our modern, Western notions of legal and social behavior? One example of the anachronistic interpretation of ancient cultures through a modern lens is when Western people hear the phrase "Athenian democracy" and naively imagine that this term "democracy" points to the same legal and social realities that it does in our own society. A similar naiveté exists about the supposed justice and humaneness that guided the decisions of good Roman rulers and prevailed in the Roman world.[5]

Let's be clear, there were no Roman emperors who had the ethical conviction of the Seleucid Era Indian ruler Ashoka the Great (ca. 304–232 BC), who converted to Buddhism and embraced respect for life after he waged a war (Kalinga War) that killed over 100,000 innocent people.[6] Even the reign of Marcus Aurelius (AD 161–80), the philosopher-king and the last of the "Five Good Emperors," reveals an administration of multiple wars and certainly no diminution of brutality against Christians. An avalanche of evidence and examples from the modern world should be enough to change such historical naiveté about whether "nice rulers" would ever harass or kill Christians (by the way, at later times "nice" Christian rulers even killed Christians).

An instructive example of urbane rulers butchering Christians can be drawn from ancient sources generally contemporary with the prophet John and his ministry to the congregations of Roman Asia. The Roman governor Pliny the Younger, for example, was respectable, highly educated, especially well trained in matters of justice and jurisprudence, and lived a life of service to the surrounding Roman society. Pliny was a religious man and devoted to the members of his family. It is not without good reason that in his work *The Christians as the Romans Saw Them* Robert Wilken entitled his chapter on Pliny, "Pliny: A Roman Gentleman."[7] In addition to donating a very large amount of money to take care of one hundred of his own former slaves, a Latin inscription erected by his grateful hometown of Como reveals that Pliny also donated over 100,000 sesterces for the building and upkeep of the city library and one half million sesterces "for the support of the boys and girls of the lower class" (*dedit in aliment pueror et*

---

5. A sobering assessment and depiction of legal violence in the Roman world can be read in Kyle, *Spectacles*.

6. Thapar, "Ashoka," 189.

7. Wilken, *Christians*, 1–30.

puellar pleb urban).[8] It is a *non sequitur* to think that a person with Pliny's temperament of generosity, thoughtfulness, and eleemosynary concern would never have been involved in judicial hostilities or pogroms against followers of Christ.

In reality, this Roman administrator was the "butcher of Bithynia" in regards to his participation in a pogrom against the maturing Christian movement in the early decades of the second century AD. Admittedly, Pliny saw followers of Christ and legal complaints against them as just one of scores of administrative difficulties for him to solve as the legate with consular power for the Roman Emperor Trajan (AD 110–12). Whatever concerns of compassion that Pliny may have had for Christians while he was killing them, it certainly never derailed his stronger devotion to Roman law and order. As Pliny writes in his letter to Trajan, these Christians deserve to die if no other reason than that they disrespected Roman law and Pliny's delegated position of authority. Accordingly, this refined and eleemosynary Roman gentleman, who possessed the power of *ius gladii* ("right of the sword," i.e., authority to execute offenders), singlehandedly decimated the established Christian population of the region of Bithynia-- Pontus. He accomplished this by means of numerous executions, some torture,[9] and calculated acts of intimidation and brutality (Pliny, *Ep. Tra.* 10.96).

Pliny's superior, the Roman Emperor Trajan, was himself regarded as one of the "Five Good Emperors." After Pliny recounts in a letter to the Emperor Trajan what he has accomplished in decimating the unrepentant Christian population of Bithynia and Pontus, the Emperor Trajan acknowledges his support for the policies and practices that Pliny used, and informs Pliny that forgiveness is to be offered to all Christians who will abandon their Christian faith by "worshiping our gods" (Pliny, *Ep. Tra.*10.97).

Perhaps the draconian measures taken by Pliny and supported by Trajan arose from geopolitical concerns about tensions and unrest in the region of Bithynia. Certainly Pliny's contemporary, the orator Dio Chrysostom, mentions seditious collegia and uprisings in Bithynia, and Trajan disallows the creation of a seemingly innocuous fire department in Bithynia because of the frequent political disturbances in Bithynia,

---

8. English translation taken from *Roman Civilization*, 2:270. Latin inscription available in Dessau, *ILS*, no. 2927 and additional details in Pliny, *Ep.* 7.18.2.

9. Harries, *Law*, 33–35.

especially its cities.[10] While this might explain the administrative justification for such cruelty to believers, it does not diminish the reality that "Good Emperors" and "Roman Gentlemen" are capable of and complicit in barbaric treatment of their subjects.

In nuce, it makes no difference how well respected, urbane, and admirable the administration of Domitian was. The Zeitgeist of the Roman Empire was built upon the values of power, tradition, domination, and authority. If any movement was perceived as a threat or challenge to these values, it could be quashed by a Roman administrator with noble Roman values. To link the "goodness" of Domitian (or some other emperor) with the issue of whether he could have allowed (or instigated) the mistreatment of believers depicted in Revelation reflects in part a colonial attitude that imagines that expansive and powerful empires such as Rome's were benign. Even the best of emperors could find themselves on the wrong side of the table in Christian history for their mistreatment of Christians.

Recently, Leonard Thompson has argued against the traditional understanding of the background of Revelation. Instead of interpreting the Apocalypse in light of some form of external duress, Thompson holds a different opinion. "In a nutshell, the conflict and crisis in the book of Revelation between Christian commitment and the social order derive from John's perspective on Roman society rather than from significant hostilities in the social environment. In this regard the book of Revelation fits the genre to which it belongs. There is a crisis orientation in the book of Revelation, but it is a characteristic of the genre, not of political circumstances occasioning the genre."[11]

This theory about John's depiction of his political circumstances and social setting is woefully inadequate. Thompson's rejection of John's testimony appears problematic because it rejects both John's significance as an eyewitness source and also the strong and supportive testimony from various authors of the New Testament (Synoptic Gospels, Acts, Pauline Corpus, and 1 Peter) and patristic period about a generally hostile context.

Thompson's animadversion on John's depiction of the "significant hostilities in the social environment" reflects some pretension in Thompson and his methods. After all, he is not only dismissive of Christian sources, but of far more significance is his attempt to comment on Christianity in the early Roman Empire while evading the unassailable testimony

10. Pliny, *Ep. Tra.*10.34–35; for references to Dio Chrysostom and other interpretive issues cf. Sherwin-White, *Letters*, 609–10.

11. Thompson, *Revelation* (1990), 175

of virtually every pagan author who addresses the issue or who reflects upon early Christianity. The pagan sources that mention the Christian faith during the first one-hundred fifty years of its history and expansion stand in sharp contrast to the conclusions offered by Thompson. Every pagan author, except Galen, who mentions the followers of Christ knows about the oppression, brutal treatment, and the selective martyrdom of Christians.

These important authors, Suetonius (biographer), Tacitus (historian), Epictetus (philosopher), Pliny (lawyer and governor), Trajan (Roman emperor), Lucian (author, satirist, and philosopher), and Marcus Aurelius (Roman emperor), mention the mistreatment of Christian believers explicitly.

PRIMARY PAGAN SOURCES

Suetonius, *Ner.* 16, "Punishment was inflicted on the Christians."

Tacitus, *Ann.* 15.44, "The confessed members of the sect were arrested; next, on their disclosures, vast numbers were convicted, not so much on the count of arson as for hatred of the human race. And derision accompanied their end: they were covered with wild beasts' skins and torn to death by dogs; or they were fastened on crosses, and, when daylight failed were burned to serve as lamps by night."

Pliny, *Ep. Tra.* 10.96–97, "I have asked them in person if they are Christians, and if they admit it, I repeat the question a second and third time, with a warning of the punishment awaiting them. If they persist, I order them to be led away for execution; for, whatever the nature of their admission, I am convinced that their stubbornness and unshakable obstinacy ought not to go unpunished."

Epictetus, *Discourses* 4.7.1–6, "What makes the tyrant an object of fear? His guards, someone says, and their swords . . . . If, then, a man really feel their presence, and that they haves swords, but has come for that very purpose, for the reason that he wishes to die because of some misfortune, and he seeks to do so easily at the hands of another, he does not fear the guards, does he? . . . . Therefore, if madness can produce this attitude of mind toward the things which have just been mentioned, and also habit, as with the Galilaeans (i.e., Christians), cannot reason and demonstration teach a man that God has made all things in the universe . . . ?"

Lucian, *Peregr.* 13, "The poor wretches have convinced themselves, first and foremost, that they are going to be immortal and live for all time, in consequence of which they despise death and even willingly give themselves into custody, most of them."

Marcus Aurelius, *Meditations* 11:3, "What a soul is that which is ready to be released from the body at any requisite moment, and be quenched or dissipated or hold together! But the readiness must spring from a man's inner judgment, and not be the result of mere opposition as is the case with the Christians (ὡς οἱ Χριστιανοί)."

As the author Galen attacked dogmatic allegiances to certain philosophic schools, he compared it with Christianity. "For one might more easily teach novelties to the followers of Moses and Christ than to the physicians and philosophers who cling fast to their schools."[12]

12. Walzer, *Galen*, 38.

Appendix B

Did John's Prophecies Fail?

VIRTUALLY ALL INTERPRETERS OF Revelation recognize that "the words of the prophecy of this book" (Rev 22:7, 10, 18) are replete with promises of coming punitive actions; this is harsh retribution promised by God in direct response to numerous sins. Not all interpreters have noticed that many times these punishments found in Revelation are contained within a paradigm of retributive justice. That is, there were specific sins committed and they called forth the wrath of God and the Lamb (Rev 6:16b), whether the punishment was historical or eschatological. At Thyatira (Rev 2:22–23) the prophetess Jezebel and her followers are to be punished for specific sins, "Beware, I am throwing her on a bed, and those who commit adultery with her I am throwing into great distress, unless they repent of her doings; and I will strike her children dead. And all the churches will know that I am the one who searches minds and hearts, and I will give to each of you as your works deserve." The divine punishment, for example, sought by the martyrs at the fifth seal is clearly retributive since it was to "avenge our blood" (Rev 6:10). There are others who are promised future punishment that includes drinking "the wine of God's wrath, poured unmixed into the cup of his anger" and being "tormented with fire and sulfur." They are threatened with this warning because they "worshiped the beast and its image" (Rev 14:9–10). The third angel, whose bowl of wrath was to turn humankind's potable water into blood, poured out his bowl of wrath specifically on the pagans who were guilty of shedding "the blood of saints and prophets." By this particular third plague, God gave "them blood to drink"; God thinks "It is what they deserve!" (Rev 16:4–6). There are numerous macabre scenes linked to the promised, future destruction of Babylon in Revelation 17–19. Part of the justification ("for his judgments are true and just," Rev 19:2a) for this horrific punishment of Rome, the "mother of whores" (Rev 17:5), is that the Lord "has judged the great whore who corrupted the earth with her fornication, and he has avenged on her the blood of his servants" (Rev 19:2b).

Since many interpreters of Scripture place an inordinate emphasis upon the predictive element of prophecy and promises given in the book of Revelation, this puts a heavy burden upon these interpreters when the promises of retributive judgment seem to be unfulfilled. In some instances, a state of denial regarding unfulfilled promises is so strong that certain interpreters cannot acknowledge the rather straightforward and explicit teaching of Scripture that God, in fact, sometimes alters his own earlier revealed decisions. This contingent nature of biblical promises can occur even when they are stated in prophetic oracles. It might strike some modern interpreters as ironic, but at times prophetic words accomplished their greatest good when they did not come to pass as promised. Sometimes the destruction that God promised was later revoked because of the repentance and change that the prophecies themselves produced. As Bauckham correctly noted on this very point, "It [biblical prophecy] leaves room for human freedom, for human response to God's will and human participation in his purpose for the world. Jonah's threat of judgment on Nineveh is not fulfilled *because* [italics mine] Nineveh responds to his prophecy by repenting."[13]

God's repeal of his previous promises and prophecies to punish and destroy must be seen in light of the fact that punitive oracles uttered in response to sin were often contingent. The following are selections from Scripture that reflect YHWH's tendency to relent of punishment and promised destruction, a tendency noted in Jeremiah (15:6) and associated with the Old Testament gospel of Exodus 34:6 by the prophets Jonah (4:2) and Joel (2:13). It is axiomatic that God's punishment is neither capricious nor unjust. Accordingly, it follows that when some specific sins are stopped, then the punishments promised by God for these same sins can be halted. In these cases, the reasons for specific judgments promised by God no longer exist.

One works under an excessive burden if he imagines that the phantasmagory of punitive actions in the visions of Revelation are always waiting for some literal, distant fulfillment, millennia after the life and ministry of the prophet John. Many of the punishment scenes of Revelation rely upon John's use of earlier biblical imagery and themes. This technique reflects

13. Bauckham, *Theology*, 149.

a hermeneutic of "typological allusion." Like biblical prophets centuries before him, John's visions utilized a rich heritage of biblical themes, language, and spiritual argot to give expression to the details of his visions.

Like the host of his spiritual predecessors, the author of Revelation was used by God to address the people of God in his own generation. John's use of prophetic imagery aligns him more with the classical prophets of the eighth through sixth centuries BC rather than with a seer called primarily to write enigmatic predictions for the remote future. Unlike the book of Daniel where the divine directive is stated, "This is a confidential report, Daniel, for your eyes and ears only. Keep it secret. Put the book under lock and key until the end" (Dan 12:4, *The Message*), in Revelation it records, "The Angel continued, 'Don't seal the words of the prophecy of this book; don't put it away on the shelf. Time is just about up'" (Rev 22:10, *The Message*).

INTERCESSORY PRAYER

It is easiest to see the contingent nature of God's decisions in the light of intercession, a spiritual discipline portrayed throughout Scripture and seen in diverse situations. Unless intercession is only artificial role playing, then God's future actions may be altered by the intercession of his people. This dynamic role of intercession can be seen in the life of Abraham, specifically in the narrative concerning the future fate of Sodom. Anticipating the destruction in Sodom's future, Abraham approached the Lord and said to him (Gen 18:23–26), "'Will you indeed sweep away the righteous with the wicked? Suppose there are fifty righteous within the city; will you then sweep away the place and not forgive it for the fifty righteous who are in it? Far be it from you to do such a thing, to slay the righteous with the wicked, so that the righteous fare as the wicked! Far be that from you! Shall not the Judge of all the earth do what is just?' And the Lord said, 'If I find at Sodom fifty righteous in the city, I will forgive the whole place for their sake.'" It is obvious in the narrative that God's plan for Sodom was altered by his interaction with Abraham.

Moses himself, as the leader of God's people, is required early on to intercede for the future and continuance of Israel. Aaron and God's people rejected the God who redeemed them in the Exodus, and they created an idol at the base of Mt. Sinai, a false god who "shall go before us." Upon discovery of this infidelity, the Lord reveals a divine plan so that, "my wrath may burn hot against them and I may consume them; and of you [Moses] I will make a great nation." Moses immediately implores the Lord, intercedes with him, pleading with God to "change your mind and do not bring disaster on your people" (Exod 32:12). There was a certain theological logic to the intercession of Moses, and the reader learns that "the Lord changed his mind about the disaster that he planned to bring on his people" (Exod. 32:14).

There are also significant examples of God relenting of his previous promises and prophecies in the lives of the prophets.

Hezekiah

2 Kgs 20:1–6 "In those days Hezekiah became sick and was at the point of death. The prophet Isaiah son of Amoz came to him, and said to him,

Promise/prophecy

'Thus says the Lord: Set your house in order, for you shall die; you shall not recover.'

Human Behavior

Then Hezekiah turned his face to the wall and prayed to the Lord: 'Remember now, O Lord, I implore you, how I have walked before you in faithfulness with a whole heart, and have done what is good in your sight.' Hezekiah wept bitterly.

God Relented

Before Isaiah had gone out of the middle court, the word of the Lord came to him: 'Turn back, and say to Hezekiah prince of my people, Thus says the Lord, the God of your ancestor David: I have heard your prayer, I have seen your tears; indeed, I will heal you; on the third day you shall go up to the house of the Lord. I will add fifteen years to your life.'"

Jonah

Jonah 3:1–10 "The word of the Lord came to Jonah a second time, saying,

Promise/prophecy

'Get up, go to Nineveh, that great city, and proclaim to it the message that I tell you.' So Jonah set out and went to Nineveh, according to the word of the Lord. Now Nineveh was an exceedingly large city, a three days' walk across. Jonah began to go into the city, going a day's walk. And he cried out, 'Forty days more, and Nineveh shall be overthrown!'

Human Behavior

When the news reached the king of Nineveh, he rose from his throne, removed his robe, covered himself with sackcloth, and sat in ashes. Then he had a proclamation made in Nineveh: 'By the decree of the king and his nobles: No human being or animal, no herd or flock, shall taste anything. They shall not feed, nor shall they drink water. Human beings and animals shall be covered with sackcloth, and they shall cry mightily to God. All shall turn from their evil ways and from the violence that is in their hands.

God Relented

Who knows? God may relent and change his mind; he may turn from his fierce anger, so that we do not perish.' When God saw what they did, how they turned from their evil ways, God changed his mind about the calamity that he had said he would bring upon them; and he did not do it.

Explicit Teaching that God Relents of Promised Behavior

Jer 18:5–8 "Then the word of the Lord came to me: Can I not do with you, O house of Israel, just as this potter has done [with this clay]? says the Lord. Just like the clay in the potter's hand, so are you in my hand, O house of Israel.

Promise/prophecy

At one moment I may declare concerning a nation or a kingdom, that I will pluck up and break down and destroy it,

Human Behavior

but if that nation, concerning which I have spoken, turns from its evil,

God Relented

I will change my mind about the disaster that I intended to bring on it."

CONTINGENT PROMISES AND REVELATION

One of the constant enigmas about Revelation is determining when the many warnings of future destruction of Rome would come about. The Preterist position looks for the fulfillment in the classic view of the "Fall of Rome," which is typically dated sometime in the fifth century AD. This view is problematic for at least two reasons. First, why would the fulfillment of the punishments occur so many generations after the mistreatment of the church in the late first century. Second, why would God wait to punish pagan Rome after it no longer existed and rather punish it after it became Christian?

Another major response to this question is provided by the Futurist view, which looks for the fulfillment of most of the promised punishments in Revelation in the period before the End. This perspective, like the Preterist position, has to abandon the typical pattern of biblical prophecy and locate the goal of the promises in the remote future, many centuries after the period when the church was mistreated during the late first century AD. Another difficulty with the Futurist outlook is that its proponents have always been wrong. Generation after generation, some representative of the Futurist interpretation will predict the fulfillments of Revelation are just around the corner. In fact, they will quote any number of events in contemporary world history to "prove" that they and their contemporaries are living in the "Endtimes."

In regard to the punishments of Revelation and the future "Fall of Rome," both the Preterist and Futurist have little regard for the historical setting of the late first and early second centuries AD, though clearly the ideas of the Futurist orientation in this regard are more egregious than those of the Preterist.

Historians know that the hostile attitudes and actions against followers of Christ varied both geographically and chronologically until the middle of the third century AD. We cannot know with certainty, however, how long harassment against believers continued in each instance. Furthermore, interpreters must guess whether the hostile actions experienced by those in John's audience was uniform in duration. Since there is often a contingent nature to biblical promises for retributive punishment, what would be the divine consequences when the hostility toward the seven congregations of Roman Asia abated before the promises were carried out? We know from the Pliny-Trajan letters of the early second century AD that a very horrific attack took place against Christians in the adjacent region of Bithynia-Pontus less than two decades after Revelation was composed, and that the suppression of Christian faith by Pliny was not long in duration. Suppression of the Christian faith was often short lived. Tertullian informs us, for example, about the short duration of Domitian's persecution of the Christian faith. "Domitian, too, a man of Nero's type in cruelty, tried his hand at persecution; but as he had something of the human in him, he soon put an end to what he had begun, even restoring again those whom he had banished" (Tertullian, *Apol.* 5). What happens to divine threats against oppressors when they cease to oppress, regardless of the reason for the cessation?

Most students of the Old Testament know that the eighth-century prophet Micah recorded a promise from God (Mic 3:12), "Therefore because of you (false leaders, priests, prophets) Zion shall be plowed as a field; Jerusalem shall become a heap of ruins, and the mountain of the house a wooded height." This noteworthy example of a contingent promise that did not come to pass as prophesied might have escaped our attention, had it not been later quoted by some (good) elders in Judah during the late seventh-century ministry of Jeremiah.

Jeremiah the prophet was facing a death sentence for treason and heresy, having prophesied (like Micah) against the city of Jerusalem (Jer 26:11b). "Some of the (good) elders of the land" (Jer 26:17), who by the way understood contingent prophecy, "arose and said to all the assembled people" (Jer 26:18–19) . . . "during the days of King Hezekiah of Judah," the prophet Micah "said to all the people of Judah: 'Thus says the Lord of hosts, Zion shall be plowed as a field; Jerusalem shall become a heap of ruins, and the mountain of the house a wooded height.' Did King Hezekiah of Judah and all Judah actually put him to death? Did he not fear the Lord and entreat the favor of the Lord, and did not the Lord change his mind about the disaster that he had pronounced against them?"

In the light of the explicit teaching on Jer 18:5–10 and the example of Micah and Jeremiah, one's opposition to contingent prophecy and promises perhaps arises from the imposition of dogma, rather than careful exegesis. It is not inconsequential that it is the biblical prophets themselves who taught John, explicitly and implicitly, that God's prophecies and promises are often conditional and have a contingent nature. Based upon the teaching about contingent promises from Scripture explained above, what prevents someone from evaluating some of the prophecies in Revelation from the biblical perspective of "the Lord changed his mind about the disaster that he had pronounced against them?"

This contingent prophecy paradigm should not undermine anyone's view of the prophetic nature of Revelation, except someone who holds the false view that biblical prophecy is fundamentally about distant predictions and that God himself is constrained by immutable words. Since it was the duress of believers pictured in Revelation that engendered God's warnings of future punishment, when the duress subsided so would the need for punishment and the revelation of the wrath of the Lamb. This approach renders Revelation no more unusable for doctrine and preaching, for example, than do the contingent prophecies of Micah.

Appendix C

Fictive Globalism

THE PRESENCE OF FICTIVE globalism is frequent in the literature of the Scriptures as well as in the Graeco-Roman world. Some authors who have addressed this phenomenon in the book of Revelation have mistaken it for a special Jewish or Christian theological perspective. In the conclusion of his work *The Theology of the Book of Revelation*, Richard Bauckham writes about what he labels "eschatological hyperbole,"[14] which includes what I have described as fictive globalism. My disagreement is that Bauckham offers this category without any interaction with the contemporary Graeco-Roman ideas and sources which seem to point to a similar use of language and global outlook without any of the Judeo-Christian eschatological theology. Certainly John's use of fictive globalism has allowed others to apply "John's" message to later situations, but it remains unclear that these words themselves mean that, "eschatological hyperbole gives these symbols intrinsic power to reach as far as the parousia."[15]

The following citations uphold the idea that this language of fictive globalism is not necessarily eschatological, either in Jewish or Christian sources. The author of Lamentations, reflecting on the very recent destruction of Jerusalem (587 BC), wrote, "The kings of the earth *gē* (γῆ) did not believe, nor did any of the world's people, that enemies and foes could enter the gates of Jerusalem" (Lam. 4:12). Clearly the Greek translators of 2 Chronicles (9:23, 28; 12:8), Lamentations (2:15), and Ezekiel (6:14; 7:4; 8:17) used this term "*gē*" in a very restricted sense, referring not to the entire planet, but to only a very small part of it.

---

14. Bauckham, *Theology*, 152–56.
15. Ibid., 156.

Fortunately there are numerous examples in the Greek Old Testament where this term *"gē"* is translated in ways that are sensitive to its regional connotations:[16]

- Gen 19:31 "Now the elder said to the younger, 'Our father is elderly, and there is no one on the earth (*gē*) who will come in to us, as is fitting in all the world.'"

- Lev 19:29 "Do not profane your daughter by making her commit fornication, and the land (*gē*) will not fornicate, and the land shall be full of lawlessness."

- Josh 6:27 "And the Lord was with Iesous, and his name was in all the land (*gē*)."

There are attempts in some translations to make the reader aware of the issue of hyperbole as it relates to concepts of globalism. An example from the translation of the Greek phrase "the whole world," *pasan tēn oikoumenēn,* πᾶσαν τὴν οἰκουμένην, reveals the depth of the problem regarding hyperbole and hyperliteralism. When these words occur in Luke 2:1, the NRSV renders the Greek "all the world." This translation reflects a hyperliteralism and is probably one of the worst possible examples of misrepresentation of globalism. The NASB is a little better by rendering this phrase "all the inhabited world." This, however, is also very misleading since neither Luke nor his readers believed that Rome was able to tax non-Roman kingdoms and empires that were part of "the inhabited world" but were far removed from Roman hegemony. A better translation of this verse is given in the NIV which renders the Greek "the entire Roman world." Even though the Greek text does not contain the term "Roman," this rendering is certainly closer to what Luke had in mind.[17]

Two brief quotations from the Augustan poet Ovid reflect the prevalence of fictive globalism: "You (Augustus) have long been father of the world (*tu pater orbis*). You have the name on earth which Jupiter holds in heaven—father, he of gods, you of men" (Ovid, *Fast.* 2.128–33). Concerning Augustus, Ovid further writes, "Need I bring to mind barbarian lands that border either ocean? Whatever lands men live on, the world over, shall all be his to rule, and the seas also. And when peace comes to all the world, his mind will turn to law and order, civil justice, and men will learn

16. *Diccionario*, γῆ, 808; Muraoka, *Lexicon*, γῆ, 129.

17. In light of the occasional nature and intended audience of Romans, it would be nonsensical to interpret the globalism of Rom 1:8 literally when Paul writes, "First, I thank my God through Jesus Christ for all of you, because your faith is proclaimed throughout the world" (ἐν ὅλῳ τῷ κόσμῳ).

from his sublime example" (Ovid, *Metam.* 15.829–33; cf. Horace, *Odes* 1.35.29–30).

Captions for Figures

Figure 1. Woodcut of Martin Luther used by permission from the Pitts Theological Library, Candler School of Theology, Emory University, Atlanta, Georgia.

Figure 2. Statue of Christopher Columbus located at Pepperdine University. Used with kind permission of Pepperdine University. Copyright © Molly R. Oster.

Figure 3. These are all of the occurrences of the term "antichrist" in the New Testament, with none in the book of Revelation.

Figure 4. New Testament enthronement texts based upon Ps. 110:1.

Figure 5. Remains of the temple to the Egyptian gods in Pergamum, gods worshipped globally. This temple complex was the largest building in the ancient city of Pergamum. Including its large courtyard, the temple complex covered an area approximately 260 meters by 100 meters. As was typical with Egyptian cults, the temple contained large pools to be used for religious purification. © copyright holder of this work is Richard E. Oster Jr.

Figure 6. Photo shows part of the upper agora in Ephesus along with the remains of the basilica. The colonnade found here comes from the Augustan period. © copyright holder of this work is Richard E. Oster Jr.

Figure 7. Coin from Roman Corinth, struck between AD 12–16. Obverse shows head of Tiberius; reverse shows goddess Nike with feet on globe and two symbols of victory, victory wreath and palm frond. Used with the kind permission of Classical Numismatic Group, Inc., http://www.cngcoins.com.

Figure 8. A personification of Italy on the left holds a cornucopia and extends a right hand to Roma, with her foot on a globe depicting the world, dated 68 BC. Used with the kind permission of Classical Numismatic Group, Inc., http://www.cngcoins.com.

Figure 9. A Roman coin showing a globe of the earth, a rudder steering it, and a cornucopia, dated 42 BC. Used with the kind permission of Classical Numismatic Group, Inc., http://www.cngcoins.com.

Figure 10. About the time that the Apostle Paul was in Corinth (AD 50), the German city of Cologne was founded as a Roman colony (*Colonia Claudia Ara Agrippinensium*). Thus, from an early date there is abundant Roman materials from Cologne and its suburbs. This sepulchral monument shows two Capricorns holding a globe of the earth. Since the emperor Augustus had taken the Capricorn as his birth sign, this depicts Augustan control of the earth. Located in the Römisch-Germanisches Museum (Roman-Germanic Museum), Cologne, Germany. © copyright holder of this work is Richard E. Oster Jr.

Figure 11. Roman aureus, with head of Augustus on obverse and *ARMENIA CAPTA* on reverse. Minted in Pergamum, dated 19–18 BC. Used with the kind permission of the © Trustees of the British Museum.

Figure 12. Denarius minted in Italy in 28 BC. Obverse with head of Augustus and *AEGVPTO CAPTA* on reverse. Used with the kind permission of © Trustees of the British Museum.

Figure 13. Sestertius minted in Rome in AD 71. Head of Vespasian on obverse with captive Judaea seated in position of mourning on reverse with words *JUDAEA CAPTA*. Used with the kind permission of Classical Numismatic Group, Inc., http://www.cngcoins.com.

Figure 14. Sestertius minted in Rome in AD 85. The obverse shows the head of Domitian, while the reverse shows German captive with hands bound and personification of Germany seated. The inscription on the reverse reads *GERMANIA CAPTA*. Used with the kind permission of © Trustees of the British Museum.

Figure 15. This Temple of Dendur was built during the early reign of Augustus in ancient Nubia as a site for worship of Isis and other Egyptian deities. The reason for its construction was to establish Roman hegemony on this border region along the Nile. On some of the walls the Roman emperor Augustus is depicted as a Pharaoh worshiping the Egyptian gods and goddesses. The temple was relocated to the Metropolitan Museum of Art in New York City and was erected in the Museum in 1978. © copyright holder of this work is Richard E. Oster Jr.

Figure 16. This Egyptian Temple of Taffeh was constructed along the Nile in ancient Nubia during the latter third of the reign of Augustus (AD 1–14). Its construction was designed to demonstrate Roman power and influence over the religious life of the Nubians. This temple was transported to the Netherlands and reassembled in the Nation Museum of Antiquities (Rijksmuseum van Oudheden) in Leiden in the 1970s. © copyright holder of this work is Richard E. Oster Jr.

Figure 17. This coin represents the emperor Trajan and the subjugation of Mesopotamia, in the center, and with the two figures leaning against urns representing the Tigris and Euphrates Rivers. Used with the kind permission of © Trustees of the British Museum.

Figure 18. This map is based upon information given in the document "Periplus of the Erythraean Sea" and is a file from the Wikimedia Commons. Copyright © PHGCOM.

Figure 19. This is a portion of the text of the *Res Gestae Divi Augusti* (*Acts of the Divine Augustus*) located on the walls of the Temple of Augustus in the ancient Galatian city of Ankyra. This very large inscription is bilingual. For those entering the Temple of Augustus the original Latin text was written on the walls. On the outer walls (more accessible today) the text was written in the lingua franca of Greek. Seen here in this Greek translation, this work of Augustus is entitled the πράξεις of the divine Augustus, using the same Greek term used for the "Acts" of the Apostles. Located in Ankara, Turkey. © copyright holder of this work is Richard E. Oster Jr.

Figure 20. In addition to this important temple in the modern city of Ankara, capital of the modern Republic of Turkey, archaeologists have found remains of another temple with a copy of the *Res Gestae Divi Augusti* in the New Testament city of Pisidian Antioch (Acts 13); see Wilson, *Biblical Turkey*, 109–18. © copyright holder of this work is Richard E. Oster Jr.

Figure 21. A Greek inscription from Assos honors the divinity of Gaius Caesar Germanicus Augustus and is typical for this region of the world in the Hellenistic and Roman periods. These kinds of accolades were fulsome in the minds of Jewish and Christian inhabitants and visitors. © copyright holder of this work is Richard E. Oster Jr.

Figure 22. An aureus of Galba issued AD 68–69; the reverse shows a woman with her foot on the globe of the world. The inscription on the reverse reads *SALUS GEN HVMANI*, whose meaning approximates the idea that Galba is the "salvation/safety of humankind." Used with the kind permission of Classical Numismatic Group, Inc., http://www.cngcoins.com.

Figure 23. A personification of Italy on the left holds a cornucopia and extends a right hand to Roma, with her foot on a globe depicting world mastery, dated 68 BC. Used with the kind permission of Classical Numismatic Group, Inc., http://www.cngcoins.com.

Figure 24. A Roman coin whose inscription proclaims the divinity of the dead Julius Caesar. The goddess Victory stands atop a globe of the world, holding a victory wreath, dated 31–30 BC. Used with the kind permission of Classical Numismatic Group, Inc., http://www.cngcoins.com.

Figure 25. Sestertius minted in Rome in AD 117. The purpose of Trajan handing the globe of the world to Hadrian was to show that the dead Trajan had indeed given the rule of the Roman Empire to Hadrian. Used with the kind permission of Classical Numismatic Group, Inc., http://www.cngcoins.com.

Figure 26. This Roman Gem, known as the "Actium Victory Cameo," shows Augustus in a chariot being drawn by four Tritons. The iconography of this image with its ocean and globe depicts Augustus as "Master of land and sea" in its celebration of the Victory of Actium. Gem located in the Kunsthistorisches Museum in Vienna, Austria. © copyright holder of this work is Richard E. Oster Jr.

Figure 27. This Ephesian monument is known as the Fountain of Trajan (*Nymphaeum Traiani*) and was dedicated to this emperor no later than AD 114. The center niche originally contained a colossal statue of the emperor Trajan. The fragmentary remains include the foot of the Emperor Trajan next to a globe representing a subservient earth. © copyright holder of this work is Richard E. Oster Jr.

Figure 28. This close up shows a Greek inscription under the statue of Trajan that stated among other things that he was regarded as "son of god." © copyright holder of this work is Richard E. Oster Jr.

Figure 29. This statue of the second century AD Roman emperor Hadrian visually conveys the Roman sense of world control. The State Hermitage Museum, St. Petersburg, Russia. © copyright holder of this work is Richard E. Oster Jr.

Figure 30. Reverse of this Greek coin has the identifying words "Of King Antiochus Epiphanes." *Nike* has her victory wreath in hand. Used with the kind permission of Classical Numismatic Group, Inc., http://www.cngcoins.com.

Figure 31. Reverse of a denarius coin issued by the new Roman leader Octavian in 30–29 BC. The nautical imagery of prow, rudder, and anchor celebrate the victorious sea battle of Octavian over Cleopatra and Mark Antony at Actium. Used with the kind permission of Classical Numismatic Group, Inc., http://www.cngcoins.com.

Figure 32. Map of Priene, Metropolis, Maeonia, Dorylaion, Eumeneia, Apameia. These are the cities in which the well-known Priene Calendar inscription have been discovered. © copyright holder of this work is Google Maps.

Figure 33. Map of Christian congregations in first century Asia Minor. © copyright holder of this work is Google Maps.

Figure 34. Hierapolis. © copyright holder of this work is Richard E. Oster Jr.

Figure 35. This Julian star coin is an instructive example of Roman astral symbolism serving as propaganda. It portrays the apotheosis of Julius Caesar, i.e., the belief that Caesar ascended to divinity upon his death. Copyright © Clint Burnett.

Figure 36. Denarius struck during the reign of Trajan (AD 98–117), using astral imagery. The goddess Eternity (*Aeternitas*) holds the heads of the sun (her right hand) and moon (her left hand), with the text reading "Eternity of Augustus" (*Aet-Aug*). This message suggests the eternity of Trajan's influence and Rome's domination. Used with the kind permission of forumancientcoins.com.

Figure 37. Sarcophagus (stone coffin) placed outside the archaeological museum for Ephesus, in the town of Selçuk, Turkey. © copyright holder of this work is Richard E. Oster Jr.

Figure 38. *Commune Asiae* coin, located in the State Hermitage Museum, St. Petersburg, Russia. © copyright holder of this work is Richard E. Oster Jr.

Figure 39. Jewish menorah found on the inner wall of the Arch of Titus, an arch constructed in Rome by Domitian to celebrate the military victory of his brother, Titus, over the Jews. The spoils of war are displayed to commemorate the total destruction of Jerusalem and the Jewish temple there (AD 70).

Figure 40. This single lamp stand is much taller than most, but it might be closer to the size of the seven lamp stands among which the Son of Man moved in John's initial vision. Metropolitan Museum of Art, New York, New York. © copyright holder of this work is Richard E. Oster Jr.

Figure 41. A golden coin issued by Domitian (AD 81–84), who employed, like John, sevenfold sidereal imagery for a divine being, his son who died in infancy. Used with the kind permission of the Trustees of the British Museum.

Figure 42. Chariot with sun god, displaying radiate iconography of the sun. Nero pictured with rays of the sun to imitate the sun god Helius, perhaps to proclaim that he was *Neos Helius*, a new manifestation of the sun god. This artifact is in the The State Hermitage Museum, St. Petersburg, Russia. © copyright holder of this work is Richard E. Oster Jr.

Figure 43. Coin of Hellenized Divine Ruler, Ptolemy III Euergetes (reigned 246–222 BC), whose divinity was highlighted by his radiate crown. Altes Museum, Berlin, Germany. © copyright holder of this work is Richard E. Oster Jr.

Figure 44. Roman's first emperor, Augustus, portrayed with radiate crown. This gem is located in the Römisch-Germanisches Museum, Cologne, Germany. © copyright holder of this work is Richard E. Oster Jr.

Figure 45. Statue of Greek god Hades, located in the archaeological museum on the site of Hierapolis, Turkey. © copyright holder of this work is Richard E. Oster Jr.

Figure 46. Sarcophagus panel with Hermes standing at the door to meet the souls of the dead and to escort them into the underworld. Third century AD. The State Hermitage Museum, St. Petersburg, Russia. © copyright holder of this work is Richard E. Oster Jr.

Figure 47. *Plutonium* discovered in 1962–65 excavations at Hierapolis. D'Antria, *Hierapolis,* 142–44.4. Photo © copyright holder of this work is Richard E. Oster Jr.

Figure 48. Bronze Jewish Prutah coin. Struck by Roman Procurator of Judaea Porcius Festus in ca. AD 58–59 under the reign of Nero (AD 54–68). The Greek on the obverse states "of Nero" (*NEROS*), while the reverse states "of Caesar" (*KAISAROS*). Used with the kind permission of Classical Numismatic Group, Inc., http://www.cngcoins.com.

Figure 49. Panorama photo of the wadi, the cliff, and cave 4 at Qumran. © copyright holder of this work is Evertt Huffard.

Figure 50. This statue represents a standard view of the Hellenistic-Egyptian deity Sarapis, with a modius on his head. The modius represented a basket/measure of grain and thus bounty. The State Hermitage Museum, St. Petersburg, Russia. © copyright holder of this work is Richard E. Oster Jr.

Figure 51. Iconic building from the early second century AD, the library of Celsus, constructed in AD 110. © copyright holder of this work is Richard E. Oster Jr.

Figure 52. This photograph comes from the writings of John Turtle Wood, the British architect who discovered the location of the temple of the Ephesian Artemis (*Discoveries*, 4). This depiction illustrates why early explorers gave reports of great desolation at the site of ancient Ephesus.

Figure 53. This is a mid-second century AD inscription that records the decision of the proconsul Lucius Antonius Albus to punish those who contributed to the harbor being nonnavigable. Inscription located at the Ephesus Museum, Selçuk, Turkey. © copyright holder of this work is Richard E. Oster Jr.

Figure 54. Aerial view showing the Roman city of Ephesus, where the ancient harbor was located by the lower agora, and the modern coastline. © copyright holder of this work is Google Maps.

Figure 55. Theater at Ephesus dated from the Hellenistic period but expanded during the reign of the Roman Emperor Claudius. This theater had a seating capacity of approximately 25,000. © copyright holder of this work is Richard E. Oster Jr.

Figure 56. Stadium from Aphrodisias, where stone seating reveals damage of earthquake; its seating capacity was approximately 30,000 spectators. © copyright holder of this work is Richard E. Oster Jr.

Figure 57. Information about ancient professions come principally from inscriptions, funerary stones, and vases. These two examples are found in the museums on Museum Island, Berlin, Germany. © copyright holder of this work is Richard E. Oster Jr.

Figure 58. Coin minted at Ephesus in AD 71 during the reign of Vespasian. Accompanying the inscription "To the peace of Augustus" is the image of Nike bearing the wreath of victory. Used with the kind permission of Classical Numismatic Group, Inc., http://www.cngcoins.com.

Figure 59. Monument depicting the goddess Nike, found at Ephesus, one of the seven cities of Revelation. © copyright holder of this work is Richard E. Oster Jr.

Figure 60. Praying youth expressing reverential posture, located in the Pergamum Museum, Berlin, Germany. © copyright holder of this work is Richard E. Oster Jr.

Figure 61. Expectations of a typical worshiper of Asclepius is that the god will answer prayers. The iconography of this artifact agrees with the sentiment of the Greeks since it is dedicated to Savior Asclepius. Rather than asking Savior Asclepius for the healing an ear, the devotee is reminding Asclepius that he is a god who hears. © copyright holder of this work is Richard E. Oster Jr.

Figure 62. Portion of temple for Athena Nikephoros, found at the Pergamum Museum, Berlin, Germany. © copyright holder of this work is Richard E. Oster Jr.

Figure 63. There is a replica in Nashville, Tennessee, of the original Parthenon Temple located on the Acropolis in Athens. © copyright holder of this work is Richard E. Oster Jr.

Figure 64. Although the temple of Zeus at Olympia was destroyed in antiquity, ancient descriptions as well as coin pictures have provided a good idea of its original size and character. This line drawing was made in 1572 by Philippe Galle. The coin comes from Tarsus of Cilicia in southeast Turkey (home of the Apostle Paul) and dates from 164–27 BC. Zeus is seated and holds Nike in his right hand and a scepter in his left. Used with the kind permission of Classical Numismatic Group, Inc., http://www.cngcoins.com.

Figure 65. Lamp with figure of Victory with wreath in right hand and palm frond in left hand; this artifact is located in the Ephesos Museum in Vienna, Austria. Used with the kind permission of Mattia Moretti.

Figure 66. Nike ornament, located in the Altes Museum, Berlin, Germany. © copyright holder of this work is Richard E. Oster Jr.

Figure 67. Nike offering libation, a liquid offering; located in Pergamum Museum, Berlin, Germany. © copyright holder of this work is Richard E. Oster Jr.

Figure 68. Two goddesses of Victory (*Nikai*) leading animals on behalf of worshipers to be sacrificed to the gods. Monument discovered at Ephesus, dated from the first century AD. In the left hand of the left Nike is an incense burner. Ephesos-Museum (an off-site collection of the larger Kunsthistorisches Museum), Vienna, Austria. © copyright holder of this work is Richard E. Oster Jr.

Figure 69. Two Nike monuments showing the goddesses in the process of sacrificial slaughter, thereby bringing these sacrificed animals into the presence of various goddesses and gods in order to complete the worship that had been initiated by devotees and worshipers. Pergamum Museum, Berlin, Germany. © copyright holder of this work is Richard E. Oster Jr.

Figure 70. Nike ("Nike loosening her Sandal") is involved in bringing sacrifices to the goddess Athena Nike to celebrate the military victory of Athens over Sparta in the Peloponnesian War in the late fifth century BC. Statue from the Temple of Athena Nike (now in "New" Acropolis Museum). Copyright © Karen Green, used with permission.

Figure 71. This image represents an Assyrian sacred tree, identified by some scholars with the idea of life. The idea of the sacred tree has a very long history in the art of the ancient Near East and shares some similarities with the Jewish tree of life, from which the prophet John derives his ideas of the tree of life. These panels are located in the Brooklyn Museum, New York. © copyright holder of this work is Richard E. Oster Jr.

Figure 72. .This Assyrian monument, the Sacred Tree, depicts two supernatural beings who take care of the sacred trees. Archaeologists suggest that in this scene the supernatural beings are pollinating the trees. These panels are located in the Brooklyn Museum, New York. © copyright holder of this work is Richard E. Oster Jr.

Figure 73. Ancient agora of Smyrna. Georges Jansoone.

Figure 74. Coin showing Noah, his wife, and the ark, minted by pagan rulers at Apameia. Used with the kind permission of Classical Numismatic Group, Inc., http://www.cngcoins.com.

Figure 75. Julia Severa, builder of Jewish synagogue, inscription, dated first century AD.

Figure 76. Roman coin minted during the reign of Nerva, following the death of Domitian. The relations between Rome and Judaism declined following the first Jewish Revolt. The Romans forced the Jews to continue to pay a temple tax, known as the *Ficus Judaicus*, but the revenue went to building a pagan temple. The harshness of the enforcement of this law under Domitian was relaxed by Nerva. Used with the kind permission of Classical Numismatic Group, Inc., http://www.cngcoins.com.

Figure 77. Monument from Ephesus depicting the several crowns awarded to an individual. © copyright holder of this work is Richard E. Oster Jr.

Figure 78. Bust of individual wearing the gold leaf crown. This item is located in the Museum of Anatolian Civilizations in Ankara, Turkey. © copyright holder of this work is Richard E. Oster Jr.

Figure 79. This typical crown is located in the Metropolitan Museum, New York. © copyright holder of this work is Richard E. Oster Jr.

Figure 80. Golden diadem located in the archaeological museum in Hierapolis, a city mentioned in the New Testament (Col. 4:13). © copyright holder of this work is Richard E. Oster Jr.

Figure 81. Pictures of burial finds with golden victory wreaths. Image on left is located in the Museum of Anatolian Civilizations in Ankara, Turkey. Picture on right is a model of a woman wearing a golden burial crown, located in the Archaeological Museum, Izmir, Turkey. © copyright holder of this work is Richard E. Oster Jr.

Figure 82. Sepulchral monument showing the deceased holding a crown of victory. © copyright holder of this work is Richard E. Oster Jr.

Figure 83. The altar of Zeus is one of the best known monuments from ancient Pergamum. Constructed in the second century BC, the dimensions of this altar are approximately 36 meters by 33 meters. This serpent's head adorns the friezes on the outer wall, depicting the well known theme of the Graeco-Roman world Gigantomachy, the battle between the Olympian gods and the Giants. © copyright holder of this work is Richard E. Oster Jr.

Figure 84. Statue representing the god Asclepius, located in the National Archaeological Museum, Athens, Greece. © copyright holder of this work is Richard E. Oster Jr.

Figure 85. Asclepius Sanctuary at Pergamum. In the upper-left-hand corner is the sanctuary's theater, with seating for 3,500. At the bottom right is a building perhaps used for medical treatment since Asclepius was the god of healing and medicine. Although this Asclepius complex did not exist in its current form during the reign of Domitian, there is no doubt that Asclepius was an important deity in the city of Pergamum at that time.

Figure 86. A model of ancient Pergamum, located in the Pergamum Museum, Berlin, Germany.

Figure 87. The great altar of Zeus brought from Pergamum and it now located in the Pergamum Museum in Berlin, Germany. This monumental structure was constructed in the mid-second century BC. © copyright holder of this work is Richard E. Oster Jr.

Figure 88. Roman coin dating from the reign of Nero, showing the façade of the macellum in Rome. These building were found throughout the Empire in cities of any size and provided the location for the sale of various foods, including vegetables, fruits, and meats. It is a structure of this type from which those who hold the "teaching of Balaam" would purchase their "foods sacrificed to idols." Used with the kind permission of Classical Numismatic Group, Inc., http://www.cngcoins.com.

Figure 89. One of the great monuments to the Emperor Trajan in Roman Asia was built on the acropolis of Pergamum during the early decades of the second century AD. It was constructed on the highest point of the acropolis during Trajan's reign but was expanded by his successor Hadrian. © copyright holder of this work is Richard E. Oster Jr.

Figure 90. Text from a pagan Greek author named Lucian that depicts the expulsion of a Christian named Peregrinus for eating food forbidden by Christianity in that region.

Figure 91. Texts from Isaiah showing the metaphorical use of the threat of the sword and of divine punishment.

Figure 92. Image of the Jewish Ark of Covenant, minted in AD 132–35 during the Bar Kochba Revolt. This scene shows the Ark placed inside the Jewish temple, which, of course, had been destroyed decades earlier. Used with the kind permission of Classical Numismatic Group, Inc., http://www.cngcoins.com.

Figure 93. This coin from Thyatira dates from the reign of Domitian. The presence of the goddess of victory along with both a victory wreath and a palm frond on the reverse of the coin certainly highlights the dramatic tension between the outlook of imperial theology and the theology that the prophet John is proclaiming. Used with the kind permission of Classical Numismatic Group, Inc., http://www.cngcoins.com.

Figure 94. Representative texts from the Dead Sea Scrolls that reflect understanding of Belial.

Figure 95. A Roman Dupondius minted after AD 16. The obverse shows the head of Augustus with the star of Venus above his head. On the reverse the wife of Augustus, Livia, is portrayed with a crescent moon above her head and a globe under her bust. The inscription on the reverse declares her *GENETRIX ORBIS* (mother of the world). Used with the kind permission of Classical Numismatic Group, Inc., http://www.cngcoins.com.

Figure 96. Temple of Artemis in Sardis, first begun in the early Hellenistic period and reaching completion in the second century AD. Its main columns were almost fifty feet tall. © copyright holder of this work is Richard E. Oster Jr.

Figure 97. Ethical teachings from a pagan cult. This particular inscription, which is pre-Christian in date, is unknown to too many students of the New Testament in general and especially the book of Revelation. There is some debate whether the *oikos* mentioned in the inscription refers to a domestic cult or to a shrine or temple. In either case, the information is helpful in adumbrating the Graeco-Roman ethical context of nascent Christianity.

Figure 98. Caryatids showing human forms as pillars in a temple. © copyright holder of this work is Richard E. Oster Jr.

Figure 99. This alliance coin between Laodicea and Smyrna dates to the reign of Nero. Alliances between cities were established to promote economic, religious, and civic relationships. Examples of these alliance coins are found in the coinage of many of the cities of Roman Asia. Used with the kind permission of Classical Numismatic Group, Inc., http://www.cngcoins.com.

Figure 100. This depiction of Jesus (*The Light of the World*) at the door was painted by William Holman Hunt (1827–1910). It is characterized by the same misconceptions as the painting by Warner Sallman.

Bibliography

PRIMARY SOURCES

American Numismatic Society. "Aegypto Capta." No pages. Online: http://www.numismatics.org/dpubs/romangeneral/.

———. "Antonius Pius." No pages. Online: http://numismatics.org/collection/1965.66.32.

———. "Armenia Capta." No pages. Online: http://www.numismatics.org/lookup.cgi?string=1944.100.39174.

———. "Civil War." No pages. Online: http://www.numismatics.org/lookup.cgi?string=1999.79.5.

———. "Germania Capta." No pages. Online: http://www.numismatics.org/lookup.cgi?string=1905.57.328.

———. "Iudaea Capta." No pages. Online: http://www.numismatics.org/lookup.cgi?string=1944.100.39981.

———. "Nero." No pages. Online: http://www.numismatics.org/lookup.cgi?string=1944.100.39417.

———. "Nero." No pages. Online: http://www.numismatics.org/lookup.cgi?string=1944.100.39419.

———. "Nero." No pages. Online: http://www.numismatics.org/lookup.cgi?string=1944.100.39780.

———. "Octavian." No pages. Online: http://www.numismatics.org/lookup.cgi?string=1937.158.439.

———. "Octavian." No pages. Online: http://www.numismatics.org/lookup.cgi?string=1944.100.39147.

———. "Octavian." No pages. Online: http://www.numismatics.org/lookup.cgi?string=0000.999.16782.

———. "Tiberius." No pages. Online: http://www.numismatics.org/lookup.cgi?string=1944.100.39242.

Aelius Aristides: The Complete Works, Orations XVII–LIII. Translated by C. A. Behr. Leiden: Brill, 1981.

The Apostolic Fathers. Translated by J.B. Lightfoot and J.R. Hamer. Edited and Revised by Michael W. Holmes, 2 ed. Grand Rapids, MI: Baker Book House, 1989.

Aristotle. *On the Cosmos.* Translated by D.J. Furley. Loeb Classical LIbrary. Cambridge, MA: Harvard University Press, 1955.

Bibliography

Augustus, *Res Gestae Divi Augusti, Text, Translation, and Commentary* by Alison E. Cooley. Cambridge University Press, 2009.

Beard, Mary, et al. *Religions of Rome Volume 2: A Sourcebook.* Cambridge: Cambridge University Press, 1998.

Blunt, P. A. and J. M. Moore, eds. *Res Gestae Divi Augusti.* London: Oxford University Press, 1967.

Braund, David C. *Augustus to Nero: A Sourcebook on Roman History 31 BC–AD 68.* Totowa, NJ: Barnes and Noble, 1985.

Burstein, Stanley M. *The Hellenistic Age from the Battle of Ipsos to the Death of Kleopatra VII.* Translated Documents of Greece and Rome 3. New York: Cambridge University Press, 1985.

Casson, Lionel, ed. *The Periplus Maris Erythraei: Text with Introduction, Translation, and Commentary.* Princeton: Princeton University Press, 1989.

Charlesworth, James, ed. *The Old Testament Pseudepigrapha.* 2 vols. New York: Doubleday, 1983.

Cicero. *De Re Publica et De Legibus.* Translated by Clinton Walker Keyes. Loeb Classical Library 213. Cambridge, MA: Harvard University Press, 1928.

Columbus, Christopher. *The Book of Prophecies, Edited by Christopher Columbus. Repertorium Columbianum 3.* Edited by Roberto Rusconi. Translated by Blair Sullivan. Berkley: University of California Press, 1997.

Dio Cassius. *Roman History.* Translated by Earnest Cary. 9 vols. Loeb Classical Library. Cambridge, MA: Harvard University Press, 1914–27.

Diodorus of Sicily. Translated by Francis R. Walton et al. 12 vols. Loeb Classical Library. Cambridge, MA: Harvard University Press, 1933–67.

Dörner, F. K., and J. H. Young. "The *Nomos* Inscriptions." In *Nemrud Dagi: The Hierothesion of Antiochus I of Commange,* edited by Donald H. Sanders, 1.206–24. Winona Lake, IN: Eisenbrauns, 1996.

Edelstein, E. J., and L. Edelstein, eds. *Asclepius: Collection and Interpretation of the Testimonies.* Baltimore: Johns Hopkins University Press, 1998.

Ehrenberg, Victor, and A. H. M. Jones, eds. *Documents Illustrating the Reigns of Augustus and Tiberius.* 2nd ed. Oxford: Clarendon Press, 1955.

Epictetus. *The Discourses as Reported by Arrian.* Translated by W. A. Oldfather. 2 vols. Loeb Classical Library. Cambridge, MA: Harvard University Press, 1925–28.

Eusebius. *The History of the Church from Christ to Constantine.* Translated by G. A. Williamson. New York: New York University Press, 1966.

Forum Ancient Coins. "Trajan." No pages. Online: http://www.forumancientcoins. com/moonmoth/coins/trajan_008.html.

———. "Radiata Corona. No pages. Online: http://www.forumancientcoins.com/ numiswiki/view.asp?key=Radiata%20Corona.

Griffiths, J. Gwyn. *Apuleius of Madauros: The Isis-Book (Metamorphoses, Book XI).* Leiden: Brill, 1975.

Head, Barclay V. *A Catalogue of the Greek Coins in the British Museum: Catalogue of the Greek Coins of Phrygia.* London: Order of the Trustees, 1906.

Homer. *Iliad.* Loeb Classical Library. Cambridge, MA: Harvard University Press, 1954–1957.

Irenaeus. *Against Heresies.* In vol. 1 of *Ante-Nicene Fathers,* translated by A. Roberts and J. Donaldson. Grand Rapids: Eerdmans, 1975.

Bibliography

Josephus. Translated by H. St. J. Thackeray et al. 10 vols. Loeb Classical Library. Cambridge, MA: Harvard University Press, 1926–65.

Josephus. *The War of the Jews*. In *The Works of Josephus*. Translated by William Whiston. Peabody, MA: Hendrickson Publishers, 1987.

[Saint] Justin Martyr. *The First Apology, The Second Apology, Dialogue with Trypho, Exhortation to the Greeks, Discourse to the Greeks, The Monarchy; or the Rule of God*. Translated by Thomas B. Falls. Fathers of the Church, vol. 6. New York: Christian Heritage, 1948.

———. *First Apology*. In vol. 1 of *Ante-Nicene Fathers*. Translated by A. Roberts and J. Donaldson. Grand Rapids: Eerdmans, 1975.

Juvenal and Persius. Translated by G. G. Ramsay. Loeb Classical Library 91. Cambridge, MA: Harvard University Press, 1918.

Lehmann, Helmut T. et al., eds. *Luther's Works*. St. Louis: Concordia, 1955.

Lewis, Naphtali, and Meyer Reinhold, eds. *Roman Civilization*. 2 vols. New York: Columbia University Press, 1990.

Lucian. Translated by A. M. Harmon et al. 8 vols. Loeb Classical Library. Cambridge, MA: Harvard University Press, 1913–67.

Marcus Aurelius Antonius. Translated by C.R. Haines. Loeb Classical Library. Cambridge, MA: Harvard University Press, 1916.

McCrumb, M., and A. G. Woodhead, eds. *Select Documents of the Principates of the Flavian Emperors: Including the Year of Revolution A.D. 68–96*. Cambridge: Cambridge University Press, 1964.

Merkelbach, Reinhold et al., eds. *Die Inschriften von Assos*. Inschriften Griechischer Städte aus Kleinasien 4. Bonn: Habelt, 1976.

Münzkabinett, Staatliche Museen zu Berlin. No pages. Online: http://www.smb .museum/ikmk/object.php?objectNR=0.

Ovid. *Fasti*. Translated by James George Frazer. Loeb Classical Library 253. Cambridge, MA: Harvard University Press, 1931.

———. *Metamorphoses*. Translated by Frank Justus Miller. 2 vols. Loeb Classical Library 42–43. Cambridge, MA: Harvard University Press, 1977–84.

Pausanias. *Description of Greece*. Translated by W. H. S. Jones et al. 4 vols. Loeb Classical Library. Cambridge, MA: Harvard University Press, 1933–55.

Philo. Translated by F. H. Colson et al. 10 vols. Loeb Classical Library. Cambridge, MA: Harvard University Press, 1929–70.

Philo. Translated by C.D. Yonge. *The Works of Philo: Complete and Unabridged*. Peabody, MA: Hendrickson Publishers, 1993.

Plato. *Euthyphro, Apology, Crito, Phaedo, Phaedrus*. Translated by Harold North Fowler. Loeb Classical Library 36. Cambridge, MA: Harvard University Press, 1914.

———. *Lysis, Symposium, Gorgias*. Translated by W. R. M. Lamb. Loeb Classical Library 166. Cambridge, MA: Harvard University Press, 1925.

———. *Phaedo*. In *The Collected Dialogues of Plato Including the Letters*. Translated by Hugh Tredennick. Princeton, NJ: Princeton University Press, 1961.

———. *Republic*. Translated by Paul Shorey. 2 vols. Loeb Classical Library. Cambridge, MA: Harvard University Press, 1935–46.

———. *The Republic*. Translated by Francis Macdonald Cornford. New York: Oxford University Press, 1976.

Pliny the Elder. *Natural History*. Translated by H. Rackham et al. 10 vols. Loeb Classical Library. Cambridge, MA: Harvard University Press, 1938–62.

Bibliography

Pliny the Younger. *Letters.* Translated by Betty Radice. 2 vols. Loeb Classical Library. Cambridge, MA: Harvard University Press, 1969.

Plutarch. Translated by Frank Cole Babbit et al. 15 vols. Loeb Classical Library. Cambridge, MA: Harvard University Press, 1948–55.

Sear, David. *Roman Coins and Their Values.* 4th rev. ed. London: Seaby, 1988.

Sherk, Robert K. *Roman Documents from the Greek East: Senatus Consulta and Epistulae to the Age of Augustus.* Baltimore: Johns Hopkins University Press, 1969.

———, ed. *Rome and the Greek East to the Death of Augustus.* Vol. 4. Cambridge: Cambridge University Press, 1984.

Strabo. *Geography.* Translated by Horace Leonard Jones. 8 vols. Loeb Classical Library. Cambridge, MA: Harvard University Press, 1917–32.

Strecker, Georg. *Neuer Wettstein: Texte zum Neuen Testament aus Griechentum und Hellenismus.* 2 vols. New York: Walter de Gruyter, 1996.

Suarez, Rasiel. *ERIC II: The Encyclopedia of Roman Imperial Coins.* Tumwater, Wash: Dirty Old Books, 2010.

Suetonius. Translated by J. C. Rolfe. 2 vols. Loeb Classical Library. 2 vols. Cambridge, MA: Harvard University Press, 1913–14.

Tacitus. *The Annals.* Translated by John Jackson. 2 vols. Loeb Classical Library. Cambridge, MA: Harvard University Press, 1937.

Tertullian. *Latin Christianity.* In vol. 3 of *Ante-Nicene Fathers,* translated by A. Roberts and J. Donaldson. Grand Rapids: Eerdmans, 1975.

The Message. Translated by Eugene Peterson. No pages. Online: http://www .biblegateway.com/.

The Orthodox Study Bible. Edited by Jack Norman Sparks et al. Nashville, TN: Nelson, 2008.

Virgil. Translated by H. Rushton Fairclough. 2 vols. Loeb Classical Library. Cambridge, MA: Harvard University Press, 1918.

Wankel, Hermann et al., eds. *Die Inschriften von Ephesos.* Inschriften Griechischer Städte aus Kleinasien 11. Bonn: Rudolf Habelt, 1979–84.

Wright, Benjamin G., and Albert Pietersma. *A New English Translation of the Septuagint And the Other Greek Translations Traditionally Included Under That Title.* Oxford: Oxford University Press, 2007.

SECONDARY SOURCES

Abegg, Martin, Jr., Peter Flint, and Eugene Ulrich, eds. *The Dead Sea Scrolls Bible.* New York: HarperCollins, 1999.

Adrados, F. R. and Elvira Gangutia Elicegui. *Diccionario Griego-Español, Vol. 4.* Madrid: Consejo Superior de Investigaciones Científicas, 1994.

Albani, Matthias. "Horoscopes." In *Encyclopedia of the Dead Sea Scrolls,* edited by Lawrence H. Schiffman and James VanderKam, 1:370–73. New York: Oxford University Press, 2000.

Arzt-Grabner, Peter. *Philemon.* In *Papyrologische Kommentar zum Neuen Testament* 1. Göttingen: Vandenhoeck & Ruprecht, 2003.

Aune, David E. "The Apocalypse of John and Palestinian Jewish Apocalyptic." In *The Pseudepigrapha and Christian Origins: Essays from the Studiorum Novi Testamenti*

Societas, edited by Gerbern Oegema and James Charlesworth, 169–92. London: T&T Clark, 2008.

———. "Intertextuality." In *The Westminster Dictionary of New Testament and Early Christian Literature and Rhetoric*, 233–34. Louisville, KY: Westminster John Knox, 2003.

———. *Prophecy in Early Christianity and the Ancient Mediterranean World*. Grand Rapids: Eerdmans, 1983.

———. *Revelation 1–5*. Word Biblical Commentary 52a. Dallas, TX: Word, 1997.

———. *Revelation 17–22*. Word Biblical Commentary 52c. Nashville, TN: Nelson, 1998.

———. "Revelation to John." In *The Westminster Dictionary of New Testament and Early Christian Literature and Rhetoric*, 399–406. Louisville, KY: Westminster John Knox, 2003.

Bäbler, Balbina. "Nike II Iconography." In *Brill's New Pauly: Encyclopedia of the Ancient World*, edited by Hubert Cancik et al., 9:755–56. Leiden: Brill, 2006.

Backus, Irena. *Reformation Readings of the Apocalypse: Geneva, Zurich, and Wittenberg*. New York: Oxford University Press, 2000.

Balsdon, J. P. V. D. *Romans and Aliens*. Chapel Hill: University of North Carolina Press, 1979.

Barr, David L. *Reading the Book of Revelation: A Resource for Students*. Atlanta: SBL, 2003.

Barton, John. "Prophecy (Postexilic)." In *The Anchor Bible Dictionary*, edited by David Noel Freedman, 5:489–95. New York: Doubleday, 1992.

Barton, S. C., and G. H. R. Horsley. "A Hellenistic Cult Group and the New Testament Churches." *Jahrbuch Für Antike und Christentum* 24 (1981): 7–41.

Bauckham, Richard. *2 Peter, Jude*. Word Biblical Commentary 50. Waco, TX: Word, 1983.

———. *The Climax of Prophecy: Studies on the Book of Revelation*. Edinburgh: T&T Clark, 1993.

———. "The Lord's Day." In *From Sabbath to Lord's Day*, edited by D. A. Carson, 221–50. Grand Rapids: Zondervan, 1982.

———. *The Theology of the Book of Revelation*. Cambridge: Cambridge University Press, 1993.

Baumgarten, Albert I. "Seekers after Smooth Things." In *Encyclopedia of the Dead Sea Scrolls*, edited by Lawrence Schiffman and James VanderKam, 2:857–59. New York: Oxford University Press, 2000.

Beale, G. K. *The Book of Revelation: A Commentary on the Greek Text*. New International Greek Testament Commentary. Grand Rapids: Eerdmans, 1999.

———. *The Use of Daniel in Jewish Apocalyptic Literature and in the Revelation of St. John*. Lanham, MD: University Press of America, 1984.

Beale, G. K., and Sean M. McDonough. "Revelation." In *Commentary on the New Testament Use of the Old Testament*, edited by G. K. Beale and D. A. Carson, 1081–1162. Grand Rapids: Baker Academic, 2007.

Beardslee, William A. "*De facie quae in orbe lunae apparet* (Moralia 920A–945D)." In *Plutarch's Theological Writings and Early Christian Literature*, edited by Hans D. Betz, 286–300. Leiden: Brill, 1975.

Beckwith, Isbon T. *The Apocalypse of John: Studies in Introduction with a Critical and Exegetical Commentary*. New York: Macmillan, 1919.

Bibliography

Begley, Vimala, and Richard D. De Puma. *Rome and India: The Ancient Sea Trade.* Madison: University of Wisconsin Press, 1991.

Bergmann, Marianne. *Die Strahlen der Herrscher: Theomorphes Herrscherbild und politische Symbolik im Hellenismus und in der römischen Kaiserzeit.* Deutsches Archäologisches Institut. Mainz: von Zabern, 1998.

Binder, Gerhard. "Banquet." In *Brill's New Pauly: Encyclopedia of the Ancient World,* edited by Hubert Cancik et al., 2:488–497. Leiden: Brill, 2003.

Black, C. Clifton. "The First, Second, and Third Letters of John: Introduction, Commentary, and Reflection." In *The New Interpreter's Bible,* edited by Leander E. Keck, 12:365–469. Nashville, TN: Abingdon, 1998.

Bonhoeffer, Dietrich. *The Cost of Discipleship.* Rev ed. New York: Macmillan, 1963.

Bonz, Marianne Palmer. "The Jewish Donor Inscriptions from Aphrodisias: Are They Both Third Century, and Who Are the Theosebeis?" *HSCP* 96 (1994): 281–299.

Boring, Eugene M. *Hellenistic Commentary to the New Testament.* Nashville, TN: Abingdon, 1995.

———. "Prophecy (Early Christian)." In *The Anchor Bible Dictionary,* edited by David Noel Freedman, 5:495–502. New York: Doubleday, 1992.

Boxall, Ian. *The Revelation of Saint John.* Peabody, MA: Hendrickson, 2006.

Boyer, Paul. "The Growth of Fundamentalist Apocalyptic in United States." In *The Encyclopedia of Apocalypticism,* edited by John Collins et al., 3:145–47. New York: Continuum, 1998.

Bremmer, Jan N. "Hades." In *Brill's New Pauly: Encyclopedia of the Ancient World,* edited by Hubert Cancik et al., 9:1076–77. Leiden: Brill, 2004.

Brooke, George J. "Prophecy." In *Encyclopedia of Dead Sea Scrolls,* edited by Lawrence. Schiffman and James VanderKam, 2:694–700. Oxford: Oxford University Press, 2000.

Brouskari, Maria S. *The Acropolis Museum: A Descriptive Catalogue.* Athens: Commercial Bank of Greece, 1974.

Bultmann, Rudolf. *Theology of the New Testament.* 2 vols. Translated by Kendrick Grobel. New York: Scribner's, 1955.

Burrell, Barbara. *Neokoroi: Greek Cities and Roman Emperors.* Cincinnati Classical Studies. Boston: Brill, 2004.

Caird, G. B. *A Commentary on the Revelation of St. John the Divine.* New York: Harper & Row, 1966.

Calvin, John. *Commentary on the Book of Isaiah the Prophet.* Vols. I-IV. Translated by William Pringle. Grand Rapids: Eerdmans, 1956.

Carson, D. A. and Douglas Moo. *An Introduction to the New Testament.* 2nd ed. Grand Rapids: Zondervan, 2005.

Chami, Felix A. "Graeco-Roman Trade Link and the Bantu Migration Theory." *Anthropos* 94 (1999): 205–15.

———. "Roman Beads from the Rufiji Delta, Tanzania: First Incontrovertible Archaeological Link with the Periplus." *Current Anthropology* 40 (1999): 237–41.

Charles, R. H. *A Critical and Exegetical Commentary on the Revelation of St. John.* Vol. 1. Edinburgh: T&T Clark, 1963.

Charlesworth, James H. "Paradise." In *The Anchor Bible Dictionary,* edited by David Noel Freedman, 5:154–55. New York: Doubleday, 1992.

————. "III. The Voice and Early Christology." In *The Old Testament Pseudepigrapha and the New Testament: Prolegomena for the Study of Christian Origins*, 128–31. Cambridge: Cambridge University Press, 1985.

Chavalas, M. W. "Balaam." In *Dictionary of Old Testament Pentateuch*, edited by T. Desmond Alexander and David W. Baker, 75–78. Downers Grove, IL: InterVarsity, 2003.

Christensen, Duane L. *Deuteronomy 21:10–34:14*. Word Biblical Commentary 6b. Nashville, TN: Thomas Nelson, 2002.

Clausen, W. V. "Theocritus and Virgil." In *The Cambridge History of Classical Literature*. Vol. 2, *Latin Literature*, edited by E. J. Kennedy and W. V. Clausen, 315–17. London: Cambridge University Press, 1982.

Clinton, Kevin. "The Eleusinian Mysteries: Roman Initiates and Benefactors, Second Century BC to AD 267." In *Aufstieg und Niedergang der römischen Welt II.18.2*, edited by Hildegard Temporini and Wolfgang Haase, 1499–1539. Berlin: de Gruyter, 1989.

————. *Myth and Cult: The Iconography of the Eleusinian Mysteries*. M. P. Nilsson Lectures. Stockholm: Svenska Institutet i Athen, 1992.

Cohen, J. M. *The Four Voyages of Christopher Columbus: Being His Own Log-book, Letters and Dispatches with Connecting Narrative Drawn from the Life of the Admiral by His Son Hernando Colon and Other Contemporary Historians*. Translated by J. M. Cohen. New York: Penguin, 1969.

Cohen, Shaye. "Respect for Judaism by Gentiles According to Josephus." *HTR* 80 (1987): 409–30.

Collins, Adela Yarbro. "Apocalypses and Apocalypticism, Early Christian." In *Anchor Bible Dictionary*, edited by David Noel Freedman, 1:288–92. New York: Doubleday, 1992.

————. "Insiders and Outsiders in the Book of Revelation." In *"To See Ourselves as Others See Us": Christians, Jews, "Others" in Late Antiquity*, edited by J. Neusner and E. S. Frerichs, 187–218. Chico, CA: Scholars, 1985.

————. "Pergamon in Early Christian Literature." In *Pergamon: Citadel of the Gods*, edited by Helmut Koester, 163–84. Harrisburg, PA: Trinity Press International, 1998.

————. "Revelation, Book of." In *Anchor Bible Dictionary*, edited by David Noel Freedman, 5:695–69. New York: Doubleday, 1992.

Collins, John. "Apocalypses and Apocalypticism, Early Jewish Apocalypticism." In *Anchor Bible Dictionary*, edited by David Noel Freedman, 1:282–288. New York: Doubleday, 1992.

————. *The Scepter and the Star. The Messiahs of the Dead Sea Scrolls and Other Ancient Literature*. New York: Doubleday, 1995.

Cramer, Frederick H. *Astrology in Roman Law and Politics*. Chicago: Ares, 1996.

Cuss, Dominique. *Imperial Cult and Honorary Terms in the New Testament*. Paradosis, Contributions to the History of Early Christian Literature and Theology 23. Fribourg: University Press, 1974.

D'Andria, Francesco. *Hierapolis of Phrygia (Pamukkale): An Archaeological Guide*. Translated by Paul Arthur. Istanbul: Ege Yayinlari, 2003.

Davidson, Maxwell John. "Angel." In *The New Interpreter's Dictionary of the Bible*, edited by Katharine D. Sakenfeld, 1:148–55. Nashville, TN: Abingdon, 2006.

Bibliography

Deissmann, Adolf. *Bible Studies*. Translated by Alexander Grieve. 2nd ed. Edinburgh: T&T Clark, 1909.

———. *Light from the Ancient East: The New Testament Illustrated by Recently Discovered Texts of the Graeco-Roman World*. Translated by Lionel R. M. Strachan. New York: Doran, 1927.

DeSilva, David A. *Introducing the Apocrypha: Message, Context, and Significance*. Grand Rapids: Baker Academic, 2002.

DiTommaso, Lorenzo. "New Jerusalem Text." In *The Eerdmans Dictionary of Early Judaism*, edited by John Collins and Daniel C. Harlow, 996–97. Grand Rapids: Eerdmans, 2010.

Dodd, B. J. "Millennium." In *Dictionary of the Later New Testament and Its Developments*, edited by Ralph P. Martin and Peter H. Davids, 738–41. Downers Grove, IL: InterVarsity, 1997.

Dolansky, Fanny. "*Togam virilem sumere*: Coming of Age in the Roman World." In *Roman Dress and the Fabrics of Roman Culture*, edited by J. Edmondson and A. Keith. London: University of Toronto Press, 2008.

Dunbabin, Katherine M. D. *The Roman Banquet: Images of Conviviality*. Cambridge: Cambridge University Press, 2003.

Engelmann, Helmut. *The Delian Aretalogy of Sarapis*. Études Préliminaires aux Religions Orientales dans L'empire Romain 44, edited by M. J. Vermaseren. Leiden: Brill, 1975.

Evans, Craig. "Mark's Incipit and the Priene Calendar Inscription: From Jewish Gospel to Greco-Roman Gospel." Online: http://craigaevans.com/Priene%20art.pdf.

Fantuzzi, Marco. "Ekphrasis." In *Brill's New Pauly: Encyclopedia of the Ancient World*. Edited by Hubert Cancik et al., 4:872–75. Leiden: Brill, 2006.

Fekkes, Jan, *Isaiah and the Prophetic Traditions in the Book of Revelation: Visionary Antecedents and Their Development*. JSNT Supplement Series 93. Sheffield: JSOT, 1994.

Feldmeier, Reinhard. *Die Christen als Fremde: Die Metapher der Fremde in der antiken Welt, im Urchristentum und im 1. Peter*. Tübingen: Mohr Siebeck, 1992.

Fiorenza, E. Schüssler. "Apokalypsis and Propheteia: The Book of Revelation in the Context of Early Christian Prophecy." In *L'Apocalypse johannique et l'Apocalyptique dans le Nouveau Testament*, edited by J. Lambrecht, 105–28. Leuven: Leuven University Press, 1980.

Fitzgerald, John, and L. Michael White. *The Tabula of Cebes: Texts and Translations*. Graeco-Roman Religion Series. Chico, CA: Scholars, 1983.

Flower, Michael A. *The Seer in Ancient Greece*. Berkeley: University of California Press, 2008.

Fraser, P. M. "The Kings of Commagene and the Greek World." In *Studien zur Religion und Kultur Kleinasiens: Festschrift für Friedrich Karl Dörner*, edited by Friedrich Karl Dörner et al., 359–74. Leiden: Brill, 1978.

Freyburger, Gérard. "Augustalia." In *Brill's New Pauly: Encyclopedia of the Ancient World*, edited by Hubert Cancik et al., 2:354. Leiden: Brill, 2006.

Friesen, Steven. *Imperial Cults and the Apocalypse of John: Reading Revelation in the Ruins*. New York: Oxford University Press, 2001.

———. "Revelation, Realia, and Religion." *HTR* 88 (1995): 291–314.

———. *Twice Neokoros: Ephesus, Asia, and the Cult of the Flavian Imperial Family*. Leiden: Brill, 1993.

Garcia Martínez, Florentino. "New Jerusalem." In *Encyclopedia of the Dead Sea Scrolls*, edited by Lawrence Schiffman and James VanderKam, 2:606–10. New York: Oxford University Press, 2000.

Garcia Martínez, Florentino, and E. J. C. Tigchelaar, eds. *The Dead Sea Scrolls Study Edition*. 2 vols. Leiden: Brill, 1997–1998.

Garland, David E. *2 Corinthians*. New American Commentary. Nashville, TN: Broadman & Holman, 1999.

Glasson, T. F. *Greek Influence in Jewish Eschatology with Special Reference to the Apocalypses and Pseudepigraphs*. London: SPCK, 1961.

Goell, K. "Foreword." In *Nemrud Dagi: The Hierothesion of Antiochus I of Commagene*, edited by Donald H. Sanders, 1:xxxix–xliv. Winona Lake, IN: Eisenbrauns, 1996.

Goldstein, Jonathan. *The II Maccabees*. Anchor Bible Commentaries 41a. Garden City, NY: Doubleday, 1983.

Goodman, Martin. "Nerva, the *Fiscus Judaicus*, and Jewish Identity." *JRS* 79 (1989): 40–44.

Gorman, Frank. "Nakedness." In *The New Interpreter's Dictionary of the Bible*, edited by Katharine Doob Sakenfeld, 1:217. Nashville, TN: Abingdon, 2009.

Grant, Robert. "American New Testament Study." *JBL* 87 (1968): 42–50.

Greene, John T. *Probing the Frontiers of Biblical Studies*. Princeton Theological Monograph Series 111. Eugene, OR: Pickwick, 2009.

Gundry, R. H. "The New Jerusalem, People as Place, not Place for People." *NovT* 29 (1987): 254–64.

Gutsfeld, Andreas. "Meals." In *Brill's New Pauly: Encyclopedia of the Ancient World*, edited by Hubert Cancik et al., 8:525–27. Leiden: Brill, 2006.

Habicht, C. "The Seleucids and Their Rivals." In *The Cambridge Ancient History*, edited by A. E. Astin et al., 8:324–87. 2nd ed. Cambridge: Cambridge University Press, 1989.

Hackett, Jo Ann. "Balaam." In *The Anchor Bible Dictionary*, edited by David Noel Freedman, 1:569–72. New York: Doubleday, 1992.

Harland, Philip A. *Associations, Synagogues, and Congregations: Claiming a Place in Ancient Mediterranean Society*. Minneapolis: Fortress, 2003.

Harries, Jill. *Law and Crime in the Roman World*. Cambridge: Cambridge University Press, 2007.

Harrington, Daniel J. *Invitation to the Apocrypha*. Grand Rapids: Eerdmans, 1999.

Harrington, Wilfrid J. *Revelation*. Sacra Pagina 16. Collegeville, MN: Glazier, 1993.

Hatzfeld, Jean. "Inscriptions de Panamara." *BCH* 51 (1927): 57–122.

Hemer, Colin. *The Letters to the Seven Churches of Asia*. JSNT Supplement Series 11. Sheffield: JSOT, 1986.

Hemp, Vinzene. "'esh." *Theological Dictionary of the Old Testament*, edited by G. J. Botterweck and H. Ringgren, 1:418–28. Grand Rapids: Eerdmans, 1974.

Herrmann, A. "Farbe." In *Reallexikon für Antike und Christentum*, edited by Th. Klauser, 7:358–447. Stuttgart: Anton Hiersemann, 1969.

Hicks, E. L. "Inscriptions from Western Cilicia." *JHS* 12 (1891): 225–73.

Hiers, Richard H. "Day of the Lord." In *The Anchor Bible Dictionary*, edited by David Noel Freedman, 2:82. New York: Doubleday, 1992.

Hoffmann, Adolf. "The Roman Remodeling of the Asklepieion." In *Pergamon Citadel of the Gods*, edited by H. Koester, 41–61. Harrisburg, PA: Trinity Press International, 1998.

Hoffmann, Matthias R. *The Destroyer and the Lamb: The Relationship between Angelomorphic and Lamb Christology in the Book of Revelation*. WUNT2 203. Tübingen: Mohr Siebeck, 2005.

Hölscher, Tonio. *Victoria Romana; Archäologische Untersuschungen zur Geschichte und Wesensart der römischen Siegesgöttin von den Anfängen bis zum Ende des 3. Jhs. n. Chr.* Mainz am Rhein: P. von Zabern, 1967.

Horbury, William. "The Benediction of the *Minim* and Early Jewish-Christian Controversy." *JTS* 33 (1982): 19–61.

Horsley, Greg H. "A 'Letter from Heaven.'" *NewDocs* 1:29–32.

Hort, F. J. A. *The Apocalypse of St. John I–III, with Introduction, Commentary, and Additional Notes*. London: Macmillan, 1908.

Howgego, Christopher et al. *Coinage and Identity in the Roman Provinces*. Oxford: The Oxford University Press, 2005.

Hubers, John. "'It Is a Strange Thing,' The Millennial Blindness of Christopher Columbus." *Missiology: An International Review* 37 (2009): 333–53.

Huffman, H. B. "Prophecy (ANE)." In *The Anchor Bible Dictionary*, edited by David Noel Freedman, 5:477–82. New York: Doubleday, 1992.

Huntingford, W. B. *The Periplus of the Erythraean Sea*. London: The Hakluyt Society, 1980.

Jauhiainen, Marko. *The Use of Zechariah in Revelation*. WUNT2 199. Tübingen: Mohr Siebeck, 2005.

International Nemrud Foundation. "?" No pages. Online: http://www.nemrud.nl/en/sc_tekst2.asp.

Kähler, Heinz. *Alberti Rubeni Dissertatio De Gemma Augustea*. Monumenta Artis Romanae 9. Berlin: Mann, 1968.

Kahn, Charles H. "Pythagoras, Pythagoreanism." In *Oxford Classical Dictionary*, 3rd ed., edited by Simon Hornblower and Antony Spawforth, 1283–85. Oxford: Oxford University Press, 1996.

Kearns, Emily. "Theoxenia." In *The Oxford Classical Dictionary*, 3rd ed., edited by Simon Hornblower amd Anthony Spawforth, 1506–7. Oxford: Oxford University Press, 1996.

Kee, H. C. "The Transformation of the Synagogue after 70 CE: Its Import for Early Christianity." *NTS* 36 (1990): 1–24.

Keener, Craig. "Lamb." In *Dictionary of the Later New Testament and Its Developments*, edited by R. P. Martin and P. H. Davids, 641–42. Downers Grove, IL: InterVarsity, 1997.

———. *Revelation*. NIV Application Commentary. Grand Rapids: Zondervan, 2000.

Keppie, L. J. F. *Understanding Roman Inscriptions*. Baltimore: Johns Hopkins University Press, 1991.

Kiddle, Martin. *The Revelation of St. John*. New York: Harper, 1940.

Kim, Kyoung-Shik. *God Will Judge Each One According to Works. Judgment According to Works and Psalm 62 in Early Judaism and the New Testament*. Berlin: Walter de Gruyter, 2011.

Kirchhoff, Karl-Heinz. "Münster." In *The Oxford Encyclopedia of the Reformation*, edited by Hans J. Hillerbrand. New York: Oxford University Press, 1996.

Klauck, Hans-Josef. *The Religious Context of Early Christianity*. Edinburgh: T&T Clark, 2000.

Klauser, Theodor. "Baum." In *Reallexikon für Antike und Christentum*, edited by Theodor Klauser, 2:1-34. Stuttgart: Anton Hiersemann, 1954.

Koenen, Ludwig. "Die Prophezeiungen des 'Töpfers.'" *ZPE* 2 (1968): 178-209.

Koenen, L., and J. Kramer. "Ein Hymnus auf den Allgott." *ZPE* 4 (1969): 19-21.

Koester, Craig R. "The Message to Laodicea and the Problem of Its Local Context: A Study of the Imagery in Rev. 3:14-22." *NTS* 49 (2003): 407-24.

Koole, Jan L. *Isaiah III*. Historical Commentary on the Old Testament 3. Leuven: Peeters, 2001.

Krafft, Fritz. "Astrology." In *Brill's New Pauly: Encyclopedia of the Ancient World*, edited by Hubert Cancik et al., 2:196-210. Leiden: Brill, 2003.

Kraft, Heinrich. *Die Offenbarung des Johannes*. Handbuch zum Neuen Testament 16a. Tübingen: Mohr Siebeck, 1974.

Krahn, Cornelius. *Dutch Anabaptism: Origin, Spread, Life, and Thought (1450-1600)*. The Hague: Martinus Nijhoff, 1968.

Kunisch, Norbert. "Die stiertötende Nike. Typengeschichtliche und mythologische Untersuchungen." Doctoral diss., München, 1964.

Kyle, Donald G. *Spectacles of Death in Ancient Rome*. New York: Routledge, 2001.

Kyle, Richard G. *The Last Days Are Here Again: A History of the End Times*. Grand Rapids: Baker, 1998.

Ladd, George Eldon. *A Theology of the New Testament*. Rev. ed. Grand Rapids: Eerdmans, 1993.

Lähnemann, Johannes. "Die sieben Sendschreiben der Johannes-Apokalypse: Dokumente für die Konfrontation des frühen Christentums mit hellenistisch-römischer Kultur und Religion in Kleinasien." In *Studien zur Religion and Kultur Kleinasiens. Festschrift für Friedrich Karl Dörner zum 65. Geburtstag am 28. Februar 1976*, edited by Sencer Sahin et al., 2:516-39. Leiden: Brill, 1978.

Landes, Richard Allen, ed. *Encyclopedia of Millennialism and Millennial Movements*. New York: Routledge, 2000.

Lattimore, Richard. *Themes in Greek and Latin Epitaphs*. Urbana: University of Illinois Press, 1962.

Lerner, Robert E. "Millennialism." In *The Encyclopedia of Apocalypticism*, edited by John Collins et al., 2:326-60. New York: Continuum, 1998.

Levinskaya, Irina, ed. *The Book of Acts in Its First Century Setting*. Vol. 5, *Diaspora Setting*. Grand Rapids: Eerdmans, 1996.

Lifshitz, B. *Donateurs et Fondateurs dans les Synagogues*. Paris: Gabalda, 1969.

Lim, Timothy, "Kittim." In *Encyclopedia of the Dead Sea Scrolls*, edited by Lawrence H. Schiffman and James VanderKam, 1:1469-71. New York: Oxford University Press, 2000.

Lindenberger, James M. "Letters." In *Encyclopedia of the Dead Sea Scrolls*, edited by Lawrence Schiffman and James VanderKam, 1:480-85. New York: Oxford University Press, 2000.

Lippold, G. "Nike." *Paulys Real-Encyclopädie der classischen Altertumswissenschaft*, 33.51: cols. 283-307. Stuttgart: Metzlersche Verlagsbuchhandlung, 1936.

Lippy, Charles H. "Millennialism and Adventism." In *Encyclopedia of the American Religious Experience: Studies of Traditions and Movements*, edited by Charles H. Lippy and Peter W. Williams, 2:831-44. New York: Scribners, 1988.

Llewelyn, S. R. "The Conveyance of Letters." *NewDocs* 7:1-57.

Bibliography

Lupieri, Edmondo F. *A Commentary on the Apocalypse of John.* Translated by Maria Poggi Johnson and Adam Kamesar. Grand Rapids: Eerdmans, 2006.

Lupu, Eran, ed. *Greek Sacred Law: A Collection of New Documents (NGSL).* Leiden: Brill, 2005.

MacMullen, Ramsay. *Christianity and Paganism in the Fourth to Eight Centuries.* New Haven, CT: Yale University Press, 1997.

————. *Christianizing the Roman Empire (AD 100–400).* New Haven: Yale University Press, 1984.

————. *Enemies of the Roman Order: Treason, Unrest, and Alienation in the Empire.* Cambridge, MA: Harvard University Press, 1966.

Mach, Michael. "Angels." In *Encyclopedia of the Dead Sea Scrolls,* edited by Lawrence Schiffman and James VanderKam, 1:24–27. New York: Oxford University Press, 2000.

Magie, David. *Roman Rule in Asia Minor to the End of the Third Century after Christ.* Princeton, NJ: Princeton University Press, 1950.

Marcus, Joel. "Birkat Ha-Minim Revisited." *NTS* 55 (2009): 523–51.

Marshall, I. H. "Son of Man." In *Dictionary of Jesus and the Gospels,* edited by Joel B. Greene et al., 775–81. Downers Grove, IL: InterVarsity, 1992.

Martin, Ralph P. *2 Corinthians.* Word Biblical Commentary 40. Waco, TX: Word, 1986.

Maximowa, M. "Un Camée commémoratif de la Bataille d'Actium." *RA* 30 (1929): 64–69.

McDonough, Sean M. *YHWH at Patmos: Rev. 1:4 in Its Hellenistic and Early Jewish Setting.* Tübingen: Mohr Siebeck, 1999.

McKnight, Scot. *The King Jesus Gospel.* Grand Rapids: Zondervan, 2011.

Mellor, Ronald. Θεὰ Ῥώμη: *The Worship of the Goddess Roma in the Greek World.* Göttingen: Vandenhoeck & Reprecht, 1975.

Merkelbach, Reinhold. "Der Rangstreit der Städte Asiens und die Rede des Aelius Aristides über the Eintracht." *ZPE* 32 (1978): 287–96.

Merrill, Eugene H. *Deuteronomy.* Nashville, TN: Broadman & Holman, 1994.

Meyers, Carol L., and Eric M. *Haggai, Zechariah 1–8.* The Anchor Bible 25b. Garden City, NY: Doubleday, 1987.

Minear, Paul S. *I Saw a New Earth: an Introduction to the Visions of the Apocalypse.* Washington: Corpus Publications, 1968.

Mitchell, Stephen. *Anatolia: Land, Men, and Gods in Asia Minor.* 2 vols. Oxford: Oxford University Press, 1995.

Momigliano, Arnaldo. "Biblical Studies and Classical Studies: Simple Reflections about Historical Method." *BA* 45 (1982): 224–28.

————. "Terra Marique." *JRS* 32 (1942): 53–64.

Morgan, David. "Warner Sallman and the Visual Culture of American Protestantism." In *Icons of American Protestantism: The Art of Warner Sallman,* edited by David Morgan. New Haven: Yale University Press, 1996.

Moulton, James H., and George Milligan. *The Vocabulary of the Greek Testament, Illustrated from the Papyri and Other Non-literary Sources.* Grand Rapids: Eerdmans, 1952.

Mounce, Robert H. *The Book of Revelation.* New International Commentary on the New Testament. Rev. ed. Grand Rapids: Eerdmans, 1998.

Moyise, Steve. *The Old Testament in the Book of Revelation.* JSNT Supplement Series 115. Sheffield: Sheffield Academic, 1995.

Müller, D. "Apostle." In *The New International Dictionary of New Testament Theology*, edited by Collin Brown, 1:126–37. Grand Rapids: Zondervan, 1975.

Muraoka, T. *A Greek-English Lexicon of the Septuagint*. Paris: Peeters, 2009.

Newport, Kenneth G. C. *Apocalypse and Millennium: Studies in Biblical Eisegesis*. Cambridge: Cambridge University Press, 2000.

Newsom, Carol A. "Songs of the Sabbath Sacrifice." In *Encyclopedia of the Dead Sea Scrolls*, edited by Lawrence Schiffman and James VanderKam, 2:887–89. New York: Oxford University Press, 2000.

Nickelsburg, George W. E. *1 Enoch 1: A Commentary on the Book of 1 Enoch, Chapters 1–36; 81–108*. Hermeneia. Minneapolis: Augsburg Fortress, 2001.

———. *Jewish Literature between the Bible and the Mishnah*. 2nd ed. Minneapolis: Fortress, 2005.

Nock, A. D. *Conversion: The Old and the New in Religion from Alexander the Great to Augustine of Hippo*. Oxford: Oxford University Press, 1933.

———. "Σύνναος Θεός." In *Essays on Religion and the Ancient World*, edited by Zeph Stewart, 1:202–51. Cambridge, MA: Harvard University Press, 1972.

Oakley, Paul. "Jesus, Lover of My Soul (It's All About You)." Kingsway's Thankyou Music, 1995.

Oberleitner, Wolfgang. *Geschnittene Steine: Die Prunkkameen der Wiener Antikensammlung*. Vienna: Böhlaus, 1985.

Osborne, Grant. "Response." In *Evangelicalism & the Stone-Campbell Movement*, edited by William R. Baker. Abilene, TX: Abilene Christian University Press, 2006.

———. *Revelation*. Baker Exegetical Commentary on the New Testament. Grand Rapids: Baker, 2002.

Oster, Richard E., Jr. "Christianity and Emperor Veneration in Ephesus: Iconography of a Conflict." *ResQ* 25 (1982): 143–49.

———. "Christianity in Asia Minor." In *The Anchor Bible Dictionary*, edited by David Noel Freedman, 1:938–54. New York: Doubleday, 1992.

———. "The Ephesian Artemis as an Opponent of Early Christianity." *JAC* 19 (1976): 24–44.

———. "Numismatic Windows into the Social World of Early Christianity: A Methodological Inquiry." *JBL* 101 (1982): 204–8.

———. "Supposed Anachronism in Luke-Acts's Use of συναγωγή." *NTS* 39 (1993): 178–208.

Pallas, D. I. et al. "Inscriptions Lyciennes trouvées a Solomos pres de Corinthe." *BCH* 83 (1959): 496–508.

Parker, T. H. L. *John Calvin: A Biography*. Philadelphia: Westminster, 1975.

Peek, Werner. *Griechische Grabgedichte, griechisch und deutsch*. Berlin: Akademie-Verlag, 1960.

Peerbolte, L. J. Lietaert. "Antichrist, ἀντίχριστος." In *Dictionary of Deities and Demons in the Bible*, 2nd ed, edited by Karel can der Toorn et al., 62–64. Grand Rapids: Eerdmans, 1999.

Peres, Imre. *Griechische Grabinschriften und neutestamentliche Eschatologie*. WUNT 157. Tübingen: Mohr, 2003.

Peters, Olutola K. *The Mandate of the Church in the Apocalypse of John*. Studies in Biblical Theology 77. New York: Lang, 2005.

Pitts, William L., Jr. "Davidians." In *Encyclopedia of Millennialism and Millennial Movements*, edited by Richard A. Landes, 113–117. New York: Routledge, 2000.

Bibliography

Potter, David S. "Julius Firmicus Maternus." In *The Oxford Classical Dictionary*, 3rd ed., edited by Simon Hornblower and Antony Spawforth, 598. Oxford: Oxford University Press, 1996.

————. "Numbers, sacred." In *The Oxford Classical Dictionary*, 3rd ed., edited by Simon Hornblower and Anthony Spawforth, 1053–54. Oxford: Oxford University Press, 1996.

Powell, Mark Allan. *Introducing the New Testament*. Grand Rapids: Baker Academic, 2009.

Price, Simon R. F. *Rituals and Power: The Roman Imperial Cult in Asia Minor*. Cambridge: Cambridge University Press, 1984.

Prigent, Pierre. *Commentary on the Apocalypse of St. John*. Translated by Wendy Pradels. Tübingen: Mohr Siebeck, 2001.

Purcell, Nicholas. "*Res Gestae* (of Augustus)." In *The Oxford Classical Dictionary*, 3rd ed., edited by Simon Hornblower and Antony Spawforth, 1309. New York: Oxford University Press, 1996.

Quek, Tze-Ming. "'I Will Give Authority over the Nations': Psalm 2:8–9 in Revelation 2:26–27." In *Early Christian Literature and Intertextuality*, edited by Craig Evans and H. Daniel Zacharias, 2:175–87. New York: T&T Clark, 2009.

von Rad, Gerhard. *Old Testament Theology: The Theology of Israel's Prophetic Traditions*. Translated by D. M. G. Stalker. New York: Harper & Row, 1965.

Rajak, Tessa. "Porcius Festus." In *The Oxford Classical Dictionary*, 3rd ed., edited by Simon Hornblower and Antony Spawforth, 1226. Oxford: Oxford University Press, 1996.

Ramsay, William M. *The Cities and Bishoprics of Phrygia: Being an Essay of the Local History of Phrygia*. Vol. 1. Oxford: Clarendon, 1897.

————. *The Cities and Bishoprics of Phrygia: Being an Essay of the Local History of Phrygia from the Earliest Times to the Türkish Conquest 1, 2 West and West-Central Phrygia*. Oxford: Clarendon, 1897.

————. *The Letters to the Seven Churches of Asia*. London: Hodder & Stoughton, 1904.

Rapp, A. "Helios." In *Ausführliches Lexikon der griechischen und römischen Mythologie*, edited by W. H. Roscher, 2:1994–2026. New York: Olms, 1978.

Rea, John. "A New Version of P. Yale Inv. 299." *ZPE* 27 (1977): 151–56.

Reddish, Mitchell. *Revelation*. Macon, GA: Smyth & Helwys, 2001.

Reitz, Christiane. "Ekphrasis." In *Brill's New Pauly: Encyclopedia of the Ancient World*, edited by Hubert Cancik et al., 4:875–78. Leiden: Brill, 2006.

Rengstort, Karl Heinrich. "ἀπόστολος." In *Theological Dictionary of the New Testament*, edited by Gerhard Kittel, 1:420–24. Grand Rapids: Eerdmans, 1974.

Rösel, Martin. "Names of God." In *Encyclopedia of the Dead Sea Scrolls*, edited by Lawrence H. Schiffman and James VanderKam, 2:600–602. New York: Oxford University Press, 2000.

Rosscup, James E. "The Overcomer of the Apocalypse." *Grace Theological Journal* 3 (1982): 272–73.

Rowe, C. Kavin. *World Upside Down: Reading Acts in the Graeco-Roman Age*. Oxford: Oxford University Press, 2009.

Rowland, Christopher C. "The Book of Revelation." In *The New Interpreter's Bible*, edited by Leander Keck, 12:503–744. Nashville, TN: Abingdon, 1998.

Ruiz, J.-P. *Ezekiel in the Apocalypse: The Transformation of Prophetic Language in Revelation 16:17–19:10*. New York: Lang, 1989.

Sandelin, Karl-Gustuv. "The Danger of Idolatry according to Philo of Alexandria." *Temenos* 27 (1991): 109–50.

Sandys-Wunsch, John, and Laurence Eldridge. "J. P. Gabler and the Distinction between Biblical and Dogmatic Theology: Translation, Commentary, and Discussion of His Originality." *SJT* 33 (1980): 133–58.

Schenck, Kenneth. *A Brief Guide to Philo.* Louisville, KY: Westminster John Knox, 2005.

Scherer, Chr. "Hades." In *Ausführliches Lexikon der griechischen und römischen Mythologie,* edited by W. H. Roscher, 2:1778–1814. New York: Verlag, 1978.

Scherf, Johannes. "Nike. I Mythology." In *Brill's New Pauly: Encyclopedia of the Ancient World,* edited by Hubert Cancik et al., 9:754–55. Leiden: Brill, 2006.

Scherrer, Peter, ed. *Ephesus: The New Guide.* Rev. ed. Turkey: Zero Prod., 2000.

Schiffman, Lawrence H. "Miqtsat Ma'asei Ha-Torah." In *Encyclopedia of the Dead Sea Scrolls,* edited by Lawrence Schiffman and James VanderKam, 1:558–60. New York: Oxford University Press, 2000.

Schimanowski, Gottfried. "Die jüdische Intergration in die Oberschicht Alexandriens und die angebliche Apostasie des Tiberius Julius Alexander." In *Jewish Identity in the Greco-Roman World,* 111–35. Ancient Judaism and Early Christianity 71. Leiden: Brill, 2007.

Schlachter, A., and Friedrich Gisinger. *Globus: Seine Entstehung und Verwendung in der Antike.* Berlin: Teubner, 1927.

Schlapbach, Karin. "Phlegethon." In *Brill's New Pauly: Encyclopedia of the Ancient World,* edited by Hubert Cancik et al., 11:132. Leiden: Brill, 2006.

Schmitt, John J. "Prophecy (Preexilic Hebrew)." In *The Anchor Bible Dictionary,* edited by David Noel Freedman, 5:482–89. New York: Doubleday, 1992.

Schuele, Andreas. "Heart." In *The New Interpreter's Dictionary of the Bible,* edited by Leander Keck et al., 2:764–66. Nashville, TN: Abingdon, 2007.

Sherwin-White, A. N. *The Letters of Pliny: A Historical and Social Commentary.* Oxford: Clarendon, 1966.

Sidebotham, Steven E., and Willemina Z. Wendrich. "Berenike: Archaeological Fieldwork at a Ptolemaic-Roman Port on the Red Sea Coast of Egypt 1999–2001." *Sahara* 13 (2001–2002): 23–50.

Skolnik, Fred. "Birkat Ha-minim." In *Encyclopaedia Judaica,* 2nd ed., edited by Fred Skolnik and Michael Berenbaum, 3:711–12. New York: Keter, 2007.

Slater, Thomas B. "On the Social Setting of the Revelation of John." *NTS* 44 (1998): 232–56.

Smalley, Stephen S. *The Revelation to John: A Commentary on the Greek Text of the Apocalypse.* Downers Grove, IL: InterVarsity, 2005.

Smith, Dennis E. *From Symposium to Eucharist: The Banquet in the Early Christian World.* Minneapolis, MN: Augsburg Fortress, 2003.

Smith, R. R. R. "The Imperial Reliefs from the Sebasteion at Aphrodisias." *JRS* 77 (1987): 115–17.

———. *The Monument of C. Julius Zoilos. Aphrodisias Papers 1.* Mainz: von Zabern, 1993.

Sokolowski, Franciszek. *Lois Sacrées de L'Asie Mineure.* Paris: Boccard, 1955.

———. *Lois Sacrées des Cités Grecques.* Paris: Boccard, 1969.

Spicq, Ceslas. *Theological Lexicon of the New Testament.* Translated and edited by James D. Ernest. Peabody, MA: Hendrickson, 1994.

Bibliography

Staehle, Karl. *Die Zahlenmystik bei Philon von Alexandreia*. Berlin: Teubner und Druck, 1931.

Stayer, James M. "John of Leiden." In *The Oxford Encyclopedia of the Reformation*, edited by Hans J. Hillerbrand, 2:350–51. New York: Oxford University Press, 1996.

Stein, Stephen J. "Apocalypticism Outside the Mainstream in the United States." In *The Encyclopedia of Apocalypticism*, edited by John Collins et al., 3:115–17. New York: Continuum, 1998.

Stern, Menahem. *Greek and Latin Authors on Jews and Judaism*. 3 vols. Jerusalem: The Israel Academy of Sciences and Humanities, 1984.

Stevenson, Gregory. "Conceptual Background to Golden Crown Imagery in the Apocalypse of John (4:4, 10; 14:14)." *JBL* 114 (1995): 257–72.

———. *Power and Place: Temple and Identity in the Book of Revelation*. Berlin: Walter de Gruyter, 2001.

Stevenson, Seth W. et al., eds. "*Coronae*." In *Dictionary of Roman Coins Republican and Imperial*, 290–93. London: Bell, 1889.

———. "*Radiata Corona*." In *Dictionary of Roman Coins Republican and Imperial*, 679. London: Bell, 1889.

Strecker, Georg. *The Johannine Letters: A Commentary on 1, 2, and 3 John*. Edited by Harold Attridge. Translated by Linda M. Maloney. Minneapolis: Fortress, 1996.

Strubbe, Johan H. M. "Curses Against Violation of the Grave in Jewish Epitaphs of Asia Minor." In *Studies in Early Jewish Epigraphy*. Arbeiten zur Geschichte des antiken Judentums und des Urchristentums 21. Edited by Jan W. van Henten and Pieter W. van der Horst. Leiden: Brill, 1994.

Stuckenbruck, Loren. *Angel Veneration and Christology*. WUNT 70. 2nd ed. Tübingen: Mohr, 1995.

———. "Revelation." In *Eerdmans Commentary on the Bible*, edited by James D. G. Dunn, 1535–72. Grand Rapids: Eerdmans, 2003.

Stylianopoulos, Theodore. "'I Know Your Works': Grace and Judgment in the Apocalypse." In *Apocalyptic Thought in Early Christianity*, edited by Robert J. Daly, 17–32. Grand Rapids: Baker Academic, 2009.

Sutherland, C. H. V. *Roman Coins*. New York: G. P. Putnams, 1974.

Sweeney, Marvin A. *The Twelve Prophets*. 2 vols. Collegeville, MN: Liturgical, 2000.

Swete, Henry Barclay. *The Apocalypse of St John: The Greek Text with Introduction, Notes and Indices*. Grand Rapids: Eerdmans, 1906.

Sylloge Inscriptionum Graecarum. Edited Wihelm Dittenberger. 4 vols. Hildesheim: Olms, 1982.

Talbert, Charles H. *The Apocalypse*. Louisville: Westminster John Knox, 1994.

Thapar, Rosalind. "Ashoka." In *The Oxford Classical Dictionary*, 3rd ed., edited by Simon Hornblower and Antony Spawforth, 189. Oxford: Oxford University Press, 1996.

Thayer, Joseph. *Thayer's Greek-English Lexicon of the New Testament*. Peabody, MA: Hendrickson, 1996.

Thomas, Robert L. *Revelation 1–7: An Exegetical Commentary*. Chicago: Moody, 1992.

———. *Revelation 8–22: An Exegetical Commentary*. Chicago: Moody, 1992.

Thompson, Leonard. *The Book of Revelation: Apocalypse and Empire*. New York: Oxford University Press, 1990.

———. *Revelation*. Nashville, TN: Abingdon, 1998.

Tosi, Renzo. "Eratosthenes." In *Brill's New Pauly: Encyclopedia of the Ancient World*, edited by Hubert Cancik et al., 5:14–20. Leiden: Brill, 2004.

Totti, Maria. *Ausgewählte Texte der Isis- und Sarapis-Religion.* Zürich: Olms, 1985.

Trebilco, Paul. *Jewish Communities in Asia Minor.* Cambridge: Cambridge University Press, 1991.

Trench, Richard Chenevix. *Commentary on the Epistles to the Seven Churches in Asia.* 6th ed. Minneapolis: Klock & Klock, 1897.

Tuckett, C. M. "Atonement in the NT." In *The Anchor Bible Dictionary,* edited by David Noel Freedman, 1:518. New York: Doubleday, 1992.

van Unnik, W. C. "A Formula Describing Prophecy." *NTS* 9 (1962–63): 86–94.

Veyne, Paul. *Die griechisch-römische Religion: Kult, Frömmigkeit und Moral.* Translated by Ursula Blank-Sangmeister. Stuttgart: Reclam, 2008.

Viola, Frank, and George Barna. *Pagan Christianity? Exploring the Root of our Church Practices.* Carol Stream, IL: Barna, 2008.

Vos, Louis A. *The Synoptic Traditions in the Apocalypse.* Kampen: Kok, 1965.

Wächter, L. "*sheol.*" *Theological Dictionary of the Old Testament,* edited by G. Johannes Botterweck et al., 14:239–48. Grand Rapids: Eerdmans, 2004.

Wainwright, Arthur W. *Mysterious Apocalypse: Interpreting the Book of Revelation.* Nashville, TN: Abingdon, 1993.

Wallace, Daniel. *Greek Grammar beyond the Basics: An Exegetical Syntax of the New Testament.* Grand Rapids: Zondervan, 1996.

Wallace, Howard N. "Garden of God." In *The Anchor Bible Dictionary,* edited by David Noel Freedman, 2:906–7. New York: Doubleday, 1992.

Wallace, J. A. *The Seven Churches of Asia.* London: Nisbet, 1842.

Walters, James. "'Phoebe' and 'Junias.'" In *Essays on Women in Earliest Christianity,* 2nd ed., edited by Carroll D. Osburn, 1:167–90. Joplin, MO: College, 1995.

Walzer, R. *Galen on Jews and Christians.* London: Oxford University Press, 1949.

Wan, Sze-Kar. "Mind." In *The New Interpreter's Dictionary of the Bible,* edited by Katharine Doob Sakenfeld, 4:90–91. Nashville, TN: Abingdon, 2009.

The Warner Sallman Collection. "Christ at Heart's Door." Anderson University. No pages. Online: http://www.warnersallman.com/collection/images/christ-at-hearts -door/.

Watts, Pauline Moffitt. "Prophecy and Discovery: On the Spiritual Origins of Christopher Columbus's 'Enterprise of the Indies.'" *AHR* 90 (1985): 73–102.

Webb, Stephen H. "Eschatology and Politics." In *The Oxford Handbook of Eschatology.* Oxford: Oxford University Press, 2008.

Weeber, Karl-Wilhelm. "Post." *Alltag im Alten Rom. Ein Lexikon.* Düsseldorf: Artemis & Winkler, 1998.

Weinstock, Stefan. *Divus Julius.* London: Oxford University Press, 1971.

———. "Victoria." *Paulys Real-Encyclopädie der classischen Altertumswissenschaft.* 2nd ser., 16:2, cols. 2501–42. Stuttgart: Alfred Druckenmüller Verlag, 1958.

Wikenhauser, Alfred. *New Testament Introduction.* Translated by Joseph Cunningham. New York: Herder & Herder, 1958.

Wilken, Robert L. *The Christians as the Romans Saw Them.* New Haven: Yale University Press, 1984.

Williamson, Ronald. *Jews in the Hellenistic World: Philo.* Cambridge: Cambridge University Press, 1989.

Wilson, Mark. *Biblical Turkey: A Guide to the Jewish and Christian Sites of Asia Minor.* Istanbul: Ege Yayinlari, 2010.

———. *The Victor Sayings in the Book of Revelation.* Eugene, OR: Wipf & Stock, 2007.

Bibliography

Winter, Bruce. *Roman Wives, Roman Widows: The Appearance of New Women and The Pauline Communities*. Grand Rapids: Eerdmans, 2003.

Witherington, Ben, III. *Revelation*. New Cambridge Bible Commentary. New York: Cambridge University Press, 2003.

Wood, John Turtle. *Discoveries at Ephesus*. Boston: Osgood, 1877.

Wright, D. F. "Docetism." In *Dictionary of the Later New Testament and Its Development*, edited by Ralph P. Martin and Peter H. David. Downers Grove, IL: InterVarsity, 1997.

Wright, N. T. *The Resurrection of the Son of God*. Minneapolis: Fortress, 2003.

Wu, J. L. "Liturgical Elements." In *Dictionary of the Later New Testament and Its Developments*, edited by Ralph P. Martin and Peter H. Davids, 661–62. Downers Grove, IL: InterVarsity, 1997.

Yegül, Fikret. *Bathing in the Roman World*. Cambridge: Cambridge University Press, 2010.

Yinger, Kent L. *Paul, Judaism, and Judgment According to Deeds*. Cambridge: Cambridge University Press, 1999.

York, H. "Heiliger Baum." In *Reallexikon der Assyriologie und Vorderasiatischen Archäologie*, edited by D. O. Edzard, 4:269–82. Berlin: de Gruyter, 1975.

Zimmermann, Klaus. "Cartography." In *Brill's New Pauly: Encyclopedia of the Ancient World*, edited by Hubert Cancik et al., 2.1138–44. Leiden: Brill, 2006.

Zuntz, Günter. *Aion: Gott des Römerreichs*. Heidelberg: Universitätsverlag, 1989.

———. *Aion im Römerreich. Die archäologischen Zeugnisse*. Heidelberg: Universitätsverlag, 1991.

Author Index

Author Index

Author Index

Subject Index

Subject Index

Index of Ancient Documents

EXTRA-BIBLICAL SOURCES JEWISH SOURCES

Apocalypse of Abraham

Apocalypse of Zephaniah

Psalms of Solomon

Tobit

Wisdom of Solomon

1 Maccabees

2 Maccabees

4 Maccabees

Papyri

Inscriptions